THE CATHEDRALS OF
SPAIN

1 SEGOVIA: view from south-west of the church, 1525–91, by Juan and
Rodrigo Gil de Hontañón; the tower lantern of 1620 and the dome of 1615
by Juan de Mugaguren

THE CATHEDRALS
OF SPAIN

by

John Harvey

London
B. T. BATSFORD LTD

First published, 1957

MADE AND PRINTED IN GREAT BRITAIN BY
WILLIAM CLOWES AND SONS, LTD, LONDON AND BECCLES
FOR THE PUBLISHERS
B. T. BATSFORD LTD
4 FITZHARDINGE STREET, PORTMAN SQUARE, LONDON, W.1

PREFACE

THE facts of geography and history have forged many links between Britain and the Iberian Peninsula, and both Spain and Portugal have long been familiar ground to the business man and the pleasure tourist from this country. And if it is Portugal with which England has been linked by treaty for nearly six centuries, it is rather Spain that has attracted the attention of students of art and architecture. To so great an extent is this true, that at least three works by Englishmen have become, in translation, standard text-books accepted in Spain itself.* For a long time insular interest in Spanish art centred upon the Moorish Alhambra at Granada and the great Sevillian painter Murillo, but in course of time appreciation has become more catholic and has widened to include the Middle Ages of Castile and Catalonia and the Baroque movement which swept the Peninsula in the seventeenth and early eighteenth centuries.† Some of the greater churches of Spain have come in for their fair share of this general interest, but by no means to the same relative extent as elsewhere in western Europe. The study of architecture in France, Italy, Germany and England has been largely a study of their major cathedrals and the architects responsible for them, and the literature is both extensive and well informed. This cannot be said of the corresponding works of Spain. Even in Spanish, modern books covering the greater churches are few, for the most part written from an historical or popular viewpoint, and inadequately illustrated. With the exception of several notable monographs,‡ little has been written of the aesthetic or the strictly architectural aspect. In English no serious general survey has been attempted since Street, apart from the unavoidably condensed references in Mr. Bevan's admirable general history of Spanish architecture. All fresh work must necessarily be brought into comparison with that of Street, and it is difficult to see how any study can seriously rival one of the most remarkable pieces of architectural research ever carried out, a masterpiece of travel literature into the bargain. The very excellence of Street's work, in spite of the limits imposed upon him by the communications of his time and

---

* G. E. Street: *Some Account of Gothic Architecture in Spain*; Sir B. F. Fletcher: *A History of Architecture on the Comparative Method*; B. Bevan: *History of Spanish Architecture*.

† The centring of interest upon the Baroque is largely due, not only in England but elsewhere, to Mr. Sacheverell Sitwell's *Southern Baroque Art* (1924).

‡ Especially those of Sr. D. F. Chueca Goitia on the new cathedral of Salamanca and on that of Valladolid.

7

the then state of historical knowledge, has indeed been a bar to any fresh covering of the same ground.

At the same time, the opening up of Spain by modern transport, the results of a century of intensive historical and architectural research, and the possibility of photographic illustration have in some ways rendered Street's book out of date; while its topographical and chronological limitations are in any case implicit. Street was able to cover only the northern two-thirds of Spain, and his chosen period closed in the sixteenth century. This essay is, then, a modest attempt to deal with the Spanish cathedral as a single architectural phenomenon, treating its historical development only in subordination to its aesthetic significance. No attempt is made to provide detailed descriptions of all that is worth seeing at each separate building, nor to cover the historical and anecdotal background, except where such facts help to reveal the conditions and thought of a place and time different from those in which we live.

My principal concern has been to appreciate the greater churches of Spain in the light of Spanish life and atmosphere. Spain is a country which differs most markedly from all others of western Europe, not merely in its intense conservatism but in its all-pervading feeling of nationality. Although its component provinces were anciently independent kingdoms, although Spain comprises extraordinary varieties of climate, soil and vegetation, every part of Spain bears the mark of its Spanishness to a degree unparalleled in the other European countries of the twentieth century.

Yet, as Mr. Bernard Bevan has said of Spain, "the history of her art is the most complicated in all Europe". Composed of elements from two different cultures, the Christian North and the Moslem South, and profoundly affected by influences from Italy, France, Africa, the Near East and the Teutonic North, it is an art which, paradoxically, remains characteristically itself. Again, it is an art which has been formed to a remarkable degree by foreigners working in Spain; but on the other hand, these same foreigners have nearly always been so deeply impressed by the *genius loci* that their work seems almost more Spanish than that of the Spaniards themselves.

Spain as a country, and her art in all its forms from music and poetry through painting to sculpture and architecture, can be appreciated to the full only by those endowed with a certain sympathy. In common with all magnets, Spain has its pole of repulsion, and it is this singularity which, to a considerable extent, must be recognised as responsible for Spain's isolation in the modern world and for the fact that at all periods, even those of her greatest glory, Spain has moved in an orbit of her own, apart from that of Europe. Spain remains absorbed within herself, sanely and surely self-sufficient, genuinely indifferent to the views of outsiders and the clamour of the world without. It is not surprising that, as has been re-marked, Spain was not normally included in the circuit of the Grand Tour. In spite of the efforts of some of the politically disillusioned "generation of '98" to force upon Spain the cosmopolitan outlook and "improve-ments" of the outside world of the twentieth century, Spain has so far retained her natural superiority complex, perhaps the only genuine national complex of this kind left in the world today.

The most generous of friends and hosts to the sympathetic stranger, the Spaniard can be harsh and uncompromising in his contempt for ways that are not his. It is profoundly to be hoped that he will never allow these sharp angles to be smoothed off by the modern cult of "all things to all men" and a false catholicity of taste which is no taste at all. Spain is the last country of discrimination; long may she retain this priceless gift. It is to this quality of discrimination, especially in matters of artistic taste, that Spain owes the extraordinary harmony and congruity of her architecture. It might be expected that an art of such diverse origins would show evident marks of discord and an unhappy clash between heterogeneous elements. That this is not so is due to the very high level, both of aesthetic inspiration and of technical quality, achieved at all periods. From the ninth century A.D. downwards, the execution of Spanish art has been marked by the coupling of refinement with force, and its aesthetic by imagination. Hence it is that we are seldom struck by incon-gruities of style: a church may consist of a Romanesque core, altered in Gothic times, and embedded in Renaissance, Baroque and neo-classic chapels, fronts and tower. Yet it still preserves a unity of feeling which is never present in a comparably heterogeneous building of France or England.

To this result Spain's passionate attachment to the Catholic Faith has no doubt contributed; yet it is precisely in the Spanishness of the Jewish synagogues of Toledo and Cordova, and the Moslem palaces of Saragossa and Granada, that this quality reaches its fullest development, almost an apotheosis. And again by a paradox, the one period for which this general truth does not hold is that of united Spain's greatest political triumphs, the age which yielded the unhappy Palace of Charles V at Granada and the Puritanism of Philip II's and Herrera's Escorial. In both cases the element of superb quality in design is present; but what is lacking is that panash of enthusiastic imagination which almost everywhere else in Spain bears away the bell.

This triumphant inspiration is by no means worked out: it is as present in Gaudí's Sagrada Familia at Barcelona and in the paintings of Sert at Vich as it was in Tomé's Transparente in Toledo Cathedral, the foreigner Gil de Siloé's masterpiece at Miraflores, or that earlier tomb of San Pedro de Osma in Burgo de Osma Cathedral. Earlier still, we meet with this fantasy not only in the Moorish vaults of Cordova, so widely copied in Christian Spain, but in the Visigothic carvings of Asturias.

It is therefore not merely permissible, but imperative, to seek a unity within the variety of Spanish art, and more especially in its highest expression, the cathedral.

The present book springs from an almost lifelong interest in Spain, grounded on the early impressions of a long childhood stay in 1913–14. More immediately it is the outcome of seven extended visits between 1948 and 1956, during which I have seen almost every cathedral, many of them on several occasions. While the historical background is taken from standard works of reference and recent monographs and articles, the view of architectural development here expressed is the result of study on the spot, and the descriptive chapters are an attempt to form a personal estimate of a remarkable art form. This attempt could not have been made without the helpful kindness of many others, notably the large number of Spaniards, both friends and chance acquaintances, with whom it has been my privilege to converse while in their hospitable country. Specifically I must record my indebtedness to my father and mother; to Dr. Xavier de Salas, Director of the Spanish Institute in London; to Mr. L. Russell Muirhead; to Mr. George F. Powell; and to Mr. Sacheverell Sitwell. My wife, who has been my companion on most of my journeys, has played a large part in the evaluation of buildings and places both by independent observations and by checking the results of analysis by means of intuitive perception. To her this book owes the deepest debt.

Winter, 1956

J. H. H.

CONTENTS

ACKNOWLEDGMENT

THE Author and publishers here express their indebtedness to the following persons and institutions for the illustrations mentioned: Mr. Bernard Bevan for figs. 44, 45, 71, 144; Club Foto, Burgos, for fig. 43; Courtauld Institute of Art, for figs. 6, 11, 27, 79, 111, 136; Dirección General del Turismo (Spanish State Tourist Department), for figs. 8, 9, 14, 16, 23, 26, 31, 38–40, 57, 66, 72, 92, 119, 121, 123, 137; Mr. Donald W. Insall, A.R.I.B.A., for fig. 7; Mr. K. C. Jordan, for fig. 2; Rev. E. Junyent, Vich, for fig. 88; Mr. A. F. Kersting, F.R.P.S., for figs. 3, 20, 41, 42, 48, 49, 58, 62, 64, 65, 68, 70, 74, 75, 77, 96, 131–3, 146; Ampliaciones y Reproducciones Mas, Barcelona, for figs. 5, 12, 15, 17–19, 22, 24, 25, 28, 30, 32, 34, 35, 37, 53–5, 63, 67, 69, 73, 80, 90, 91, 97, 103–5, 112, 113, 115–18, 120, 122, 134, 135, 139, 140, 145; Herederos de la Vda. Pla, Barcelona, for fig. 21; Messrs. Paul Popper Ltd., for fig. 138; Sobrino de L. Roisin, Barcelona, for figs. 4, 29; Sr. Truyol, Palma, for fig. 95; O. Wunderlich, Madrid, for figs. 1, 56.

Editorial Espasa-Calpe, Madrid, for figs. 50, 81, 93, 108, 109, 129, 148 (from V. Lampérez: *Historia de la Arquitectura Cristiana Española*, 1930); and for figs. 102, 106 (from E. Tormo: *Guía Regional Levante*, 1923); Editorial Plus Ultra, Madrid, for figs. 10, 33, 82, 89, 98, 101 (from *Ars Hispaniae*, V, 1948; VII, 1952). Figs. 13, 46, 47, 59–61, 83–7, 94, 99, 100, 110, 114, 125–7, 142, 143, 147 are from G. Dehio and G. v. Bezold: *Die kirchliche Baukunst des Abendlandes*, 1901; figs. 51, 141, 149 from O. Schubert: *Geschichte des Baroks in Spanien*, 1908; figs. 52 (after a plan in E. Lambert: *L'Art gothique en Espagne*, 1931), 78, 107, 124, 129 and 130 (after a plan in V. Lampérez: *op. cit.*) are from line-drawings by the Author; figs. 36, 76 are from photographs in the Author's collection.

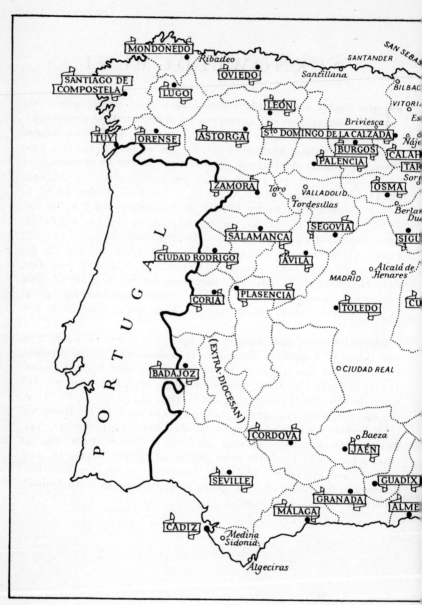

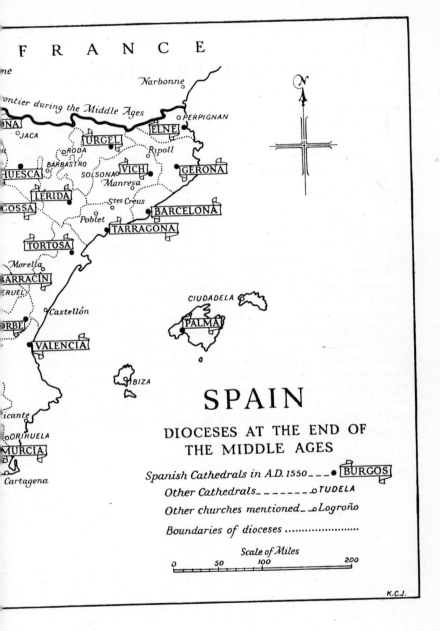

FRANCE

Narbonne

frontier during the Middle Ages

O PERPIGNAN

NA
ºJACA

URGEL
ELNE

ºRODA
Ripoll

BARBASTRO
SOLSONAº
VICH
GERONA

HUESCA
Manresa

LÉRIDA
Stes Creus

GOSSA
Poblet
BARCELONA

TARRAGONA

TORTOSA

Morella

ARRACÍN
ERUEL

ºCastellón

CIUDADELA

RBE
PALMA

VALENCIA

IBIZA

icante
ºORIHUELA

MURCIA

Cartagena

SPAIN

DIOCESES AT THE END OF
THE MIDDLE AGES

Spanish Cathedrals in A.D. 1550 ___ • BURGOS

Other Cathedrals _____ ºTUDELA

Other churches mentioned __ ºLogroño

Boundaries of dioceses ....

Scale of Miles

0   50   100   200

K.C.J.

15

THE ILLUSTRATIONS

THE half-tone plates have been chosen from mostly recent photographs to cover as far as possible the aesthetic aspect of Spanish cathedral architecture, placing some emphasis on the less well-known cathedrals; a number have been specially taken for this book by Mr. A. F. Kersting. Further illustrations will be found in S. Sitwell: *Spain* (1950); B. Bevan: *History of Spanish Architecture* (1938); and in the volumes of *Ars Hispaniae* (see Bibliographical Note, p. 265).

The map (pp. 14, 15), specially drawn by Mr. K. C. Jordan, shows all places of importance mentioned in the text and the mediaeval dioceses into which Spain was divided. The plans are on a uniform scale of 1:2000 (20 metres to 1 cm.; 500 feet to 3 inches); plans of all the English cathedrals to this scale will be found in Sir Banister Fletcher's *History of Architecture*, and of many Gothic buildings in J. H. Harvey's *Gothic World* (1950). In a few cases (Astorga, Coria, Osma, Oviedo, Plasencia and Valencia) published plans have been corrected from personal observation, and it is believed that these are the most adequate plans of these cathedrals yet published. The sections are on a uniform scale of 1:800 (8 metres to 1 cm.; 200 feet to 3 inches), as in *The Gothic World*. The best collection of plans and sections of Spanish churches is that by Lampérez (see p. 266), while plans and some photographs appear in the official catalogue *Monumentos Españoles*. In the sketch of the central tower of Cuenca (fig. 124) later blocking has been omitted from the windows, the better to show the original design.

LIST OF ILLUSTRATIONS

The numerals in parentheses in the text refer to the *figure numbers* of the illustrations

LIST OF ILLUSTRATIONS

LIST OF ILLUSTRATIONS

LIST OF ILLUSTRATIONS

GLOSSARY

THIS short glossary is intended to cover only the technical meanings of words occurring in the text; for English architectural words reference should be made to one of the standard works such as T. D. Atkinson: *A Glossary of Terms used in English Architecture* (6th ed., 1946).

Aparejador. Assistant to the mediaeval *Maestro Mayor* (*q.v.*) and in his absence responsible for the conduct of building works; nowadays a clerk-of-works or site architect.

Artesonado. Timber panelled ceiling shaped like an inverted trough (*artesón*); often in Moorish style.

Atrio. Porch, vestibule.

Capilla Mayor. Sanctuary containing the high altar, presbytery.

Churrigueresque. Name given (from José Churriguera, 1650–1723) to the extreme Baroque style in Spain, flourishing *c*. 1660–1760.

Cimborio. Lantern, usually octagonal and placed over the crossing.

Colegiata. A collegiate church.

Coro. Choir, in Spain usually screened off with walls in two or more bays of the nave, and closed on the west with *Trascoro*.

Isabelline. Name given to the florid Gothic style current in Spain under Isabel I the Catholic (1479–1504).

Maestro Mayor. Chief master mason, architect.

Meseta. Plateau or tableland, especially that of Castile.

Mezquita. Mosque, especially the Great Mosque, now Cathedral, at Cordova.

Mozárabe. Spanish Christian under Moslem rule; style of arabised art employed by such; the religious use surviving from Visigothic times and still employed, e.g. in the Capilla Mozárabe of Toledo Cathedral.

Mudéjar. Spanish Moslem under Christian rule; style of art produced by such, especially in Aragon.

Plateresque. Name (literally meaning like silversmith's work) given to the latest filigree Gothic and earliest Renaissance art of Spain, especially to those buildings of the early sixteenth century where the two styles are mixed.

Puerta. Door, gate.

Reja. Wrought-iron screen, as of *Coro*, *Capilla Mayor* or other chapels; generally of larger scale than a *verja* (*q.v.*).

Retablo. Altarpiece, reredos, retable.

Retablo Mayor. Altarpiece or reredos of the high altar.

Sagrario. Sacristy, room where the holy vessels are kept; but in Spain often distinct from the *Sacristía*. Both rooms usually contain important furniture, paintings and treasures.

Transparente. Architectural feature in which a sculptured altarpiece is lit theatrically by a window cut through the vault above, as in the most famous example in Toledo Cathedral.

Trascoro. Screen or wall closing the west side of the *coro*, sometimes solid, sometimes pierced with one or two doorways, as in the English *pulpitum*.

Verja. Wrought-iron railing round a tomb or the like; usually of smaller scale than a *reja* (*q.v.*).

Introduction

IN Spain as elsewhere in western Europe, the organisation of the Christian churches followed the lines laid down by existing local government. The Roman Empire was divided into provinces, and it was a matter of convenience that the Church should be divided likewise, with the result that to the present day the term "province" is applied to the area governed by an archbishop or metropolitan. Under Roman rule the whole of the Peninsula was shared between three provinces of very unequal size: Baetica in the south, roughly corresponding to Andalusia; Lusitania in the south-west, taking in Portugal south of the Douro as well as Extremadura in western Spain; and Tarraconensis covering all the rest. During the third century the provinces were re-arranged by Caracalla and Diocletian. The north-west, including modern Galicia, northern Portugal, Asturias and part of Leon, formed the new province of Gallaecia; a great region covering most of central Spain and the Mediterranean coast from Almeria to Valencia became Carthaginensis, taking its name from Cartago (Cartagena); while the unwieldy province of Tarraconensis was reduced to the basin of the River Ebro and the mountainous area of the eastern half of the Cantabrian coast. The Germanic peoples from North, who in the fifth century overran the Roman Empire, were eager to use as much of the existing organisation as they could, and in Spain these old provinces continued as the basis of administration.

The capital of each province naturally became the seat of the archbishop: for Baetica, Hispalis (Seville); for Lusitania, Emerita Augusta (Mérida); for Tarraconensis, Tarraco (Tarragona), whence it took its name. The capital of Gallaecia was placed at Lucus (Lugo), while that of the remaining province was the chief city of the whole West Gothic (Visigothic) kingdom, Toletum (Toledo). At each of these cities a principal church was built, or already existed, where the metropolitan archbishop of the province had his seat, or see. Each province comprised a number of smaller units of local administration, and the chief town of each naturally became the site of a church ruled by a bishop, subordinate to the metropolitan of the province. These lesser churches also, from containing the throne (*cathedra*) of a bishop, were known as cathedrals, and the area controlled from each was its diocese.

So far, the history of the Church in Spain had run parallel to that in the other western provinces of the Roman Empire. But early in the eighth century the Peninsula was attacked by the new power of Islam. The Moslems had already conquered North Africa and reached the Straits of Gibraltar, from beyond which they received reports of a land of extraordinary riches and fertility. Their spies reported the tottering state of the Visigothic kingdom, weakened by internecine feuds. King Witiza (697–710) died most opportunely, perhaps murdered at the instigation of his rival Roderick, who was able to secure the throne by a rigged election. Witiza's family and supporters took refuge at Ceuta across the Straits, the last African town in Christian hands, and under the governorship of one Julian, who remained loyal to Witiza's interests. His loyalty was not matched by an adequate grasp of the situation, for he proceeded to organise an invasion of Spain by Moslem troops, intended to secure the restoration of Witiza's heirs. As he might have expected, the success of the invasion placed the whole country at the mercy of the conquering Berber general Tarik. Within three years the Arabs were in control of the Peninsula south of the Cantabrian Mountains and the Pyrenees, and soon afterwards great armies were striking terror into southern and central France.

Had the Moslems possessed a determined high command, they might at that moment have been able to take control of the whole of Christian Europe. That they did not do so was due in part to a natural decrease in impetus, but also to the immensely attractive field for settlement offered by the new country. Notwithstanding their theoretical commitment to spread the gospel of Mohammed by the sword, the conquerors made no attempt at forcible conversions; on the contrary, by fixing a moderate poll-tax to be paid by Christians, they provided themselves with a vested interest in refraining from missionary activity. The slaves and the underprivileged benefited enormously by the change, as did the Jews, who had been suffering an embittered persecution. Nor can it be said that the Visigothic aristocracy suffered greatly, for the family of Witiza and many other nobles received enormous fiefs and retained a degree of power which for several generations almost amounted to independence.

3 CORDOVA: the Capilla de Villaviciosa of 961–69, showing the ribbed vault; transformed into the Capilla Mayor of the first cathedral

4　JAÉN: the west front of 1667–88, by Eufrasio López de Rojas

5　LA SEO DE URGEL: the west front of *c.* 1175

THE WIDE FRONT: EARLY AND LATE

In general, the Christians were allowed to retain their churches, and continued to form a majority of the population. Within a short time they were speaking Arabic as their second language, and many even became Moslems of their own free will. From the eighth century to the eleventh, Moslem Spain was for much of the time the freest, as it was by far the most highly cultured, country in western Europe. It was destroyed by its lack of unity: paradoxically enough, not by the division into Moslems and Christians, but by the inextinguishable tribal and national hatreds of the various Moslem peoples who should have formed the governing class. Occasionally power would be seized by a Moslem fanatic, whose persecution resulted in the flight of loyal Christians northwards, but it was not until much later that the Church in southern Spain disintegrated under a systematically anti-Christian policy. Meanwhile there had grown up a great nation of Christians who accepted Moslem rule and used Arabic as well as debased Latin, whose art and cultural life had become preponderantly Arabic. These were the Mozárabes (*mustarib*, arabised), who were to give their name to a remarkable style of art, in which elements of Roman and Visigothic origin were dominated by Saracenic pattern.

Like the Romans and the Visigoths before them, the Moors never really conquered Spain. From remote antiquity the natives of the Peninsula have possessed an indomitable tenacity that, whatever the temporary circumstances, will not permit them to confess ultimate defeat. The hard core of tribes that refused to admit the supremacy of Rome had long been settled in the mountains of the North, whence they had set the Visigoths at defiance for three hundred years before the coming of the Moslems. These northern mountaineers, who had already been converted from paganism to Christianity but retained their own language (Basque), were now joined by those Visigothic nobles and other refugees from southern Spain who would not accept Arab rule. Between the Cantabrian ranges and the sea and along the line of the Pyrenees there came into existence a tenuous buffer-state, or rather series of principalities, dividing Carolingian France from the Moslem amirate and later caliphate of Cordova. These little principalities, inspired by a fierce love of independence, had no more love for the French than for the Moors, and it was the Basques who inflicted on Charlemagne's rearguard the defeat of Roncesvalles which lives on in song and legend.

The arrival of Visigothic princes among these primitive mountaineers provided the leadership needed to form a politically effective community. And from that time forward, that is to say from the middle of the eighth century, the history of Spain has been the story of the fortunes of this small nucleus of leadership, reinforced as time went on, and its ultimate extension of rule over the whole of the Peninsula. An understanding of the course of this process, the Reconquest, is necessary for the appreciation of the Spanish character and also to the comprehension of the complex web of Spanish art.

In the first rush of Arab conquest organised resistance collapsed and the usurping king Roderick lost his life. Many courtiers remained to make their peace or were supporters of the party of Witiza, still nominally on the side of the invaders. But a smaller number of the nobility retreated northwards behind the Cantabrian range. The Moors, to give them the name by which they have since been known, burst through the passes in pursuit and spread over the coastal plain of Asturias. But Asturias is difficult country, where all the advantage lies with the native who knows the terrain. To one narrow and hardly accessible valley came a little band of Christian warriors under the leadership of the Visigothic prince Pelagius, or Pelayo. Said to have been only 300 strong, they made their headquarters in a large cave, later famous as Covadonga.

The Moors detached a force of considerable size to deal with Pelayo's band, but thanks to the awkward approaches to the Cave and, so it was believed, to the direct intervention of the Virgin, were utterly routed. Pelayo was proclaimed King by his followers and advancing down the valley took an oath to restore the Christian monarchy of Spain. Dim and legendary as are the details of these events, it is certain that about the year 718 the Moorish advance was checked, and the Moslems retreated south of the mountain range. The Christian future of Asturias was assured, and therewith the possibility of the future reconquest.

By the end of the eighth century, at the height of Charlemagne's power, Christian Spain had become consolidated into a narrow strip extending from Galicia continuously to the Mediterranean, some five hundred miles. But the breadth was nowhere more than about seventy-five miles, in places twenty miles or less. Although geographically continuous, the Christian territory possessed no through communications and neither a common government nor a single

7 BURGOS: the Nave of 1243–60, by Maestro Enrique

6 SALAMANCA: the Lantern of the Old Cathedral, c. 1180, by Dominico

9 TOLEDO: looking east from the Choir, 1226–

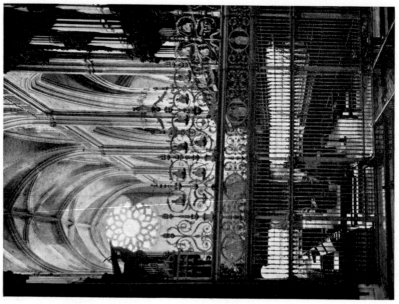

8 SEVILLE: looking west along the Nave of 1402–32,

language. At its centre was the country of the Basques, covering
modern Navarre and rather more than the three Basque provinces
of the present day, as well as a large area on the French side of the
Pyrenees. Though Christian and ready to fight for their independence, the Basques remained intensely suspicious of all their neighbours. To the east lay the Spanish March consisting of the southern
foothills of the Pyrenees, and nominally under the suzerainty of
Charlemagne's son, Louis the Debonair, who succeeded in expelling
the Moors from the rich lands of Catalonia and appointed a count
as his governor. It is to this early connection with the Carolingian
Empire that Catalonia owes its distinct outlook from that of the
rest of Spain. Whereas the years of adversity taught the northern
mountaineers the hard lesson of self-reliance, the Catalans looked
for assistance to the great neighbouring power of France. Besides,
the Mediterranean seaports of Spain had always been great centres of
trade, and Barcelona soon regained its old commercial importance.

Before the year 1000 the foundations had been laid of all the
mediaeval kingdoms of Spain. The Asturian kings had made their
capital at Oviedo, in 850 were able to recapture León, and early in
the tenth century fixed their court there. By that time their eastern
neighbours the Basques had come under the rule of a count whose
capital was Pamplona, and this county soon afterwards became the
kingdom of Navarre. Eastward again another Pyrenean realm, that
of Aragon, developed in the high valleys, while beyond this lay
the county of Barcelona, independent from 874 when Charles the
Bald gave it to Wilfred *el Velloso*, called "the Hairy" not from his
personal appearance but from the scrub-covered lands of the Spanish
March which he ruled.

Although all of these states took part in driving the Moors southwards, the main impetus was from Asturias. After taking León the
Asturian kings established firm rule over the whole country to the
north of the Duero, including Galicia and what is now northern
Portugal. Late in the tenth century they were able to press forward
again, and before the end of the eleventh had reached the crest of
the Guadarrama range. At the same time the Moors were still in
possession of eastern Spain up to within twenty or twenty-five miles
of France. The short-lived occupation of Valencia from 1096 to
1102 was due to the Cid, Ruy Díaz de Vivar, an exiled nobleman
from Burgos, and it was not for more than another century that
the forces of Aragon and Catalonia, joined by the marriage of their

rulers in 1137, finally drove southwards and pushed their common frontier with Castile as far as the sea.

It is unnecessary here to recount the dynastic history of the mediaeval Peninsula. All that is relevant to the architecture of the period is that the country became divided into several independent states with frontiers more or less settled until the end of the Middle Ages, and that within each of these states the arts developed with relatively slight interchanges. The old Asturian-Leonese kingdom was absorbed by Castile, its former offshoot, but at the end of the eleventh century lost Portugal. Eastern Spain formed the kingdom of Aragon, smaller than Castile, but with immensely valuable sea trade and interests in Italy and throughout the Mediterranean, which were to have a profound effect upon the Aragonese-Catalonian styles of painting and sculpture. Between Castile and Aragon lay Navarre, a region with an intense architectural individuality due in part to its Basque popular traditions and much more to the close links of its dynasty with France.

The founding or refounding of cathedrals everywhere followed the political reconquest, and successive campaigns are to some extent reflected in the dates of the churches which now survive, though subsequent rebuilding and the later founding of new sees have complicated the picture. Disregarding the fragmentary remains of archaic periods, the Spanish cathedrals belong for the most part to four main phases: the Romanesque, built before the great southward expansion of the late eleventh century; the Transitional, founded or rebuilt as a result of that campaign; the High Gothic, outcome of settled conditions after the Moors had been pressed back to the far South; and the Late, partly in Gothic and partly in Renaissance style, built after the unification of Castile and Aragon and the expulsion of the Moors from Granada. Few indeed are the major works begun after 1600, other than additions of fronts or towers to existing churches.

While the strict definition of a cathedral is a matter of simple fact, it is not easy to apply this definition in an historical study. At the present time the actual cathedrals of Spain include a number which were not built for the purpose and have only within the last few years achieved that status. On the other hand several very important cathedrals, architecturally speaking, are no longer bishops' sees. Furthermore, to a proper understanding of the development of the architectural form of the cathedrals designed for the purpose it is necessary to have some acquaintance with other great churches, particularly those of monasteries, which were neither intended to be cathedrals nor have ever become such. And here it must be remarked that the cathedrals of Spain, unlike those of England, have always been secular, that is to say served by canons and not by monks of a regular order. On the other hand, the Spanish chapters provided for their life as a community by the erection of cloisters, chapter-houses and other subsidiary buildings, which often give much the impression of a monastery to the group of constructions. At this stage it may be convenient to summarise the outstanding characteristics of Spanish cathedrals, in which they differ markedly from those elsewhere.

On approaching a Spanish cathedral, the impression received is almost invariably that of a cubical block, or more often, of a series of cubical blocks closely piled together. To some extent this results from the Spanish habit of adding chapels, sacristies and other buildings around a church until its own outlines are smothered in the irregular mass. This again means that Spanish cathedrals can seldom be fully appreciated as works of art from without. Apart from the building of richly carved fronts and noble towers and lanterns, there is indeed little sign that Spanish architects were much concerned with the outside view of their work. This is, after all, a natural result of designing for a set of conditions where all the main importance, and that a transcendental one, is given to the interior.

Yet the cubical impression of Spanish cathedrals, and for that matter of all Spanish churches, is not merely the outcome of accident. The earliest buildings, it is true, show the least tendency in this direction, while it is most pronounced in work of the sixteenth and seventeenth centuries. But this is due to the steady emergence of what may be called a national style: a true Spanish architectural aesthetic. The early cathedrals were based closely upon foreign models and built by masters fetched from Lombardy, from Languedoc, from Aquitaine, from the Ile-de-France. In most cases even these early works show signs of being affected by the local atmosphere, and are not pure specimens of the foreign style they represent. As time went on, the Peninsular characteristics became more and more pronounced, reaching their complete enunciation in the great new cathedrals designed after the unification of Spain at the end of the fifteenth century.

In these late cathedrals can best be seen another of the essential Spanish characteristics: emphasis on area. Whereas in England the greater churches impress by their sheer length, and in France by sheer height, it is the amount of ground covered that is striking in Spain. Not only is this a matter of actual fact, but it is heightened by special characteristics of Spanish church architecture which have the effect of devices giving the appearance of yet more space stretching out in all directions. Everywhere are screens, the wrought-iron *rejas* which form so notable an art of their own, and the carved image-walls of stone and marble which surround the choir and sanctuary. The later addition of still more chapels and dependencies tends even to exaggerate this effect, which is most notable when coupled with the wealth of displayed pictures and other works of art. By the eighteenth century, designers were even using the trick of the *Transparente* to produce the illusion of a further vision beyond the limits of the material plane, an interpenetration of the earthly cathedral by the heavenly city, a concentus of the terrestrial and celestial choirs.

In employing such theatrical tricks of the Baroque, Spanish architects were influenced by the precedents set by Bernini and other Italians, but even more by the profound impress left on Spain by the painting of El Greco. Again, it may be said, a foreign influence through a Byzantine Greek trained in Italy; but it is precisely in this aspect of his art that El Greco is most akin and conformable to the Spanish soul. Spanish tomb-sculptures from as far back as the thirteenth century show tendencies in the same direction. What was always and everywhere a matter of dogma to the mediaeval Christian, became in Spain a living reality to the mystics and a factual rather than an imaginative truth to the ordinary layman. This is another facet of that hard, ironic common sense found in the multitude of Spanish proverbs, a profound realism moved to the acceptance of hidden truths by their presentation in tangible form. Spain alone has preserved from the Middle Ages the full panoply of religious fraternities devoted to the production of the Drama of the Passion, the processional exhibition of lifelike (or deathlike) carvings, the dressing and coiffure of sacred images. Spain reveres most the bodily Resurrection of her Lord at Easter, His triumph through the streets on the Feast of Corpus, His Blessed Mother full of power even to subvert the force of gravity.

This aspect of the Spanish outlook is best seen, historically, in the extraordinarily realistic quality of Spain's sculpture from the twelfth century onwards. The realism is distinguished from that of Germany, which in some ways it resembles, by a lack of the tendency to exaggeration and over-emphasis, particularly in the direction of sentimentality, to which Germanic art is prone. A Spanish carving, and for that matter a Spanish painting, are portrayals of an objective reality even when they are most imaginative. It is this capacity to accept life as it is, so disconcerting to the stranger taught to consider Spain a land of fantasy, that sets the keynote of all Spanish achievement from the Stoicism of Seneca and Marcus Aurelius down to the unconventional train* invented by Colonel Goicoechea.

Some have seen in Cervantes's romance of *Don Quixote* an allegory of the two types of Spaniard: the fantastic aristocrat imbued with chimerical notions, and the sturdy peasant facing hardships with an ironic scepticism and a sly jest. But the lives of the Spanish saints, and of most outstanding Spaniards of all classes and periods, show that these apparently opposed qualities reside in the same person. The Spaniard is at one and the same time Quixote and Sancho; stranger still, he is Castilian and Catalan, Andaluz and Gallego, a mass of paradoxical antipathies which add up to a single human being; much more human, be it said, than those who live by the rule of an arbitrary consistency.

Within the Spanish cathedral the most noticeable outcome of this paradoxical attitude is to be found in the *coro*, a separate structure blocking up the nave and destroying the unity of conception with which the building was endowed by its architects. Reminiscent of the schemes of the White Knight, as the White Knight himself is a reminiscence of the ingenious hidalgo of La Mancha, this conflicting duality of outer and inner shells is the answer to a practical problem. Street rightly assumed that the independent *coro* had not been an original feature of the greater Spanish churches, but had been introduced during the course of the Middle Ages. But it was the result of an insistence upon the maximum of dignity and comfort combined in the conduct of the choir services for which such churches were built. They were not intended primarily for the attendance of a lay congregation, nor for the aesthetic satisfaction of the sightseer, but for the due performance at stated hours of a precise ritual.

* The Talgo.

35

Elsewhere it was found possible to keep the Service of the Choir linked to the Sacrifice of the Altar by the provision of lengthy presbyteries, where the whole of the main aisle of the church to the east of the transept was given over to the dual purposes. But in Spain the sanctuary was never extended in this way, and the reason must be that it was felt unfitting that its transcending importance should be shared by any lesser function. The places for canons and choir had therefore to be elsewhere, yet in a position where suitably dignified access to the altar could be had. This access was secured by linking *coro* and *capilla mayor* by a passageway of screens, sometimes at the full width of the central aisle, more often only of the width actually needed for the procession.

A further example of paradox in the arrangement of Spanish cathedrals is the provision of a *cimborio* or central lantern, normally placed above or just in front of the *capilla mayor* and where it will let a flood of light down upon the altar, and the small windows and resulting gloom of most Peninsular churches. In a country where, during a part of the year at least, the heat and light of the sun can be almost unbearable, this darkness is perhaps a physical necessity, but it takes on a symbolic aspect when it is made evident by the contraposition of the central stream of light from above.

While the interior of some Spanish cathedrals, notably Barcelona, is but darkness made visible, the rule is not quite universal in its application. The great cathedrals of the latest Gothic, Segovia and Salamanca, are adequately lit, and the transplanted French church at León preserved the ample windows of its country of origin. For this reason, and because of the consequent emphasis laid upon the exquisite stained glass which those windows contain, León cannot be regarded as typically Spanish. In plan, section and detail it bears the stamp of France, although rather the France under the rule of the King of England than the Parisian realm. But León is important largely for its extraordinary survival: alone among the greater thirteenth-century churches of the fully developed Gothic of Europe, León has kept practically the whole of its amazing windows. Nowhere else is it possible to appreciate to the full the glory of the High Middle Ages, when the dim, religious light of the semi-Romanesque Chartres had been left behind, and the almost secular brilliance of King's College Chapel was yet to come. And notwithstanding, or possibly because of, this foreign idiom, it was to León Cathedral that the mediaeval proverb awarded the palm of beauty:

Sancta Ovetensis, Dives Toletana, Pulchra Leonina, Fortis Salamanca;
Oviedo the holy, Toledo the rich, León the lovely, strong Salamanca.

Judged purely by their plans, Spanish cathedrals would appear far
more French than they in fact are. The sanctuary of three parallel
apses is found in the churches of the earliest Romanesque period
(eleventh century), to be replaced by the apsidal plan with an
ambulatory and radiating chapels. Little distinguishes early examples
from their prototypes in France except their smaller dimensions
and a tendency to lengthen the transepts beyond the customary
French proportions. But alongside the French plans there was a
survival of the much earlier square sanctuary, both in Castilian and
Catalan Spain. The very wide distribution of the square sanctuary
over the whole of northern Europe deserves a much closer study than
it has yet received. It has been customary to attribute its spread
largely to Cistercian influence, but this is manifestly disproved by
the pre-Cistercian date of the many smaller churches in which it
occurs in Celtic Britain, in Scandinavia and the Baltic, and scattered across northern Spain from Galicia to Catalonia. The greatest
concentration is in Asturias, where the type was normal in the
pre-Romanesque period, but other groups occur in southern
Galicia, in the south-eastern parts of the old kingdom of Leon and,
far off, in eastern Catalonia.

There seems little doubt that the square sanctuary of these early
churches is a feature taken over from the cella of the pagan temple.
In a number of instances in northern Europe excavation of the sites
of early churches has revealed that beneath them exists the foundation of a pre-Christian sanctuary. This simply bears out the documentary evidence that many of the missionaries found it expedient
to utilise the old temples as churches in order to preserve a continuity of religious experience among their flock. But whereas in
England the adherence to the square sanctuary became coupled with
the tradition of an eastern window looking towards the morning
sun, the Spanish counterparts are generally blind, and in the early
examples small and dark. Another contrast concerns orientation:
England perhaps paid greater attention to correct orientation than
any other country; Spain probably less. Spanish churches and chapels
may face in any direction, and the orientation of subsidiary altars
seems to have been regarded as quite immaterial. This disregard
had its effect in increasing the complexity of Spanish plans, which

are seldom submitted to the restraint of symmetry or regular pattern.

It was customary in Spain to provide structural chapels for a very large number of subsidiary altars, and these were in some cases an integral part of the original plan. This was more especially the case in Catalonia, where the outer walls were placed in line with the outer ends of the buttresses, thus forming a series of cellular chapels spatially linked to the interior. This resulted in a most economical disposition of materials, taking advantage of the necessary buttresses instead of leaving them a functional excrescence. Though Catalan in origin, this spreading of the internal space between the interstices of the buttresses, as it were, and its bounding by an unbroken ring of outer walls were to become a part of all later Spanish planning, a contributory factor to the solid and cubical appearance of the Spanish church.

Owing to the political disunity of mediaeval Spain, and even more to the repeated introduction of foreign motives and foreign masters, no main line of historical development can be traced through the successive phases of Romanesque and Gothic architecture. All that can be discerned is a steady and growing tendency towards assimilation, in which foreign introductions become naturalised and regional differences grow less. Even as late as the eighteenth century, however, there was marked regionalism in style, notably in Galicia. Because of this lack of cohesion in the subject it is impossible to consider the cathedrals of Spain as presenting a single aesthetic problem, or to summarise their growth as a whole. All that can be done is to enumerate, chronologically, what remains and then to follow out in detail the descent of style within the separate component regions.

Nothing remains of an architectural character of cathedrals earlier than the eleventh century, apart from the fragmentary crypt of Palencia begun in 673, and the much rebuilt Cámara Santa at Oviedo, dating from about 802. Foundations have been discovered which have been attributed to the Visigothic cathedrals of Egara, beneath Santa María at Tarrasa, and of Setabis, beneath the church of San Félix at Játiva, as well as to the early cathedral of León founded in 916. The latter was not a new building, however, being formed from the old royal palace, which had itself employed a substantial part of the Roman thermae of the city of Legio.

The oldest Spanish cathedrals above ground are those of Roda de Isábena (1063–67) and Jaca (1054–1150), both in the modern province of Huesca; and the earliest parts of Santiago de Compostela, where work started in 1075. All of these, and the plan of the second cathedral of León (1065–73), belong to the period of great Romanesque expansion during the leadership of Cluniac monasticism and are contemporary with the first Norman churches in England such as Edward the Confessor's Westminster Abbey (1049–65), Hereford Cathedral (1079–1145) or St. Albans (1077–1115). Other Spanish churches of the same character which still survive are San Isidoro in León (1063–1149) and

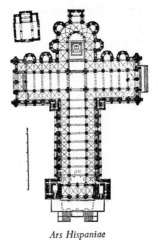

Ars Hispaniae

10 Santiago, 1075–1128, by Bernardo

the monastery of San Salvador de Leyre (1090–98), while the abbey church of Ripoll (1020–32) is somewhat earlier, as is the former cathedral of Elne (1042–68), now on French soil (*82*).

Roda and Jaca are both small churches with three parallel eastern apses immediately beyond the crossing, while Ripoll belongs essentially to the same type, though its seven apses in a range produce a long transept of tau-plan. Roda and Ripoll are both, in their architectural style, conservative works of an archaic type; Jaca, placed on one of the great pilgrimage roads from France to Compostela, shows signs of a newer, lighter touch. But it is at Santiago de Compostela that the full force of the Cluniac artistic movement was first felt in Spain. Here the plan (*10*) itself is modelled upon the recent monastic churches of France, and the whole conception radically different from anything previously known to the south of the Pyrenees. The plan is a Latin cross with a long nave of eleven bays, transepts of six bays each, and an eastern arm comprising three bays and an apse surrounded by an ambulatory. Off transepts and ambulatory open apsidal chapels, as in the French exemplars of this type, such as Sainte-Foy at Conques begun before 1065. The piers are relatively slender and built of accurately dressed and carefully laid blocks. The sanctuary of Santiago represents in fact the first great building enterprise in Spain of the renascent Middle

Ages, emerging from the chaotic conditions which had succeeded to the power of old Rome.

For many years controversy raged over the nationality of the plan and design of the cathedral at Compostela. Its obvious French affiliations and extremely close similarity to St. Sernin, Toulouse, at first suggested to French archaeologists that the Spanish church was virtually an exported copy. This hypothesis, strongly resisted by many Spanish antiquaries, had to be abandoned when it was proved that, while St. Sernin had not started before 1080, Santiago was begun by 1075 and its foundations marked out earlier, possibly in 1071. On the other hand, no antecedent school of work existed in Spain, while there are ample and immediate architectural ancestors of the design in France. There can be no doubt that Santiago and St. Sernin both stem from the same French sources, but the Spanish cathedral is distinctly the finer and more accomplished work notwithstanding its earlier date. This provides an interesting parallel to a proportion of the contemporary Norman buildings of England, both larger and stylistically more advanced than those south of the Channel. The masters evidently found a great opportunity in the "colonial" opening up of Spain and England, and at important shrines took advantage of the very large funds available to build in the best manner and on an immense scale.

At Santiago we are told that the "wonderful master" (*mirabilis magister*) of the work and the chief stonemason bore the names of Bernard and Robert respectively: names at that date typically French. Bernard is described as "the Old", probably to distinguish him from the canon Bernardo Gutiérrez who a little later had administrative control of the building organisation. Since the Codex Calixtinus, our authority for the conduct of operations, also specifies the abbot and treasurer as composing the administrative committee in charge, there is no question that both Bernard and Robert were the actual architects or else that Bernard was sole architect and Robert the head of the working masons. Bernard's age suggests that he was already well known for his architectural work, and it may be that there is here a clue to the authorship of those great churches of central France built in the same style a little before the start of work at Compostela.

It is fitting that there should be so detailed a record, from an almost contemporary source, of the organisation which produced the first of the great cathedrals of mediaeval Spain. We are left in

no doubt that the designers and builders were individual persons
with names worthy of record, and that they were distinct from the
clerics who had charge of the funds and controlled the administration of the works. At the cathedral of Santiago, in some ways the
most important surviving monument of the High Romanesque,
built at the threshold of the Gothic Age, there is already no notion
of anonymity, of a stupendous work being exuded like coral or the
wax cells of the honey-bee from the spontaneous exertions of a
multitude in the throes of a deep religious experience. Nor is there
any suggestion that the responsible builders were monks or even
secular priests. Responsibility for the architectural character of the
building is plainly given to Bernard, "the marvellous master" able
to design something hitherto undreamed of in Christian Spain.

At this point it may be as well to summarise the normal methods
of conducting large-scale building works in the Middle Ages, which
are applicable to Spain as much as to France, Germany, Flanders or
England. The king, bishop, abbot or other patron or client of the
works would usually appoint one or more officials to take financial
and administrative charge, assigning to them specific sums of money,
the rents of certain properties, or the authorisation to invite sub-
scriptions. Either the patron or the administrator, or administrative
committee where such existed, would then choose their architect:
normally a master mason of repute who was not merely skilled in the
cutting and laying of stone but also in the geometry of design
according to the canons of proportion laid down by his traditional
code. These codes of aesthetic practice differed from one country
to another, and to a less extent in different regions of the same
country. Essentially similar to the codes of proportion which
governed the classical orders of architecture, these mediaeval
codes went further in that they succeeded to an increasing extent
in relating the proportions of all buildings, however widely they
might differ in size, to the constant actual scale of the human body.
We can form some idea of the geometrical methods involved by
study of the early thirteenth-century diagrams of Villard de Honne-
court, master of the church of St. Quentin, of the account which
has come down of the disputes between Italian, French and German
masters as to the proper proportions for Milan Cathedral, of several
German treatises of the late Gothic period, and of the manual of
planning and design prepared from older sources by the Spaniard

Simón García in 1681. This last source, avowedly taken for the most part from a book which had belonged to Rodrigo Gil de Hontañón (died 1577), one of the last great Gothic architects of Spain and descendant of a family of distinguished master masons, discloses the whole of the setting-out employed to produce plan and section of the several main types of Spanish church: with one, three or five aisles.

The master responsible for design was in earlier times often in sole charge of a single work, but in the course of the Gothic period there is increasing evidence of the specialisation of certain masters in design. This placed them in much the position of the modern architect responsible for the design and general supervision of a number of works at once. Since there had to be someone with adequate technical knowledge in charge on the site, this led to the appearance of the warden, the master's deputy, of considerably higher standing than a builder's foreman, and corresponding more closely to a modern site architect or clerk of works. The warden was called *apparellator* in mediaeval Latin, *appareilleur* in French and in Spanish *aparejador*, the term still in use today. For Spain has preserved the mediaeval system of control, and the *aparejador* in the twentieth century is a person of some consequence, whose name appears after that of the architect and before that of the contractor in all architectural publicity.

The modern contract system developed during the course of the Middle Ages. At first it was usual for work to be carried out by direct labour, the administrative chief buying materials and hiring craftsmen and labourers at the charges of the building fund. The actual appointment of suitable craftsmen and their discharge if found unsuitable was naturally delegated to the master or his warden, who possessed the necessary technical knowledge. Gradually the practice grew up of certain craftsmen with a shop or some capital of their own undertaking to carry out specified tasks for sums fixed in advance. So many feet of stone were to be dressed at a settled price, the craftsman who undertook the work paying his own overhead expenses and engaging his own assistants. From the craftsman's point of view the incentive was, of course, the middle-man's profit which he could derive from organising the transaction. But the method appealed to the client, because competition in prices for tasks tended towards lower costs; and to the administrator of the building fund, who thus solved the organisational problems involved in the supply of materials and labour for a big job.

In the early Middle Ages, up to the thirteenth century, the prevailing economy was one of subsistence; but later there was a rapid transition to a system based on money. Artists and master craftsmen commanding relatively high rates of pay were in a favourable position to amass capital, and so could undertake larger and larger contracts and engage in the supply of shop-made objects of art or what we should term prefabricated parts for buildings. By the later fourteenth century the building trade especially was organised on a basis that was in almost all essentials modern. The only major difference lay in the fact that mediaeval contractors were normally bound to their own trade: the mason to supplying masonry, the woodworker to the provision of carpentry or joinery. Thus, even when a whole building was made by contract, the work was not executed by a single contractor. Several separate agreements had to be made for the stone walls, for the timberwork, for tiling or lead roofing, for plastering or decoration.

Spanish records are exceptionally full of facts as to the methods used, and a large proportion of the most interesting documents relate to cathedrals. Many architects and other artists are named and there is abundant information as to the cost of works. They prove the extensive use of drawings, a few of which survive, and the fact that there was on occasion competition between architects as well as between contractors. For example, Tortosa Cathedral has preserved a dated plan of 1345 made by one Antonio Guasch and an elevation by Benito Basques, but the church was actually built to a different plan by Benito Dalguayre under a contract of 1346; the first stone was not laid until a year after the contract had been made. This gives a valuable clue to the lapse of time which would be likely to occur between the initiation of a given project and the actual beginning of works. Presumably anything up to one year would be taken up with the preliminary discussions and preparation of the plan and small-scale designs; another year might elapse before a contract had been entered into or materials and labour brought to the site; yet a third, or even more, might go by while the foundations were set out and dug, until the work was ready for the formal laying of the first stone on a date recorded by the local chroniclers. This lag of up to three years or more between design and construction is of importance in working out the development of style and in comparing the dates historically assigned to different buildings. The historians and chroniclers were usually concerned with notable public acts such as a ceremonial laying of foundation stones by royalty or clergy, and the consecration of a church for services. These dates may differ by several years or even widely from those of design and structural completion.

Something more may be said as to the methods by which the imaginative design in the mind of a given architect was, in the Middle Ages, translated into concrete form. The master mason, having produced a plan and, when required, other drawings or diagrams to satisfy his clients as to the general appearance of the work, had to interpret these small-scale drawings to the manual craftsmen. The foundations were marked out with lines on the ground, and the excavators set to dig out the trenches, while the masons in their banker or "lodge" hewed stones, both plain squared ashlar and moulded bases and capitals, rounded pieces for the shafts of columns and the rest. For the plain work, mere dimensions and a description of the style of tooling would be sufficient, but moulded, skew and circular work had to be set out to its full size. This was done either on a large board or table made for the purpose, on a boarded floor, or on a slab of plaster-of-Paris specially laid for the purpose. The actual curve of an arch or vault rib would be marked out with large "beam"-compasses or string, and templates cut for the guidance of the masons. Other templates, known as moulds, were cut by the master to show the intended cross-section of every moulding. These were generally made of thin wainscot boards, but sometimes of lead sheets, and in more modern times have been of zinc. It is because the moulds were cut by the master himself, or at least the mouldings drawn by him upon them, that the mouldings of a mediaeval building are its most revealing feature. They are not merely the evidence of date, but are comparable to the painter's brush-strokes as evidence of artistic personality.

In Spain, possibly more than elsewhere, it was customary to call into consultation a number of architects of reputation to advise upon an intended project or upon some major structural problem. This consultative committee or *junta* was not collectively responsible for design, though it might agree upon certain main features. In other cases, as in the famous discussion of the nave of Gerona

Cathedral in 1416, the masters were not all of one mind and the chapter which consulted them had to make its own decision as to which expert advice it would follow. In other cases arrangements were made for an architect to travel to inspect existing buildings in order to obtain the best ideas for his new design, as happened in 1414 when Pedro Balaguer was paid for his journey to see the towers and belfries of Lérida, Narbonne and elsewhere, in order that he might imitate from them the most elegant form for the crown of the campanile or Micalete of the cathedral at Valencia.

We have already seen that the surviving Spanish cathedrals of the eleventh century culminated in the introduction of Cluniac Romanesque from south central France at Santiago de Compostela. This was only one of many direct importations of foreign designs and masters from abroad. In the next century the cathedral at La Seo de Urgel (1131–82) was vaulted by Raimundo, a Lombard, and it is evident that Lombardy exerted a very great influence upon Catalan architecture as a whole at that date. Further influences from France were entering all parts of northern Spain and followed the flag of the Reconquest southward. Notable works of late Romanesque and Transitional character were produced everywhere, and in many cases survive.

In Castile are Sigüenza (1156–69), Zamora (1151–74), the old cathedral of Salamanca (1152–c. 1200); the eastern arms of Ávila (1157–68), Ciudad Rodrigo (1166–88), Santo Domingo de la Calzada (1168–80), and Cuenca (1197–1208); and the crypt of Santander (c. 1217–19). To the west Galicia was building Lugo (1129–77), Orense (1132–94), Tuy (1145–1225) and the marvellous Pórtico de la Gloria of Maestro Mateo at Compostela (1168–88); while in Navarre the beautiful collegiate church of Tudela was begun (1194–1204). Eastern Spain had seen work on La Seo at Saragossa, of which small fragments remain (1119 onwards), Tarazona (1152–1235), Solsona (1161–63) and Tarragona (1171–1230), as well as important cloisters at Gerona (1180–1210) and Vich (after 1150), followed by that of Tarragona (1200–50).

Various sources in different regions of France can be assigned to these works, Burgundian feeling being strong at Santiago and, through it, in the other Galician cathedrals; and a remarkable style derived from Perigord at Zamora and Salamanca, built with central lanterns based on the Katholikon dome of the church of the Holy

Sepulchre in Jerusalem finished by the French master Jourdain in
1149. But regional styles were becoming less easily distinguishable,
and it would seem that in many cases the imported masters brought
with them an eclectic style to some extent based on what they had
seen during their travels. Besides, not all the masters by any means
were Frenchmen. There seems good reason for claiming Maestro
Mateo of Compostela as a born Spaniard, and we know that the
Raimundo who designed Lugo was himself a Galician. On the other
hand, Fruchel, the architect of Ávila, was almost certainly French,
and there can be no doubt of the origin of Ricardo, designer of the
Cistercian convent of Las Huelgas at Burgos (1184–1230), in the
parts of France under English rule.*

The building of Las Huelgas marks a turning-point, the appearance of true Gothic as distinguished from the still heavy Transitional Romanesque. The new style was especially linked with the
arrival in Spain of the Cistercian Order, and the monastery church
of La Oliva (1164–98) already demonstrates much of the structure
of Gothic, though still coupled with the use of round arches and
very massive supports. The two great Catalan Cistercian abbeys of
royal foundation, those of Poblet (c. 1166–81) and Santes Creus
(1174 onwards), are similarly heavy. But with the new style of
Las Huelgas the supports become more refined, the mouldings
sharper, the shape of arches and vaults more aspiring. Its character
was still further developed, probably by Ricardo himself towards
the end of his life, in the earliest parts of Burgos Cathedral (1222–
30), of which little now remains that is not cloaked by later
additions.

The most complete and unspoilt Spanish cathedral of this period
is that of Salamanca (11), fortunately preserved beside the late
Gothic church which superseded it. Here we can see, unimpeded
by alterations and additions, the essential character of a great
church of the second half of the twelfth century. Still heavy in the
scale of its supports and appearing heavier still through the small
size of its windows, its pointed arches and ribbed vaults mark the
trend towards the lighter grace of a few years ahead. Its unusual tall
lantern, the famous "Torre del Gallo", lets in a flood of light before

---

* Ricardo, already architect of Las Huelgas before 1203 and still in charge in 1226,
was certainly designer of the Gothic church and chapter-house, for which a later
dating is now untenable. He may well also have produced the slightly earlier first work
at Cuenca Cathedral.

11   SALAMANCA: Old Cathedral. Looking east in the church of 1152–1200,
by Petro Petriz

12 TARRAGONA: the Sanctuary, begun 1171, and the transept of 1200–30, seen from the Choir; the stalls, begun 1478, by Francisco Gomar

the sanctuary, and now upon the fifteenth-century painted altarpiece which lines its walls. Not unlike in character is the little cathedral at Ciudad Rodrigo, but this has been much altered; it has none the less a distinctive vault treatment, evidencing a change of design during the course of the works. Originally meant for a Burgundian Church with barrel-vaulted nave and groin-vaulted aisles, the domical ribbed vaulting actually built over the whole church proves the arrival either of a master from Aquitaine, or of drawings of this new and beautiful type of vault.

In eastern Spain the finest representative of the age is Tarragona (12), though comparatively little of it was completed before 1200. Tarragona adheres, even more than the western cathedrals, to the solidity of Romanesque work, and the impression is heightened by its darkness and by the large expanse of blank wall intervening between the arcades and the clerestory. For in none of these churches is there a triforium gallery or range: the bay design of a single unit divided between arcade and clerestory had already been reached, because the stone roofs of the aisles could be laid on the vaults and no considerable height for the slope of an aisle roof of timber was required. At Tarragona, built in two phases, the bay had not been properly co-ordinated, but at Tudela in Navarre is a magnificent example of adroit handling, together with the appearance of clerestory windows which are definitely Gothic.

The achievement of truly Gothic detail in Spain came late, so that it was not until well into the thirteenth century that Spanish churches reached a stage of development comparable with that reached in France and England more than a generation earlier. In some districts, notably the highlands of Catalonia, local schools were even more conservative. The old cathedral of Lérida (96–7), built between 1203 and 1278, still retains the heavy proportions and immensely massive piers of Romanesque work, with round arched doors and windows, though its main arcades are pointed and its vaults typically Gothic.

In Galicia, too, churches remained old-fashioned, though in a different way. Compostela had set a precedent derived from the French galleried church, where the triforium was intended to take the overflow of enormous congregations of pilgrims. This scheme, unknown in the rest of Spain, was followed at Lugo and was intended at Tuy, where it was abandoned in favour of a blind triforium arcade beneath a clerestory. The triforium at Tuy produces a northern effect, while the plan with double-aisled transepts of three bays and square sanctuary (though this latter may not represent the original form) is reminiscent of the original scheme at Wells. It would seem likely that Tuy was affected by influence from the early Gothic of western France. At Mondoñedo, not begun until about 1219 and in Cistercian Gothic, the Galician gallery was still retained but without its rampant vaulting, which was reduced to a series of hidden flying buttresses beneath the roof.

I have left to the end of this discussion of the cathedrals of the twelfth century the unusual chevet of Ávila (*13*). It is singular for several reasons: as a great semicircular tower projecting beyond the line of the city wall; as a rare example of a double ambulatory in a church of three aisles and at so early a date; and as a precocious instance of Gothic slenderness in a building still largely of Transitional character. Begun about 1160 by Fruchel, an architect sent by King Alfonso VIII and probably French, the design is of a strange and awkward character, yet the slim shafts which encircle the apse, based upon the ambulatory of St. Denis, have an endearing quality of youthfulness like the hesitant legs of a colt (*16*). Slender too are the vaulting shafts between the bays and the tall twin-lights of the triforium with horseshoe heads betraying local influence on the designer.

It may be as well to state that the horseshoe arch in Spain is not a Moslem introduction but goes back to Visigothic times, and as a decorative motive to the second century A.D. Derived from the Near East through Syria, it became a constructional feature in the buildings of the Gothic kingdom, and only later was reinforced by fresh introductions of the arch in slightly different shapes by the Mohammedan invaders. Though the horseshoe arch does occur elsewhere in Europe at an early date, notably in Italy and southern France, it is solely as an exotic rarity. But it had become a distinctive feature of Spanish architecture for more than five centuries at the time of the first onset of the Gothic style.

Ávila was designed with a large triforium gallery vaulted, or intended to be vaulted, with a ramping half-barrel swept around the ambulatory. If this was ever actually built, it was later pulled

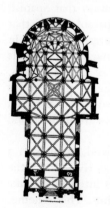

13 Ávila, c. 1160–1211, by Fruchel

down and the present series of double flying buttresses substituted. The result is to give to the eastern arm an appearance not unlike that of an apsidal Norman church such as Norwich or Peterborough, a type otherwise rare in Spain. Later work at Ávila did not live up up to the promise of its original east end, and as a whole the church possesses greater historic interest than beauty. But it remains of importance as the first Spanish example, so far as its ambulatory is concerned, of true Gothic emancipated from the clumsy piers and round arches of the Romanesque.

Much of the early Gothic entering Spain came with the Cistercians, who sent out colonies from mother-houses in France. But this Cistercian Gothic was still of a conservative and Transitional character, as at Veruela in Aragon, begun about 1170, Poblet (c. 1166–81) and Santes Creus (c. 1174–1271) in Catalonia, and La Oliva in Navarre, already mentioned. Even well into the thirteenth century, at Mondoñedo in Galicia, the cathedral of 1219–48 preserved the heavy piers and shafts of Romanesque type to support its modern sharply pointed arches and ribbed vaults. The arrival of a purer style, probably first seen at Burgos, belongs to the thirteenth century, and it was not until a date relatively late when compared with the developments in England that any complete Gothic churches were to be seen in Spain.

The two outstanding monuments of this period are the metropolitan cathedral of Toledo (9), whose chevet was built by Maestro Martín between 1227 and 1238, and the exquisitely detailed cathedral at Burgo de Osma (19), begun in 1232 by one Lope. As an example of style, that of Osma is the more valuable, for it was almost entirely completed within two generations and has not suffered much alteration internally, as has Burgos. Toledo's western nave was still building until c. 1400, and it too has suffered from alterations of style though not to the same extent. It is then to Burgo de Osma that we must go to see a complete cathedral of early Gothic character.

Of the French High Gothic there is a perfect example at León (14), whose chevet was built in 1258–77 by the same master Enrique who was responsible for the completion of Burgos from 1235. He was probably a Frenchman, certainly very well informed as to what was happening at the greater French cathedrals and especially those of the south-west such as Bayonne. But León is essentially a French work transplanted into Spain. Very different was the unusual cathedral of Valencia (*107*), now so cloaked with the classical veneer of 1774–79 that its design can only be guessed. It had a singular chevet, two chapels corresponding to each bay of the apse, and the bays of its central nave were square on plan (*106*). Quite unlike the Catalan hall-churches and differing markedly from the northern Gothic introduced to Castile, it evidenced a strong counter-current from Italy, while its first architects, Arnaldus Vitalis and Nicolas de 'Autona', may really have been Arnaldo Vitale and Niccolò di Ancona.

Far more original is the vast cathedral of Palma de Mallorca (*15*), capital and see of the Balearic Islands. The history of the first parts of the existing church is obscure. It is uncertain how much survives of the chapel begun for James I in 1230, or of the work at the east end started in 1270. It would seem, in any case, that the design of all the rest dates from the very last years of the thirteenth century and may be due to that same Jaime Fabre who had charge of Barcelona Cathedral from 1317 and who had certainly been architect of the church of Santo Domingo in Palma from a considerably earlier date. Both plan, with its square eastern chapels and regular setting-out, and monumental elevation punctuated by two tiers of buttresses bear the marks of genius.

Palma Cathedral more than any other Spanish building of the Gothic age was intended from the beginning to be a satisfying work of art not only within but outside as well. Even more than elsewhere, internal effect was emphasised in Spain at the expense of outward show. It was the impression upon the worshipper already inside the shrine that counted: external appearance was relatively unimportant. But the designer of Palma was clearly unsatisfied with this fundamental disunity of aesthetic aim, and determined that the composition and massing of his work should be appreciated from afar. The result is among the most impressive of the world's great buildings, whether seen from a distance by the sea traveller or at close quarters from the city beneath. What is striking at Palma is not mere size, though the nave is higher than Amiens and wider than York and the side aisles taller than the central nave of any English cathedral. The great bulk is beautifully proportioned and all its parts shaped to display to the best the unity of the great conception.

Barcelona Cathedral (*85–7*) was begun in 1298, and it was not until almost twenty years had elapsed that Jaime Fabre was brought from

14 LEÓN: the Chevet of 1255–77 by Maestro Enrique; south tower by Jusquín, 1458–72

15 PALMA DE MALLORCA: the south side, c. 1306–27, and Puerta del Mirador by Pedro Morey, 1389–1422

17 BARCELONA: the western Lantern, 1418–30,
by Bartomeu Gual

16 ÁVILA: the Ambulatory by Fruchel, c. 1160–1200

19 BURGO DE OSMA: interior looking east,
    designed by Maestro Lope, 1232–1300

18 OVIEDO: the Capilla Mayor of 1388–1412,
    and Nave of 1487–97

20 MURCIA: the west front of 1737–54 by Jaime Bort y Meliá, and the tower with the upper stage and

Majorca to take charge of the work. The original plan and conception were quite different from those of Palma, and from those of Barcelona's other church of cathedral scale, Santa María del Mar, built from 1329 to 1383. The cathedral has an apsidal chevet surrounded by nine chapels, an adaptation of the normal French plan, but its aisles are tall in the usual Catalan fashion. Its piers are shafted and thus give a very different impression from the plain octagons of Palma and of Santa María del Mar; the arches are only slightly pointed and those of the arcades almost semicircular. To every bay of the nave correspond two side-chapels constructed on the cellular pattern, and the cloister and other dependencies seem to have been laid out from the start, so regularly do they correspond to the church and to the block comprising the site. Completion was delayed until modern times, and a long succession of architects presided over the works: Bernard Roca, responsible for the western nave begun in 1365 and the earlier parts of the cloister from 1382; Bartomeu Gual, who built the lantern at the west end of the nave (1418–22); and Andrés Escuder, who finished the cloister in 1448.

The fourteenth century was enormously productive in eastern Spain: the little cathedral of Orihuela was built (1305–55); the chevet of Gerona (83) begun in 1312 by Enrique and continued until 1347 by the Narbonne master, Jacques Favran; La Seo at Saragossa (109) was practically rebuilt (1316–1412); the great church of Manresa begun (1322–53) to the design of Berenguer de Montagut of Barcelona; and the first work of Tortosa Cathedral (103), by Benito Dalguayre, built between 1347 and 1441. At Tarazona extensive alterations were started in 1362. Far less was done in Castile, apart from the steady continuance of long-term building projects as at Toledo; but the old church at Plasencia (130) was built during the century, and in 1321 Palencia (40) was begun at the east end. Notable are the great town churches produced late in the century at Vitoria (1370–1400) and Bilbao (1379–90), both now cathedrals. Even more important are the greater undertakings of towards 1400: the chevet of Oviedo (1388–1412), the cathedral at Murcia (108) started in 1394, and above all the stupendous project of Seville (146), whose designs were produced about 1400. Work did not actually begin, starting from the west end, until 1402.

These fourteenth-century churches have a mellow warmth and a suavity of line which demonstrate the mastery that had been achieved. It is difficult to understand the lack of appreciation which has so freely applied the term decadent to this young and virile art just shaking itself free from subservience to French models and achieving a unity and a national aesthetic all its own. Although many more foreigners were to enter Spanish service after 1400, their personalities were to become imbued more and more with the spirit of Spain, their separate contributions to be less and less characteristic of the countries from which they came.

But before the full development of the completed Spanish Gothic there was one further borrowing from France: the new cathedral of Pamplona (32–3) in Navarre, much of it built in the thirty years from 1397 to 1427, though left unfinished and now with an eighteenth-century front by Ventura Rodríguez. Pamplona is an unusual and exciting church, the outcome of original invention working upon an eclectic selection of material derived from French models. At the same time it bears no obvious marks of transplantation and has been subtly adapted to its position in the capital of an ambiguous frontier state ruled by French princes yet looking towards Spain. It is among the most successful works of a great period and ranks with the contemporary beauties of Canterbury and Winchester as a peak of High Gothic style.

For nearly a century no new cathedral church was begun, though there were important individual works such as the west fronts and towers of Toledo (1418–52), Oviedo (1431–) and Burgos (1442–58). All these employed foreign architects: Hanequín de Egas from Brussels, eclectic designer of the Toledo spire (131), and Hans of Cologne at Burgos. Pedro de la Tijera, who began the Oviedo steeple (179), may have been Spanish, but the character of the work is pronouncedly Franco-Flemish. The new cathedral of Astorga (42), begun in 1471, seems itself to have been designed by Simón de Colonia, son of Hans, and its plan is an interesting compromise between German and Spanish models. But the magnificent vertical lines of its apses and its soaring vaults, springing from many-shafted pillars without capitals, are augurs of a new era in Spanish architecture. Deriving something from Seville and a good deal from León, Astorga is none the less a work of great original genius, displayed by its author also in the Capilla del Condestable added in 1482–94 to Burgos Cathedral. Nothing else of comparable importance was done for a generation, though Calahorra (36) began to rebuild its nave in 1485 under a certain Maestro Juan, and the church of Sta. María in Logroño (now the titular cathedral) was built between 1480 and 1510.

From the marriage of Ferdinand and Isabella in 1469, and still more from their accession five years later, the artistic leadership of Spain passed rapidly to Castile. Though the latest Gothic churches incorporated much of the traditional scheme of Catalonia, the architects came from the Castilian realm. Between 1483 and 1534 the little cathedral of Segorbe was rebuilt to the designs of Juan de Burgos, while Huesca (116-7) in Aragon had as architect for its important works of 1497–1515 one Juan de Olózaga from the Basque provinces, the home also of Baltasar Barazábal, builder of the collegiate church and later cathedral of Barbastro (1500–33). Communications throughout the Peninsula rapidly improved, and architects could and did swiftly obtain information as to the most recent works in all parts of Spain.

Just as in England a preponderant part of the country's major works had been carried out by the King's Master Masons Henry Yevele and William Wynford, so in united Spain a small group of architects under Court patronage became responsible for all the great new constructions of the age which saw the conquest of Granada, the discovery of America, and the rise of the Crown of Castile very nearly to the hegemony of the known world. We have seen that the family of Hans of Cologne became acclimatised at Burgos, where in the third generation Francisco de Colonia was responsible for the lantern begun in 1540. Enrique, son of Hanequín de Egas, the Brussels master of Toledo, in his turn became architect to Toledo Cathedral and before he died in 1534 had had responsibility for important works at Jaén (1492–1519), Toledo (1494–), Plasencia (1497–), Granada (1504–), Málaga, Seville and Santiago de Compostela, where he built the great Hospital Real (1501–11). Juan Guas (fl. 1453–d. 1496), who had been a pupil of Hanequín de Egas, worked on the north porch of Ávila (1458–72) and the cloister of Segovia (1472–91) and also designed the collegiate church of San Juan de los Reyes in Toledo (1478–92) and the castle of Manzanares (1480) as well as numerous other works incorporating both Gothic and Mudéjar motives. Juan Gil de Hontañón, who died in 1526, had designed the cloister of Palencia, the lantern at Seville (1513), the new cathedral of Salamanca (1513) and also that of Segovia (1522), while his son Rodrigo not only continued his father's works but designed the new sanctuary of Ciudad

Rodrigo (1538–50) and the Gothic scheme for the great church of Valladolid (1527), and built the nave of Astorga (1530–59). Possibly the greatest genius of all, Juan de Álava, worked from 1505 on Salamanca University, from 1510 at Santiago, had charge of Plasencia (1513–37), built the south chapels of Salamanca Cathedral and designed San Esteban there (1524–).

This little company of architects, with a few others, made up an unparalleled galaxy of genius during the last two generations of the Gothic age. Together they sat upon commissions to decide the form that new projects were to take, and to recommend one of their number as architect for each of the greater buildings. Though they apparently had no organisation corresponding to the lodges of the German masons with their jurisdiction from the Rhine to the Carpathians, these Spanish designers wielded jointly a greater power than has perhaps ever before or since fallen to followers of their art. Their versatility was extraordinary, for many of them practised not only in the traditional Gothic in which they had been brought up, but also in the newly introduced Renaissance style based on Roman models. What is more, Spanish work of the early Renaissance is often of remarkable quality and free from the disproportions and failures in taste that so frequently disfigure work of the period in the North, notably in England. But the most curious feature of this capacity for making the best of both worlds is the survival in Spain and in Spanish America of many features of Gothic style in the new canon of Renaissance design. It is as though the architects could not bring themselves to abandon altogether the beauties of stellar vaulting, of flying buttress and pinnacle, of vertical line.

Even while the great Renaissance cathedrals were already in progress, a major reconstruction at Coria (129) could bring to its logical conclusion the ultimate design of a Gothic cathedral as a rectangular vaulted space of a single aisle, the direction in which so many experiments had been tending from the time of the Sainte-Chapelle of St. Louis onwards. In England this final outcome was reached only in the collegiate chapels, though it may be permissible to regard the chapel of King's College, Cambridge, as the English counterpart of Coria in the sequence of cathedral design.

Among the early Renaissance cathedrals, those of Jaén (140–1) and Guadix (139) stand out by the beauty of their proportions and the verticality of their lines. Designed as a single order of slender grouped shafts, Jaén (1540–73) by Andrés de Vandaelvira owes much to the lessons of Gothic verticality and space, and represents a great advance from the clumsy superimposed orders of, for example, Granada. Even the strictly classical church (afterwards made cathedral) of Valladolid (56–7), designed by Juan de Herrera in 1580–85, accepted an earlier Gothic ground-plan as its basis and preserves a somewhat mediaeval effect in its curiously panelled groined vaults. But Valladolid may be regarded as the furthest divergence from the traditional Spanish cathedral, although in its cubical exterior it interprets at least one major feature which had emerged from the Gothic development of space according to Spanish notions and custom.

The only complete cathedrals begun after the sixteenth century are the new cathedrals of Cadiz (1720–1838), designed by Vicente Acero, and Lérida (1760–90) by Pedro Mártir Cermeño, and the almost total rebuilding of Vich (22) in 1780–1803 by José Morató. None of these can be regarded as outstanding, though Cadiz (145) has a certain grandiose character. Far more significant are the Baroque additions made to many of the cathedrals during the earlier part of the eighteenth century. In its rich decorative quality, in its spatial fantasy, and in the vertical treatment of many of its features, Spanish Baroque was in some senses a continuation of the Gothic spirit working its way out from beneath the burden of static classicism which Herrera and the stricter Renaissance masters had attempted to impose upon it. Though its most fantastic manifestations are not to be found at the cathedrals, major works of Baroque occur in several of them.

Fronts were added at Mondoñedo (1705), Murcia (1737–54) by Jaime Bort, and Santiago (1738–50) by Fernando Casas y Nóvoa. Great towers were incorporated in the fronts or built separately, as at Murcia (1765–92) by Juan de Gea (20), Burgo de Osma (1739–44) by Domingo Ondátegui (53) and perhaps best of all at Santo Domingo de la Calzada (1762–67) by Martín de Beratúa (34). Here the spired and pinnacled character of the Gothic steeple is echoed as it had been in England by Wren a century earlier. There followed the neo-classical reaction towards purity of Roman detail, a reaction fortunately but little represented among the Spanish Cathedrals, though it is found in Ventura Rodríguez's front to Pamplona (1775–83) and in Morató's work at Vich. With equal good fortune Spain escaped the excesses of the Gothic revival, marked among her cathedrals by the project for the Almudena at

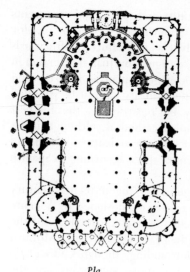

Pla

21 Barcelona: church of La
Sagrada Familia, 1882–, by
Antonio Gaudí

Madrid, started in 1880 to the designs of the Marqués Francisco de Cubas, and the new cathedral of Vitoria (1906–), whose architects were Javier Luque and Julián Apraiz. Perhaps the most successful work of the period is the west front of Barcelona Cathedral, added by José Mestres and Augusto Font in 1890–92, but this was based upon the design of 1408 made by a French master, Charles Galter of Rouen.

Although not strictly within the scope of this study, it is impossible to omit all mention of the great church of the Sagrada Familia at Barcelona (21), a cathedral in all but name. Begun as a conventional neo-Gothic design by Francisco del Villar in 1882, the direction of the works soon fell to Antonio Gaudí y Cornet, the most profound architectural genius of modern times. The strange character and often inadequate execution of much of Gaudí's detail and surface decoration have blinded many critics to the fundamental rightness of Gaudí's views on constructional design. It is one of the darkest reflections upon the Spain of the late nineteenth and early twentieth centuries that it failed to provide the funds to complete this amazing conception during the lifetime of its creator. But after some twenty years of almost total dereliction it seems that the project is at last to be realised and the models (destroyed in the civil war) have been remade, showing the originality and the beauty which the church holds in promise. As the product of creative imagination working upon materials and traditions both old and new, Gaudí's Sagrada Familia is at once the culmination of the Spanish cathedral and the link which holds together its past and its future.

CHAPTER ONE

Navarre and Biscay

O<small>UT</small> of France and into Spain, over the hills and back again: nonsense words of a children's rhyme that once expressed an historic truth, when the pilgrimage to the shrine of St. James the Great, Santiago de Compostela, was the most fre-quented in Christendom and ranked only after those to Jerusalem and Rome in the calendar of the devotee. For to reach Spain overland the hills, the great Pyrenean and Cantabrian chain, have somewhere to be crossed, whether it is by struggling up the steep valleys of the Basque Country or by surmounting the high passes or the cordillera. In the early Middle Ages few travellers attempted to reach Compostela by way of Biscay, for the Basques had a dubious reputation. They did not welcome strangers, their tongue was out-landish, and they owned no allegiance to the Kings of the Franks or the princes of the Peninsula. Hence the beaten track of the modern tourist, following the flat coastal plain from Bordeaux through Bayonne to Hendaye and San Sebastián, was not that of the pilgrim.

The great road, one of the most highly organised of all mediaeval routes, drew pilgrims through two main branches. One tapped the western side of France and reached Spanish soil at Roncesvalles; the other, from Toulouse and the east, climbed over the Somport (*Summus Portus* or topmost passage) to Canfranc and Jaca. Beyond Jaca this branch turned westwards and in Navarre joined the first road which had already passed through the capital, Pamplona. The course of the road gave great religious significance to Navarre itself, comparable to its political importance as the key to Spain. At an early date the principality had, indeed, been outstanding among the realms of the reconquest and its ruler, Sancho the Great (1000–1035), achieved a hegemony over the Christian kingdoms. In his time Navarre proper already included a part of France and extended beyond the Ebro to the mountains of Burgos, while its influence reached across the Basque provinces to the sea coast from Fuenterrabía to Bilbao. Later events were to curtail Navarre's greatness and she lost the race for the Mediterranean, shut in between Aragon and Castile. The Rioja, the rich province west of the Ebro, with the tombs of her early kings in their church at Nájera, was absorbed by Castile; but Navarre lived on until the end of the mediaeval period, a land with a strong personality and a rich endowment of artistic talent.

For our present purposes it is convenient to consider Navarre at its widest extent, including even the old Aragonese capital of Jaca. Jaca lies on the River Aragón which gave the later kingdom its name, but whose watershed divides it from the greater part of the realm of Huesca and Saragossa and throws it into the Navarrese basin. This area of the upper valley of the Ebro forms in fact a distinct geographical province, intermediate in character between European France and Spain proper with its feeling of Africa. On this natural foundation later dynastic history was to build a political entity intermediate in character, interpreting to one another the two great nations of the Atlantic seaboard.

The mediaeval traveller from south-western France, entering upon the pilgrimage road, was faced by the mountain barrier across his path, broken up into giant fingers stretching northwards into the plain. Between these rocky fingers lay, and still lie, green fertile valleys entirely typical of northern Europe. Rich vegetation of deciduous trees, orchards and meadows, all were what he would find familiar. Looking back, even from the top of the pass, he would have seen, as we can see today, the panorama of his homeland if he were a Frenchman; or if he were not, still a picture familiar in its essentials. Turning his back and setting his face to the south, he climbed down, not just into a different country, but another continent, a changed world. We may still experience this by crossing the Somport itself, or feel the contrast yet more sharply after passing through the long blackness of the railway tunnel. On both sides are deep valleys overshadowed by lofty peaks sprinkled with snow; but those on the north are lush with the sap of a temperate climate, on the south the slopes are bare rock, the colours dusty. No great feat of imagination is required to picture the dry and stony deserts which do exist not many miles to the south.

The contrasts of the road from St.-Jean-Pied-de-Port through

22 VICH: the Nave of 1780–1803, looking eastward; by José Morató

23 SARAGOSSA: El Pilar, begun in 1677 by Francisco de Herrera el Mozo, and altered 1753–66 by Ventura Rodríguez

24 MURCIA: vault of Capilla de los Vélez, c. 1495–1507, perhaps by Juan de León

25 GRANADA: the Capilla Real of 1504–21, by Enrique Egas and Juan de Mena

27 GRANADA: the west front of 1667–1703, designed by Alonso Cano

26 VALENCIA: the west front, 1703–13, by Konrad Rudolf and Francisco Vergara

28　JACA: the Nave of 1063–1100, with aisle vault of 1495–1520, by Juan de Segura, and high vault of 1598 by Juan de Bescós

Valcarlos and past Roncesvalles are rather less sharp, and I have already said that Navarre has an intermediate character. It is Spain with a trace of the France of the *ancien régime* added. As befits such a buffer state, the cathedrals of the Navarrese region are not yet altogether Iberian in their characteristics. Internally, at least, they betray a more airy grace but a less robust strength than those we shall meet to the south and west. This is true even of Jaca, the earliest of existing Spanish cathedrals, a product of the full flood of the Romanesque eleventh century.

Approached from all directions but the north, Jaca stands high on a neck of land above the valley of the Aragón. From the north the ancient road, parallel to the river and the modern railway, enters the town on the level across an isthmus, which has been commanded since 1592 by the fortifications of Philip II's citadel, the least altered specimen of this period of military architecture in Spain. At the edge of the township stands the cathedral, an irregular mass of greyish stone surmounted by a low and massive tower at the west end. The cloister and subsidiary buildings cloak the north side, but the eastern apses can be seen: the central apse beyond an elongated sanctuary being an eighteenth-century adaptation. The style is one of extreme simplicity but the masonry is remarkably sound and well built for its early date.

On the south a low portico on elegant columns is apparently built of re-used materials which may be those of a predecessor on the same site. Within is the south doorway of simple round-arched orders. The main entrance is at the west end, where a singular but impressive porch of unusual height stands out from the tower, partly supported upon it. The porch is barrel-vaulted, with stout cross-arches of rectangular section, now much flattened at the crown. This is the great door which King Ramiro I himself recorded in 1063 that he had begun, to support a tower for the eight bells, four of which were to be large, two middling and two small. The king also specified that the roof was to be of stone over all three aisles, and though these original vaults have gone we may suppose them to have been intended as barrel vaults like that of the porch. The setting out of the internal bays, however, with alternating compound piers and circular shafts, suggests that by the time the church was finished it had groined instead of barrel vaulting.

The delay in completion is not likely to have been very great, and the Lombardic and even classical character of the bases of the piers and columns (28), and the simple carving of their capitals, indicate a date at latest very close to 1100. The present vaults are substitutions of the sixteenth century: those of the aisles having been inserted between 1495 and 1520 by Juan de Segura, architect also of Barbastro Cathedral and the Lonja at Saragossa, and that of the nave completed by Juan de Bescós in 1598. In both cases the design is restrained for its late period, and it is evident that Segura and Bescós were at pains to suit their additions to the character of the old work. Segura's star vaulting is eminently satisfactory and recalls the success of the Perpendicular vault added to the Norman structure at Norwich. The crossing at Jaca is covered by an unusual domical vault with ribs of square section intersecting at the centre. This is considered by Sr. José Camón to be of the late eleventh century and thus earlier than the first ribbed vaults in France; he further suggests a connection of some kind between Jaca and Durham, whose ribbed vaults also antedate those of France. One curious feature, perhaps indicating a very early date in the experimental history of ribbed vaulting, is that the ribs are at the middle of the faces of the octagonal dome, not beneath the groin lines. It cannot be doubted that there is a link between these ribs of the late eleventh century at Jaca and those of the Great Mosque at Cordova, whose relevant bays (3) were built a hundred years earlier; and, if so, the derivation of the ribbed vault from Islamic sources may be regarded as proven.

The eastward view towards the sanctuary, with its elegant saucer-dome painted by Manuel Bayeu in 1792, and its flanking apses of the original work, is restful and pleasing. Here, on the threshold of Spain, is a notable instance of the happy relations which exist between works of various periods. No careful pastiche of Romanesque style could have been so successful as an extension to the sanctuary as is this plain classical treatment carried out with a distinguished simplicity. We may also be grateful for the sixteenth-century clerestory windows of the nave, which admit enough light for the proper appreciation of the interior, a rare occurrence in Spain. Modern alterations, too, which have removed the obstructive *coro* and its huge organ, have enabled the pleasing proportions of the original design to be seen. The church is so small that there is no question here of the opening of vistas, but simply of disencumbering its volume of space.

The stone of walls and piers is very hard, but in spite of a harsh texture appears softened at a little distance on account of its delicate grey colour. The later vaults are of a much lighter, creamish, stone. Among the fittings is a good late Gothic altarpiece of sculpture and painted panels in the chapel at the west end of the south aisle, while there are several re-used sections of a fine early wrought-iron screen. This is of the same type as the gates in Winchester Cathedral now at the entrance to the south choir aisle, and the screens inserted by the Crusaders in the Dome of the Rock at the time that it was converted into a church. Another important example exists at the church of Iguácel, a few miles to the north-east of Jaca, where the building is precisely dated to 1072. There, and in the cases of Jaca and Winchester, the screens need not be contemporary with the building, but are probably not very much later, while the screens at Jerusalem must belong to the early years of the twelfth century. Examples elsewhere in Spain, and in France, all appear to be of later date, and the source of this remarkable school of design in blacksmith's work remains to be found.

Beyond Jaca the pilgrims' road runs almost due west, following the course of the Aragón, which it crosses at Puente de la Reina. Further on is the strange village acropolis of Berdún, and just after crossing the boundary of Navarre the monastery of Leyre, high up on the right, perched like a swallow's nest on the cliffs. Its ancient church of San Salvador has a sanctuary of three aisles with parallel apses, built in 1090–98, and with piers and vaults of much the same type as the western porch of Jaca. To the west was added, about the end of the thirteenth century, a nave of four bays of a single span. Since Leyre was the royal pantheon, the Westminster Abbey of Navarre, this singular disposition may well have suggested the later application of the single nave on a grand scale at Gerona, as we shall later see.

Soon after Leyre the road leaves the Aragón and crosses its tributary the Irati, climbing over high ground before dropping towards Pamplona. Some miles short of the city, in a fertile open valley between two ranges of steep hills, the pilgrimage route bears to the south from the modern road, which continues direct for the capital. The countryside is impressive, with distant views of sudden peaks and the strange cleft to the north-west, between the Two Sisters, marking the way to the coast. The city lies on a hill, steeply rising above the green valley with its rows of poplars lining the river banks. Coming from the north, as the French pilgrims had done, the traveller sees ramparts rising high and bluff from the water's edge, and above them the bulk of the cathedral with its sharp-edged apse like the prow of a ship, backed by the transepts forming a liner's bridge. To the left runs the high line of the cloister broken by the noble silhouette of the old chapter-house or Capilla Barbazana. The whole exterior is essentially Spanish in its cubical proportions and large areas of blank walling.

The approach to the main front from within the town is an anticlimax, for the west end shows nothing of the mediaeval church within. Completed to a design by Ventura Rodríguez in 1783, this façade's main interest is as a late and academic specimen of the wide-spreading front with towers outside the aisles whose distant ancestry can be traced back to the English model of Old St. Paul's. The Pamplona towers are crowned by bell-turrets recalling those of Wren's St. Paul's and contrasting strangely with the church behind them. Once through the doors and one is in a different world (32). Pamplona Cathedral is internally the finest example in Spain of unity of design, although two main builds can be distinguished by the differing details of piers and bases. Begun at the east end in 1397, perhaps by the French mason Jacques Pérut, the chevet, transept and part of the nave aisles and chapels were finished only thirty years later. This is enough to prove the architect possessor of a most original brain, whose project was fulfilled by another as accomplished. This latter was certainly Janin Lomme of Tournai, who was working for the Crown of Navarre as early as 1411 and was *maestro mayor* of the cathedral in 1439. Meanwhile he had made, from 1416 onwards, the magnificent alabaster tomb of Charles III the Noble and his queen which, surrounded by carved weepers, now stands in the middle of the nave. For here again the choir seating has been banished, less defensibly than at Jaca, for the sanctuary is short and as Street pointed out, certainly planned with the intention of placing the *coro* in the nave.

None the less, the beauty of the interior can now be felt to a degree impossible while the large and obstructive *coro* remained, and the unity of the church's design can be fully appreciated. The windows are relatively small, and filled in many cases with good early Renaissance glass of fine colour; but there is sufficient light to see the exquisite details of moulding which owe much to French precedent of the period. The bases of the nave piers are mostly

29 TUY: the
west front of
1225–87

HUESCA: the
west front. The
portals of *c.*
1300–13; upper
stage *c.* 1497–
1515, by Juan
de Olózaga

31 TUDELA: the Nave of c. 1205–65

built of a warm cream stone of smooth texture, while the shafts
and walls above this level are of a cool grey limestone. Whether
this too is a matter of personal intention on the part of Janin
Lomme, or simply a question of convenience in the supply of
materials, it enhances the effect of the subtly proportioned shafts.
Towards the nave a triple moulding, representing three shafts of
the pier's inward angle, is carried up the wall to the springing of
the vault, at the level of the sill of the clerestory windows. Horizontal connection between the bays is provided by a simple moulding
carried along at some slight distance above the arches of the main
arcade. The high placing of the small clerestory windows, and the
(for Spain) unusually steep pitch of the aisle roof, produce an unfortunately large belt of plain walling in the place of a triforium.
This has to be regarded as the chief defect in a design which is
otherwise of outstanding harmony and refinement.

Most distinctive is the plan of the east end (33), derived from
that of Soissons in that the apsidal chapels form a single structure
with the ambulatory, but with the individual feature of a single
medial pier. There are only four chapels, those adjacent to the
transepts being curiously and awkwardly distorted in plan. It has
to be remembered that when the new cathedral was built, the site
may not have been entirely cleared, especially close to the north
walk of the cloister, built earlier in the fourteenth century by the

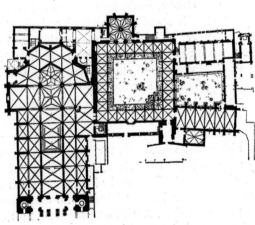

Ars Hispaniae

33 Pamplona, 1397–c. 1525; cloister, 1317–;
west front 1780–83, by Ventura Rodríguez

old Romanesque cathedral whose only remains are a series of exquisitely cut capitals now in the Museo de Navarra. Whatever the cause, the actual plan of the church is asymmetrical in detail, though regular in principle. The transepts are unaisled, but that next to the cloister doorway is extended westwards through two bays. Through this door we proceed down into the cloister, one of the finest of the whole Gothic period. The doorway itself is divided by a pier on which stands, facing the west walk of the cloister, an exquisite statue of the Virgin and Child, Nuestra Señora del Amparo, the object of continuing devotion.

Devotion to the Virgin is indeed strong at Pamplona, and the great church is never more impressive than during the evening service when, in fading daylight and carrying lanterns and banners, the confraternity of Our Lady, men, women and small children, go in procession chanting *Ave Maria*. The untrained voices of the children alternate in the service with the harsh Spanish bass of the men, a poignant and unforgettable contrast. It is easy to recapture the spirit of popular devotion of the Middle Ages, while the less spectacular routine of the mediaeval Church continues in the morning and afternoon choir services of the canons, maintaining as century follows century the work of God in this cathedral church which is also a royal shrine.

Several of the chapels have good mediaeval altarpieces and the iron screen of the sanctuary, made by Guillermo Ervenat in 1517, is outstanding. Behind it stands the high altar beneath a modern Gothic canopy of silver, of admirable proportions and one of the very few recent works of church art which can be said to justify revivalism in style. Sculpture of the fourteenth and fifteenth centuries is notably represented, not only by the recumbent effigies of Charles the Noble and his queen, but by the outstanding series of works in the cloister and its dependencies. Besides the statue of Our Lady of Succour already mentioned, and the remarkable Dormition in high relief which fills the tympanum above it, there is the equally notable Puerta Preciosa, and an interesting group of the Adoration of the Magi of the end of the fourteenth century by the French mason-sculptor Jacques Pérut, who may have been also the architect of the cathedral. Architecturally the Capilla Barbazana attracts attention by its height and by its ingenious adaptation of an octagonal vault to the square plan, with charming miniature vaults beneath the squinches across the angles. Another delightful feature

of the cloister is the little chapel at its south-western corner, projecting into the garth, and screened by iron grilles made from the
famous chains taken at the battle of Las Navas de Tolosa in 1212,
chains which appear on the shield of arms of the kingdom of Navarre
and thus in the quarterings of Spain.

Truly wonderful wall-paintings, formerly in the cathedral and
cloisters, have now been transferred to canvas and are to be found
in the Museo de Navarra. Among them the principal comes from
the old refectory, now the Capilla de San Francisco Javier; it is a
retablo of the Passion, inscribed with the date 1330 and the painter's
name, Johannes Oliveri, as well as the arms of Navarre and those
of Gaston II, Count of Foix and Béarn. The style is remarkably close
to that of contemporary English miniature painting and has suggested that the artist was an Englishman. He may have been identical
with the "Joan Oliver" who was working for King Peter the
Ceremonious of Aragon in Barcelona in 1364, and who was dead
before 1377, but this is by no means certain. But the close relations
of England, through Bordeaux and Bayonne, with Béarn and Navarre
at the time make the painter's English origin highly probable.

From Pamplona it is a short and scenic journey to the sea at San
Sebastián, but the cathedral there is of less architectural interest
than any other in Spain. It was built as a parish church on a large
scale in neo-Gothic style and is noteworthy only for its tall steeple,
a landmark in the new city. Nor need we spend much more time
on the equally neo-Gothic cathedral of Vitoria, begun in 1906.
Its works were suspended from 1914 until 1946, but are now once
more in full swing. While it is a welcome sign of Spain's vitality
that she should multiply cathedrals in modern times, it is doubtful
whether the costly and painstaking imitation of an historical style
or any other extensive new building project is justifiable at Vitoria.
For there is an admirable ancient Colegiata de Santa María which
at present serves as the cathedral and is a most distinguished work of
the late fourteenth century. Its style is Navarrese, with notable
resemblances to work at Pamplona, and this must be explained as
the result of its having been built during the short occupation of
Vitoria by the kings of Navarre from 1366 to 1413, a date which
both general character and details in any case support.

The church is not impressive outside, apart from the unusual
western portico with a tall open arch to the south and an apse
towards the north, covered with good late stellar vaulting of about

1500. Sheltered by this lofty vestibule are the three doorways o
the main west front, the central being one of the very finest o
Gothic portals, flanked with statues and with an elaborately carvec
tympanum in four scenes of the life of the Virgin. The richly
moulded orders of the surrounding arch are provided with two
series of small statues in niches following the curve, and foliage
is carried round the main arch and the doorways. But the special
beauty of the entrance is its central mullion bearing a standing
figure of the Virgin, closely resembling Our Lady of Succour in the
Pamplona cloister. Internally the church is stayed by a series of
shallow arched struts, which interfere with a full appreciation of
the design. The plan is unusual for the period, with a three-aisled
nave of five bays, a wide-spreading transept of three bays on each
side, and a five-sided central apse opening immediately off the
crossing and surrounded by three hexagonal chapels and the trape-
zoidal chapels of the east side of the transept. The circular piers with
moulded shafts growing from their surface resemble those of the
chevet at Pamplona, as do the wall-shafts which carry the simple
bays of ribbed-vaulting; but the walls are here diversified with a
continuous triforium.

Vitoria is an ancient town of considerable interest, with many
mediaeval mansions and half-timbered houses of a type which suggests northern Europe rather than Spain. It lies on a sudden hill
in the middle of a broad plain divided by streams and marked by
rows of tall poplars. To the north lie the mountainous ranges of
Biscay, and through these runs the road to Bilbao. All three of the
Basque provinces now possess cathedrals, which none of them had
in the Middle Ages. At Bilbao, as at Vitoria, a collegiate church of
the late fourteenth century has been advanced in rank. This is
Santiago, the largest church of the old town and a simple but
elegant example of the best work of its time (c. 1379–1404).
Again its character is closely related to that of contemporary building in Navarre and is clearly inspired by models in south-western
France. Some degree of English influence, either coming through
Bayonne or direct by sea, is suggested by details though the plan,
with its fully developed chevet and relatively broad proportions, is
altogether Franco-Spanish.

The remaining cathedrals of the Basco-Navarran region lie west
of the Ebro and close, on one side or the other, to the old frontier
with Castile. Three in number, one of them (Tudela) held cathedral

rank only from 1738 to 1851, while the others, Santo Domingo de la Calzada and Calahorra, share a single diocese between them. Of the existing buildings the earliest is Tudela (31), built under Sancho the Strong of Navarre as a collegiate church, by far the most important in the southern part of his kingdom. The eastern end, three parallel apses between two square chapels opening from the transept, was begun in 1194 and completed some ten years later, while the four bays west of the crossing were carried on more slowly and the west front finished about 1265. There are slight differences in detail and the form of the clerestory windows, but the whole church is essentially homogeneous in its Transitional style and unusually light and elegant for its time. The bay design is interesting in that it completely eliminates the triforium, and in the nave has windows of Gothic bar-tracery, closely above the pointed arches of the main arcade. In the transept fronts are triple lancets and in their side walls circular windows and windows with unusual plate-tracery of larger and smaller circles and trefoils. Around the main arches, of very plain section, runs a moulding enriched with dog-tooth ornament.

The special beauty of Tudela is its late Romanesque cloister, one of the most richly carved in Spain and a rival to that of the abbey of Santo Domingo de Silos, though of a single stage only. Among the most interesting of the very many miniature figures on its capitals are some in the east walk of soldiers in mail carrying long pointed shields with armorial bearings indicated by cross-hatching, an unusually early instance of the use of heraldry in iconographical illustration. The other architectural feature of outstanding value is the great portal in the west front, the Puerta del Juicio, consisting of eight pointed orders divided into 116 sections carved in high relief with scenes of the Last Judgment. The church contains a lovely thirteenth-century statue of the Virgin, standing by the south-east crossing pier, and a large altarpiece painted in 1489–94 by Pedro Díaz of Oviedo, elaborately framed in wood with canopies and buttresses of filigree carving. In the most southerly chapel of the transept, behind a finely wrought screen, is the tomb of the Chancellor Francisco de Villaespesa who died in 1421, and a great painted retable. The tomb bears lifelike figures of the Chancellor and his wife and a notable series of realistic weepers and scenes in relief, among the most important of their period for the details of costume and expression which they show.

Tudela, with its narrow streets of ancient houses and its long stone bridge crossing the Ebro, is one of the most attractive cities of northern Spain and must always have been of considerable importance. Its commercial and strategic standing were echoed in the quality of its architecture and art, which benefited from the characteristics of the three adjoining kingdoms, Navarre, Aragon and Castile. Ascending the valley, the southern bank soon becomes Castilian and the cathedral of Calahorra appears at a distance of little more than twenty-five miles from Tudela. Calahorra had ecclesiastical jurisdiction for centuries, not only over the Rioja on the right bank of the Ebro, but over almost the whole of the Basque provinces. Navarrese in political origin, the diocese soon came under Castilian influence but kept in touch with both Aragon and Navarre.

Calahorra now gives no impression of a cathedral city, being a little market town on a hill set among the wide rice-fields for which the district is famous. The pace of life is still unhurried and in a side street one may find a wheelwright's shop turning out brand-new farm wagons, splendidly painted in apple-green and orange, with patterns and lines picked out in contrasting colours. The cathedral is not large and attracts little attention, though its oblong tower is a curiosity. Externally the one feature that calls for notice is the early Renaissance north door, an attempt to translate the framework of a great Gothic portal into terms of Roman detail. A pair of doorways with elliptical heads support an entablature, surmounted by a great tympanum with moulded orders, one of which contains a range of small figures as in the mediaeval model; the great arch is framed between Ionic attached columns standing upon the lower order of Corinthian pilasters surrounding the doors, and the spandrels above the arch contain large figures of angels in low relief, apparently blowing flame through trumpets. The main west front, added in 1680–1704, is an insignificant piece of provincial Baroque, and there is a good deal of similarly dull work inside. The architecture of the nave (36), however, is good, surviving from the general rebuilding begun in 1485 under Maestro Juan. The great piers are octagonal in plan, with simple mouldings emphasising the vertical angles as in the Marienkirche of Danzig, and from these both arcades and vaults spring freely without capitals. The stellar vaults are of excellent patterns and their ribs, and indeed the mouldings generally, are extremely well proportioned. Unfortunately the eastern arm was again rebuilt in two phases beginning in 1561 and 1621, and the *capilla mayor* is covered, apart from its Gothic vaulting, by Renaissance detail and a large but inferior reredos.

Continuing up the valley, the next important town is Logroño, capital of the modern province and titular see. In fact, the two cathedrals of Calahorra and Santo Domingo de la Calzada are unlikely to be replaced, but the church of Santa María la Redonda in Logroño claims to be the head of the diocese and is a noble specimen of the local type of hall-church built at the end of the fifteenth century. Tall round pillars diversified with four slender shafts on the cardinal points bear the lace-work vaults of five bays, while the east end terminates in three three-sided apses. At the west end a remarkable rotunda was added in 1742–60, while a deep Baroque entrance between flanking steeples was finished in 1769 to the designs of Martín de Beratúa, whom we shall meet also as architect of the tall steeple of La Calzada.

At Logroño the pilgrimage road crosses the Ebro and runs almost due west towards Burgos. Santo Domingo de la Calzada lies on the road some thirty miles to the west of Logroño and, like Calahorra, though much smaller still, is a simple country town. But here the cathedral is dominant to the whole landscape, for it possesses one of the finest steeples in Spain (*34*), designed by Beratúa and built in 1762–67. Isolated from the church, the tower stands on a very tall blind story which carries it to a level above the neighbouring roofs of the town; this has simple pilasters at the angles and above it rises another square stage, more complex in design, with four Baroque pilasters on each face and a single small window within a heavy architrave. This stage ends in a heavy entablature carrying pinnacled cupolas at the angles surrounding an octagonal lantern which is continued as a richly ornamented steeple. The skilful disposition of the enrichments, which decrease in scale and increase in number as they rise, is probably unequalled in the eighteenth century, and may fairly be compared with the best of Wren's London spires.

The church belongs mainly to two building periods, the earlier Transitional from 1158 when the first stone was laid until 1235 when the nave was completed; and the second during the first half of the sixteenth century. Of the original church three bays of the nave, the north transept, and the ambulatory with its central apsidal chapel remain; the crossing and the bay to the west, with the south transept and the adjacent vaults, are of the latest Gothic internally and externally Renaissance plateresque. The ambulatory and its chapels, ready for service in 1180, are still almost purely Romanesque, but the *capilla mayor* and the nave are clearly later, no doubt designed at the end of the twelfth and built early in the thirteenth century. The vaults of the transept and nave have ridge ribs, probably a signal of English influence which may have come from Burgos soon after 1200. The eastern crossing piers have large paired shafts on the cardinal faces, and narrower nook-shafts at the angles of the central block of masonry. The monumental effect is grand and happily completed by the star vaulting of the *capilla mayor*, added about 1529 by Juan de Rasines, possibly to the designs of Felipe de Vigarni of Burgos, a Burgundian, who is known to have made the drawings for the saint's shrine in the south transept, undertaken by Rasines in 1513. But Juan and his brother Pedro de Rasines were notable designers in their own right, Juan building the fine Colegiata of Berlanga de Duero in 1526–30, and Pedro the church of Santo Tomás at Haro (1564).

Architecturally the best work in the church is the daring south transept of this same period, where an area of 58 feet by 40 is vaulted in two enormous spans of lierne pattern, resting on the rebuilt south-west pier of the crossing. This great expansion of the transept was for the purpose of providing a worthy position for the shrine of the saint, a local shepherd of the eleventh century who in later life became a noted engineer of roads and bridges and made the great new causeway (*calzada*) which gives a surname to his city. This was a direct road, specially built for the Compostelan pilgrims, improving upon the more circuitous Roman way which had linked Logroño to Burgos and by the time of Santo Domingo had become almost impassable.

On the west side of the south transept, and opposite to the shrine, is a feature unique in Christian architecture: an enriched chamber with a grilled opening and access doorway for the keeping of a live cock and hen (35). This chamber belongs, like the shrine itself, to the work of Vigarni and Rasines begun in 1513, but the keeping of a cock and hen in the cathedral appears to go back to a considerably earlier date. The custom is founded in the tradition of a miracle attributed to the saint's powers: a young pilgrim, wrongly accused of theft from the inn at Santo Domingo where he was staying on his way to Compostella, was condemned and hanged, but after his

34   The chevet of 1158–1200 and the Tower
of 1762–67, by Martín de Beratúa

35   The loft for cock and hen in the South
Transept of 1513–29, by Felipe Vigarni
and Juan Rasines

SANTO DOMINGO DE LA CALZADA

37 PLASENCIA: the Transept by Juan de Álava,

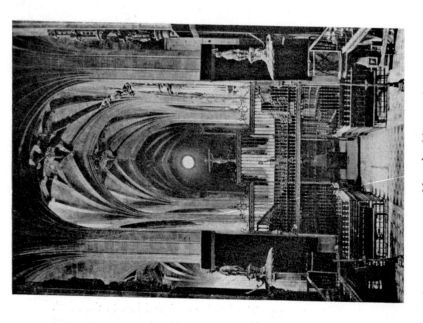

36 CALAHORRA: Nave by Maestro Juan, 1485—

death appeared to his parents, who thereupon went before the justice who had condemned him and related their son's miraculous resuscitation and his version of the facts. The judge, who was seated at table about to eat his dinner, answered that it was as true that their son was alive as that the roast cock and hen upon the platter in front of him were. Whereupon the birds left the dish, became reclothed in all their feathers, and sang. The judge, convinced, went with the boys' parents and the whole population to the gallows, where the youth was cut down alive, and all gave thanks to the saint in the cathedral. The date was the 13th of October, on which the miracle has ever since been commemorated, while a pure white cock and hen are replaced in the chamber every year.

The great Plateresque altarpiece was begun in 1537 by Damián Forment, and completed by the time of his death in 1541, though not set in position until afterwards. Far less satisfactory than his works in Gothic style, it is none the less a remarkable achievement for a master at the end of his career experimenting in a fresh fashion. Much more successful are the splendidly carved choir stalls and bishop's throne of 1521–26, made by Andrés de Nájera and Guillén de Holanda, assisted by several others including "the Burgundian", supposed to be Felipe de Vigarni. The design and direction of the work seem to have been given by Nájera, who also carried out the closely similar stallwork of 1525 for the monastery of San Benito in Valladolid, now in the National Museum of Sculpture there.

A cloister at Santo Domingo was built for Bishop Juan del Pino, who died in 1346, but the present work is of 1517–1550, and of relatively little interest, though it contains several monuments of historical importance, notably that of the heart-burial of Henry II of Trastamara, King of Castile, the bastard brother of Peter the Cruel. Henry died here in 1379 after a reign of ten years; his body was taken to Toledo. It was left to his successor to deal with John of Gaunt, who was in the meantime claiming to be King of Castile in right of his second wife, daughter of Peter. Gaunt seriously invaded Spain in 1386 and conquering Galicia was for a few months able to reign in Compostela. After the failure of the Anglo-Portuguese campaign of 1387 the English troops were allowed to march through Castile to Bayonne, doubtless along the pilgrims' road which saw also many ambassadors and messengers passing until peace was concluded with the marriage of Lancaster's daughter to the heir of Castile, made Prince of the Asturias in imitation of the English royal usage of the Principality of Wales. It may be due to these English contacts that there is at La Calzada, behind the high altar towards the ambulatory, a stone screen with reticulated tracery of English appearance and carvings (apparently of about 1400) of similarly insular style. But it is equally possible that the work was done by some sculptor on his return from the pilgrimage, or forced by poverty to work his way.

CHAPTER TWO

Old Castile and Leon

OLD Castile is the cradle of Spain, and an understanding of Castile is the key to the Spanish character. It is an area with a certain geographical and climatic unity, it corresponds to a definite and important step in historical development, and it is and has been for many centuries peopled by the speakers of the Spanish language in its greatest purity. For this reason, the Spaniards themselves call their language Castilian, even if they are Aragonese or from Leon; and still more, if they come from the Spanish-speaking world overseas. Dr. Menéndez Pidal has shown, and illustrated with a remarkable series of phonetic distribution maps, the origins and growth of Castilian as a language distinct from the ancient Romance language of the Peninsula, which was a decayed Latin possessed of those characteristics which Catalan and Provençal to the east, and Galician and Portuguese to the west, still share with one another. This was the speech of Iberia when it was invaded by the Moors, and of the eighth- and ninth-century rulers of the reconquered kingdom of Leon. The story of Spain since that time has been the outcome of an explosion: the successive outward waves of expansion of the Castilians and their language together, until a point approaching saturation was reached. Castilian institutions and tongue have gone hand in hand from the Bay of Biscay to the Atlantic and the Mediterranean, and political unification has brought a single speech everywhere, even though not to the exclusion of older languages such as Basque and Catalan, or dialects like Galician and the Bable of Asturias.

Castile began as a "march", a border district dotted with castles to protect the eastern frontiers of the old kingdom of Leon. Its first recorded counts were subjects of the Leonese king, but by the tenth century already exercised an effective independence. As their power grew they not only enlarged their territory and with it the area in which the budding Castilian tongue was spoken, but also spread the rule of their own customary laws, driving out the written law of the Visigothic Code. In these respects there are close parallels with the early history of France and England. Castile was a country, like England, where the way of life was based upon the living experience of common law, constantly reinterpreted in the light of changing conditions. It was also, again like mediaeval England and northern France, a country of communal agriculture where enormous open fields were divided in strips among the members of a free community. The remains of this open-field system of agriculture can still be seen throughout Castile and in the parts of Spain colonised by Castilians during the centuries of the Reconquest. The free status of the early Castilians is to this day echoed in the pride of the Castilian peasant, a pride which is not shown in an arrogance of bearing but in a courtesy that goes deeper than conventional forms, and an attachment to the purity of speech after the Castilian fashion.

The centre of the early county and later kingdom of Castile was Burgos, and it was there that a single bishop's see was created in 1075, when Alfonso VI gave the site of his palace for the building of the cathedral. It was finished by 1096, but no trace of it now remains. What we have is a Gothic church begun in 1221, and only finished in the structural essentials that we now see in 1568, on the completion of the central lantern. The effect of Burgos Cathedral as a work of art is therefore to some extent the accident of a long-continued growth and not to be set down to a single design organised in its entirety from the start. But a certain degree of unity was given to its external composition by the relationships of its towers and pinnacles, all of them products of its last century of growth. For this unity there is a special reason: the fact that the architects in charge from 1442 to the end were three generations of the same family, father, son and grandson. So it is that the tall pinnacles and filigree spires on the western towers found a balancing mass in the octagonal chapel of the Constable added to the east end, and finally the central lantern came to provide a harmonious focal point between the two extremes.

The effect of these three groups of pinnacles, pale yellow spires forcing their way upwards into a sky of solid blue, is unforgettable. A distant view of Burgos is a sight of a fairy building from lands of romance and chivalry. Even more than Lichfield or Regensburg,

38 BURGOS: the Capilla del Condestable of 1482–94,
by Simón de Colonia

39 The Nave
1450–1516,
Bartolomé
Solórzano, loo[
ing to the Tr.
coro of c. 150[
probably
S i m ó n [
Colonia

40 The Ambulatory of 1321–1424

PALENCIA

Looking east in the
Nave of 1530–39,
by Rodrigo Gil de
Hontañón

42   View from south-east of the chevet of 1471–1524, probably
by Simón de Colonia

ASTORGA

43 BURGOS: the north Ambulatory of 1222–60, perhaps by Ricardo of
Burgos and Maestro Enrique

Burgos transports us instantaneously to that imagined era of picturesque activity conjured up by the term of the Middle Ages, a dynamic interlude between the static solemnity of classical times and the humdrum contemporary world. At night, too, the tracery of the western steeples is thrown in silver relief against black velvet by floodlighting, so that even the passing traveller in the night express may catch a glimpse of what Burgos meant, and means, to Spain. For the cathedral is a symbol of the place, and that in turn as we have seen is inextricably bound up with the origin and growth of Spain's essential greatness. In recent years also, Burgos has regained

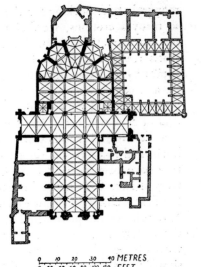

44 Burgos, 1222–60, probably by Ricardo and Enrique

much prestige owing to its temporary position as the capital of Spain during the Civil War, and shares in the aura of heroism which to many Spaniards surrounds what they regard as the latest episode of the Crusades. Burgos is in more than a merely historical sense the city of the Cid Campeador, and anachronistically enough the cathedral is its emblem.

Examined in detail, Burgos cathedral (44) is less satisfying than it seems from a distance. The main front was seriously damaged in the eighteenth century by the substitution of frigidly classical doorways for its magnificent portals; the openwork masonry of the spires by Hans of Cologne (Juan de Colonia) betrays the German origin of their designer by a certain crudity; the lantern is overloaded with an unhappy mixture of florid Gothic and plateresque Renaissance details. All three entrance fronts are surmounted by tall galleried screen-walls without any structural or aesthetic justification and rendered entirely pointless by the cathedral's low-pitched roofs. Inside too it is difficult to appreciate the spatial effects owing to the narrowness of the nave while the colossal crossing piers, rebuilt after a collapse in the sixteenth century, are lumpy and awkward besides being overlaid with ill-proportioned detail in a mongrel style. Seeking for the early Gothic design hidden beneath so many accretions, we find a church of considerable though immature attractions (43). Some features, notably the grouping of shafts round a cylindrical core and the plate-traceried triforium, appear to be drawn from Bourges, but the plan and design are eclectic and by no means a mere importation from France, though the plan of nave and transepts may owe something to the Norman cathedral of Sées which had just been set out, and Coutances Cathedral and the Cistercian Abbey of Pontigny also contributed features. The horizontal ridge-ribs of the nave, distinctively English in character, may have been derived from Coutances or from the English contacts of Ricardo, the royal master mason, who was almost certainly the first architect and must have come from Aquitaine.

In spite of the poor detail of the crossing, the upward view into the lantern is a fine one, closed by the double stellar vault inlaid with a lacework of minor ribs. But this is hardly so beautiful as the simpler one over the Constable's Chapel (38), added at the east end in 1482–94 by Simón de Colonia, son of the architect of the western towers and spires. The chapel, one of a group of comparable polygonal buildings of the same period, is an unusually pleasing treatment of a difficult problem and a happy instance of the incorporation of rich sculpture into architectural design without a disastrously indigestible result. Both inside and out the weight of enrichment decreases upwards while its complexity of detail increases, and while strength and solidity are suggested by the horizontal string-courses which link the walls together, a sufficiently dominant verticality is introduced by the finely moulded attached shafts in the angles, from which spring the sharply intersecting vault-ribs with piquant effect.

Burgos is so rich in chapels, monuments and contained works of art that it is impossible to give any short description. But apart from the church, the storied cloisters and old chapter-house, both of the first half of the fourteenth century, deserve a visit, the former especially for the tapestries and other collections of the diocesan museum which they contain. Nor is it possible to leave the cathedral without a mention of the two other churches of the front rank which stand outside the city in opposite directions: the early Gothic nuns' church of Las Huelgas with its royal tombs and amazing museum of precious fabrics found in them; and the Charterhouse of Miraflores, where Juan de Colonia worked from 1454, containing the magnificent tomb of John II and his queen by Gil de Siloé.

Following the line of the pilgrims' road, only two more cathedrals are met in Castile: León and Astorga. After the wide expanse of scorching plains and notwithstanding its own torrid climate, León has the stamp of a northern capital, an almost Aberdonian air. This is heightened by the un-Spanish appearance of the cathedral (45–7), one of the half-dozen most precious monuments of Gothic art on account of the nearly perfect preservation of its stained glass. It is in fact the only Gothic cathedral of the best period in which it is possible to appreciate fully the intentions of its builders. The masonry of Chartres is too early, the glass of Bourges too late and incomplete, while at York both architecture and glazing stand apart from the main stream. León belongs entirely to the peak of the metropolitan French tradition in design, though mellowed and improved by passing through the regions under English rule, where it lost the last stiff remains of Romanesque classicism and picked up its wide front with external towers, and the typically Norman trick of narrow lancets flanking wider openings, found in England in the thirteenth-century work at Lincoln. The main inspiration in plan and elevation comes from Rheims and proves that the work begun in 1204 cannot be the church we possess.

It seems likely that the present building was not set out before about 1255 and that Enrique, known to have had charge of the work

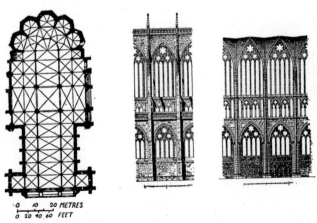

·0   10   20 METRES
0   20 40 60   FEET

45, 46, 47   León, 1255–1303, by Enrique

95

at Burgos from 1235 until his death in 1277 and who here directed
the whole of the first work, was the author. At León, as at Burgos,
he was succeeded by Juan Pérez, who died in 1296, when the church
was nearing completion, though the north transept was not ended
until 1448 and the south tower completed only in 1458–72. These
fifteenth-century additions, with the walls of the cloister and the
coro begun in 1464, were all designed by a master named Jusquín,
apparently the Joosken from Utrecht in Holland, who had worked
at Toledo in 1429 and at Tordesillas in 1430–35, at the latter place
with Guillén de Ruán (Rouen), his predecessor (d. 1431) at León.
Still later came the chapter staircase of 1525–34 and the strangely
unbeautiful cloister vaults (c. 1538–40) by Juan de Badajoz the
younger, whose father had built the Capilla de Santiago (1492–
1507).

The outside of Léon (14) does not make its appeal from a distance,
as does Burgos, for the western spires are relatively low, and the
high roofs for which gables were built have never been provided.
This has left a curious impression of ruin, but in other respects
León appears as one of the best composed of Spanish churches,
with a clear outline punctuated by the well-proportioned pinnacles
of its flying buttresses and its transeptal turrets. Both west and south
fronts have notable triple portals of the type of those of the Chartres
transepts, filled with statuary and carvings. A curious feature of
both the main fronts is the isolation of the nave or high transept
respectively, and the abutment given by flyers springing in the one
case from the towers outside the aisles, and in the transept from
corner turrets. In this respect, as well as in certain details, the
south front in particular has points of resemblance to the elevation
for a church front with triple porches, found in the well-known
Rheims palimpsest of c. 1250.

Internally, and it is within that are all the chief glories of the
place, the impression is exquisite (48). Though neither large nor
tall by French standards, the church has a slim elegance seldom
matched elsewhere in its period and the windows occupy almost
the whole of the wall space. The bay design is excellent, with an
openwork triforium architecturally linked to the clerestory and
itself glazed in an outer plane. Although the horizontal string-
courses beneath triforium and clerestory are carried round the
vaulting shafts, the capitals of the main arcade are not, with considerably increased vertical emphasis and refinement of line as

48 LÉON: looking north-east from the south transept; work of
1255–77 by Enrique of Burgos

49   ASTORGA: looking east in the south aisle of the Nave, 1530–59,
by Rodrigo Gil de Hontañón

compared with the model of Rheims. The fact that the *coro* takes up only the two eastern bays of the nave, while there are four bays to the west, enables an adequate vista to be seen from the main entrance. The *trascoro*, designed by Juan de Badajoz the younger about 1570, is fortunately provided with a central triumphal arch instead of the solid wall usual in Spain. This is apparently due to the fact that it stood originally beneath the eastern arch of the crossing, the *coro* being in the two western bays of the presbytery until 1746, an interesting proof of Street's thesis that Spanish choirs were not originally intended to block up the nave in the way most of them now do. The richly carved stalls themselves had been made in two series, both by Flemings: from 1467 to 1476 by Juan de Malinas, and thenceforward to 1481 by Diego Copín de Holanda.

Of the glass whole books might be written. By no means all belongs to the original scheme, and a substantial proportion of the total is modern glass inserted in the great restoration at the end of the last century to fill gaps. But the work was done with great care and with material harmonising with the old in colour and texture, so that only careful examination will reveal the insertions. However objectionable this may seem to the archaeological purist, aesthetically it is as it should be. For so much of the ancient glazing survived that it was possible in this way, as nowhere else in the world, to recreate wholly the glowing atmosphere of light which all the Gothic churches of northern Europe were meant to hold. Here at León, alone out of the several hundred surviving greater churches of the high Middle Ages, can we penetrate the veil (paradoxically a veil of harsh white light) which hides from us the intentions of the greatest artists our continent has known.

An exemption from taxes granted to the building staff in 1277 shows that in addition to the twenty masons, there were then a glazier and a smith at work, and there is an extensive series of windows of the late thirteenth century in the chevet and nave clerestories, in the eastern windows of the transepts and in the north aisle of the nave. Those on the west of the transept, with the north rose and several other windows in the south transept, are works of 1419–25 made by Juan de Arquer, possibly from Angers in France, There is also fifteenth-century glass in part of the nave triforium, and in the nave aisles, some of which was begun about 1451 by one Nicolás. In the Capilla de Santiago, a splendid late Gothic room to the south-east of the cloister, is glass of 1524 by Diego de Santillana,

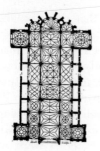

(*Lampérez*: *A. C. E. Espasa-Calpe*)

50 Astorga, 1471–1559, by Simón de Colonia and Rodrigo Gil de Hontañón

while Rodrigo de Herreras in 1565 painted that which fills the windows of the central chapel of the ambulatory.

Not much more than thirty miles to the west of León lies Astorga, a very ancient city still surrounded by the remains of enormous Roman walls. A Romanesque cathedral was consecrated in 1069 and another in the middle of the thirteenth century, but of these nothing is left. A fresh start was made in 1471, probably under Simón de Colonia, the chevet was glazed in 1524–27, and the nave built in 1530–59 by Rodrigo Gil de Hontañón (49). The west front, imitated in its general scheme from that of León, was not carried out until the Baroque period and the northern tower never was finished, the works coming to a stop in 1704.*

Considerably smaller than León, Astorga is not a large cathedral, but is tall for its size and impressive in scale both in its towered main front and in its buttressed polygonal apses at the east end, a plan which it shares with the contemporary Santa María la Redonda at Logroño and the later Barbastro.

The internal bay design (41) consists, as usual in such late works, of arcade and clerestory only, united by the moulded vaulting shafts which continue from base to springing without capitals; but here the cross-arches and ribs all spring from the shafts with a marked interpenetration of mouldings. The early bays at the east end retain rudimentary capitals, hardly more than a band of carving, upon the shafts of the main arcade and towards the aisles, but these are abandoned in the nave, where the piers are of simpler and more robust plan. The arches of the arcades, most singularly, are four-centred of the Tudor fashion though with less difference in radius between the larger and smaller arcs. This treatment seems to be almost unique in Spain, and once more suggests the presence of an English mason as a pilgrim on the road, though at Astorga no English details appear, and the four-centred arch could be merely the recollection of something shown in a sketch-book.

Astorga is a strange and lonely city, facing westwards towards the heaped ranges of mountains which divide Spain from Galicia,

* Work on the completion of the north tower has now begun (1956).

whither the pilgrimage road led on. Some of the smaller churches have kept traces of mediaeval work, especially San Julián, which has a good late Romanesque doorway, but for the most part the local style is Baroque of the seventeenth century, the last age of prosperity before decay set in. Now the city is one of the most melancholy and lost in Spain, in spite of its position on the main road and railway to Corunna and the fame of its little cakes called *mantecadas*. But for those interested in the later history of the cathedral as an art form, Astorga must always remain a place of pilgrimage in its own right.

The time has now come to leave the pilgrims' track in order to describe those cathedrals of Old Castile and the ancient kingdom of Leon which lie to the south of its course. They fall into several groups both chronologically and topographically. In the open valley of the Pisuerga are Palencia and Valladolid; close to the northern slopes of the great mountain chain are Burgo de Osma, Segovia and Ávila; west of this and bordering on Portugal are Zamora, Salamanca and Ciudad Rodrigo. The last three belong to the southward extension of Leon before its final union with Castile; the rest fall within the region conquered piecemeal by Castile from Islam before the end of the eleventh century. The frontier between Christian and Moslem Spain as it was about the year 1100 has a singular significance: north of it lie lands of ancient settlement with long individual histories of slow expansion southwards, but with highly individual characteristics such as local dialects and local types of building. Beyond the Guadarrama, all this gives place to a new world, relatively undifferentiated, of immense spaces and sparsely set towns. I use the words "new world" advisedly, for this is precisely what southern Spain was to the aggressive northerners of the early Middle Ages. Once they had flooded across the ranges they were able to take over enormous districts of land, build fresh cities and towns, and artificially plant them with colonists drawn from various parts of their old country to the north. Long before Spaniards set foot in America, they had had experience of colonisation in their own country.

Palencia, lying just off the main road and the main line of railway between Burgos and Madrid, is a city undeservedly underrated. Capital of a rich province, it contains a series of fine churches and a cathedral which, if not one of the first flight, is of large scale and possessed of a pleasant atmosphere of its own. Its character is largely determined by the warm creamy stone of which it is built, covered in part with a rich orange-brown patina apparently identical with that which covers the similar cream-coloured stone from the Isle of Wight of which Winchester College was made. The generic likeness is heightened by the fact that Palencia is a cathedral of the mature Gothic of the fourteenth and fifteenth centuries. This is the reason for Street's low estimate of the building, an estimate which must have had much to do with its neglect. Strictly correct as are the separate counts of Street's indictment, his verdict does much less than justice to a building of noble proportions and grand general impression. The outside is not striking apart from the good tower with its strangely asymmetrical buttresses and bell turret. The chevet, begun in 1321, has externally rather lean details and spidery flyers with pinnacles of inadequate mass. The chapels and the high apse have a singular frieze imitating tile-hanging, under the cornice which carries the parapet.

Beneath the *coro* in the middle of the structural nave is a crypt, the only relic of a basilica begun in A.D. 673, and entered through a barrel-vaulted apsidal chamber of the eleventh century. No doubt the Romanesque cathedral stood here, on the site of the existing nave, the work of the east end begun in 1321 being started on open ground. This explains the two distinct stages in the development of the Gothic church. The first, consisting only of the ambulatory with its five chapels and central high apse, was provided on its west side with a sort of false transept or pair of lateral porches; these are only of the height of the aisles, though each has an external doorway. This eastern work lasted for more than a century, the vaults being completed in 1424–29 by the mysterious master Isabrante, probably the same who was consulted at Saragossa in 1417 and at Seville in 1434. The detail of this build (40) is developed from that of Burgos and, apart from the vaulting, is typical of fourteenth-century work of a conservative character. The transept (c. 1440–50) was added by Pedro Jalopa, a master who had already worked at Huesca in Aragon.

The western bays (39) of the cathedral are quite different and were not begun until after 1450 and finished in 1516. The principal architect was Bartolomé de Solórzano, who died in 1507. In spite of the large scale and rather crude character of much of his detail, Solórzano must be given credit for a forceful design with bold and well-marked shafts and mouldings, sharply pointed arches and a well-designed Flamboyant triforium. The rather cramped clerestory is the weakest feature, but is more than ample for lighting by Spanish standards. Intermediate in date between the chevet and the nave are the tower and the Capilla de San Jerónimo, east of the south and north transepts respectively, and begun about 1435 by Gómez Día de Burgos. The *trascoro* of *c.* 1499–1519 is attributed to Simón de Colonia and its carvings to Gil de Siloé; it is a well composed but florid work, in which Gothic and Renaissance elements make somewhat uneasy bedfellows. Far more successful is the contemporary cloister by Juan Gil de Hontañón, an elegant work of simple mouldings and stellar vaulting, unfortunately spoilt by the walling up of all its arcades.

Valladolid had no cathedral in the Middle Ages, and the great church begun in the sixteenth century was not made the seat of a bishop until 1595. None the less it has to be considered among the most important of Spanish cathedrals, architecturally speaking, on account of its immense scale and the fame of its designer, Juan de Herrera. In his plan (51), however, Herrera largely followed what had been laid down as early as 1527 by Rodrigo Gil. Had the church been built as planned it would have been only five feet shorter than Seville and among the largest cathedrals in the world. Even as it is, cut in half and finished off according to the discordant ideas of several successive architects, it does not lack a quality of strict and puritan stateliness emphasised to the full by its cold grey stones (56–7). Its proportions and detail are even grimmer than its author's work at the Escorial, and seem to express the emotions appropriate to the met-

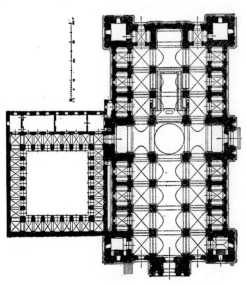

Schubert

51 Valladolid, 1580–, by Juan de Herrera; still unfinished

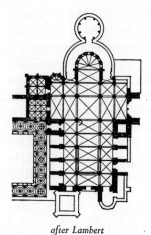

after Lambert

52   Burgo de Osma,
1232–c. 1300, by Lope;
cloisters 1510–23, by Juan
de la Piedra; west tower
1739–44   by   Dom.
Ondátegui

ropolitan church of a country run as a
penitentiary and with a population not
of warders and prisoners, but of prisoners alone.

It seems that the great but abnormal
mind of Philip II, for whose taste Herrera
worked, did indeed conceive of this
world in such terms, himself but the
first captive of the greatest state on
earth. Herrera's genius in interpreting
this view cannot be denied, any more
than the convincing simplicity and perfect lines of his work. Yet we may
doubt whether he and his king were
right in this neo-Cistercian view of
aesthetics, returning a blank negative to
the search for beauty in the work of
man's brain and hands. Our doubt is
accentuated by the marked clash between
the spirit of this cathedral and that of the
city in which it stands. For Valladolid
still bears the unmistakable imprint of a capital city, not only on its
buildings, but on the faces of its inhabitants; here the aristocratic
spirit reigns, and is exemplified in the fantasies of late Gothic and
Plateresque at San Pablo and San Gregorio, in the earliest Renaissance of the Colegio de la Santa Cruz, and in the Baroque of the
University. In this scene Herrera's solemn design is out of place,
and we welcome the twist of fate which decreed that the frontispiece
above his main portal should be completed by Alberto Churriguera.

It is from Valladolid that Burgo de Osma may most easily be
visited, and few greater architectural contrasts are to be imagined.
At Osma the whole church is of the purest Gothic, to which only
one major structural addition has been made: the tower of 1739–44
by Domingo Ondátegui, one of the finest products of Spanish
Baroque (53). It is hard to understand the neglect of this cathedral
by most writers, considering the very high quality of the building
and its unspoilt condition. Begun in 1232, Osma is a type specimen
of the Gothic cathedral of the first half of the thirteenth century,
and is moreover of substantial scale. Its plan (52) is derived from
that of Cuenca, but its construction and details mainly from Burgos,

with improvements. Here too can be seen the original proportions and design unaltered and crowned throughout by the vaults for which the compound piers were built (*19*). The arches are sharply pointed and all the mouldings of excellent section. It is a slight weakness in the bay design that the vaulting shafts are interrupted by a thin series of mouldings at the springing level of the arcades, but this is common to almost all work of the time, even in France. The triforium is a blind wall, but not unduly heavy, although the clerestory windows are kept above a string-course at the springing of the high vaults. In the chevet the windows are single lancets, while the normal bays have a two-light window with an uncusped circle in the head.

Four years after the start of the work a document mentions Don Lope as master of the work of the cathedral, and Johan de Medina as *cantero* or stonemason. The Spanish description *maestro de la obra* is normally applied to the master mason or actual architect, while *cantero* means a working mason; the inference here is that Medina was the leading hand or possibly the resident master in charge, while Lope may have been only an occasional visitor. Medina, the Arabic word for a city, is not revealing, though it may well stand for Medinaceli, less than sixty miles to the south-east of Osma and close to Sigüenza. In any case there can be little doubt from their names that the two men were Spaniards, and this is borne out by the whole character of their work, which has none of the foreign feeling of Cuenca and is substantially more acclimatised than Burgos. Though shorter and lower than Burgos, Osma has a wider span.

Burgos is certainly responsible for the character of the great portal of the south transept, imitated from the corresponding doorway, the Puerta del Sarmental, in the capital. At Burgos the transeptal fronts were in hand by 1257, and the work here is no doubt substantially later but was probably finished well before the end of the century. The statuary in this porch is of very great beauty and grace, some of the figures being equal to the best of Burgos and León. But of even greater interest and extraordinary rarity is the tomb, in the north transept, made for the local saint, San Pedro de Osma, in 1258 (*54–5*). This seems to be unique in two respects: the figure of the saint is treated with complete naturalism carried to an extreme, his head lying sideways upon a tilted pillow held by angels; while the sides of the chest are wholly filled with scenes of the saint's life, miracles and death in high relief, entirely without any containing architectural framework. The reliefs are carved with immense gusto and include many valuable portrayals of costume and contemporary life.

Leaving the church itself, several of the dependencies are worth seeing, including the large cloisters begun by Juan de la Piedra in 1510 and of extremely refined design and detail. At their southeastern corner, opening off the north transept, is the vestry, a square chamber divided into nine bays of ribbed vaulting supported upon four slender columns; this dates from before 1281. Above it and approached from the transept by a double staircase is the curious Renaissance chapel of San Pedro built in 1530-47, forming an extraordinary contrast in style with the neighbouring cloisters begun less than a generation earlier. Late in the eighteenth century an ambulatory was constructed by cutting through the two inner apsidal chapels of the transepts, and at the east a large circular chapel was built in honour of the Venerable Juan de Palafox, Bishop of Osma, to the designs of Juan de Villanueva advised by Luis Bernasconi. This again is curious rather than beautiful, but the Baroque tower (53) deserves serious study. Earlier than that of La Calzada, it is obviously one of the sources from which Beratúa was rather later to draw his inspiration. Here Ondátegui produced a sturdy and masculine steeple of very simple treatment, reducing the classic orders to panelled pilasters, broken pediments and cornices and an adaptation of the triglyph. The tall lower stage is almost unadorned and is crowned with a strong entablature, balustrade and corner pinnacles; above this comes a smaller square stage with pairs of windows in which the bells are hung, again finished with entablature, balustrade and pinnacles, and supporting a small dome which itself bears a pinnacled and domed lantern, abutted by a series of inverted consoles. The pinnacles in their own idiom brilliantly echo those of the Isabelline buttresses below. The total height is 236 feet, only 9 feet more than the spire of St. Bride's, Fleet Street, but the tower at Osma dominates the whole city and the countryside, for no other high building exists as far as eye can see.

Of the cathedral at Ávila something has already been said,* but it is impossible to pass this fantastic city of another age without comment. If Burgos symbolises the romance of chivalry, it is Ávila that brings home the grimness, fear and fanaticism that went hand

* See p. 50.

53 BURGO DE OSMA: the Tower of 1739–44, by Domingo Ondátegui,
seen above the south chapels, begun c. 1494

54, 55 The Shrine of
San Pedro de
Osma, ordered
in 1258

BURGO DE OSMA

56 The west front,
begun in 1580;
upper stage by
Alberto Churri-
guera, 1730–33

Interior of the Nave,
1580–85, by Juan de
Herrera

VALLADOLID

in hand with the heroic ideal. Seen from a distance, as for example from a passing train, Ávila has the startling impact of a fairy-tale suddenly come true. The great wall with its drum towers looks now as it has done these eight centuries and more and, in spite of suburbs old and new, still keeps the city isolated on almost all sides from the world without. This is no over-restored museum piece like Carcassonne, but a genuine survival from a world of savagery as cruel, if less mealy-mouthed, than our own. It was left for the cathedral, the great House of God of this city of refuge, to build the greatest and most warlike bastion of all in which to shelter its sanctuary. Here, in sharp juxtaposition, we see the two sides of the medal again exemplified in the personality of the saint of Ávila, St. Theresa. There seems even to be a faintly ironic symbolism in the fact that while the walls and houses of Ávila are built of a pale yellowish stone, sometimes tinged with gold, the cathedral (58) is a cold dark grey.

Less than three hours from Ávila, Segovia differs from the sister city to an astonishing degree. Both are fortresses of the mountain range, both abound in Romanesque churches; yet how changed is the air and the spirit. Segovia is more self-consciously picturesque in its romanticism and has suffered more from the hand of the well-intentioned restorer, yet its human atmosphere is charged with warmth and a sprightliness which may reflect the time when Segovia was a royal residence. Here was not the serious and restrained courtliness of Valladolid, but the gaiety of noblemen bent on sport with hawk and hound, breathing the fresh mountain air and scanning the immense panorama seen from the turrets of the Alcázar. Some of this freedom is caught by the great cathedral, splendidly set on the hill-top and seen from all sides.

Before the cathedral came to be built, there had been added to its predecessor a new cloister (63) designed by Juan Guas, a Frenchman long settled at Toledo, and built in the twenty years 1472–91, which is filled with the gay abandon that the florid but

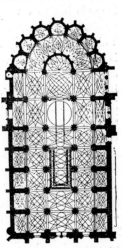

59 Segovia Cathedral, 1522–, by Juan Gil de Hontañón

still pure and undebased Gothic of that time can best portray. So beautiful was it thought fifty years after (surely a bitter test!) that it was taken down and re-erected stone by stone to accord with the plan of the new church. It is still as beautiful, one of the most poetic of cloisters with its simple vaults, sharp and elegant mouldings, and airy traceries. The church is less poetic or at least less lyrical in its outburst. It is as much the product of thought as of feeling, yet it demonstrates the power which could be reached by design according to the complex code of the last mediaeval masters. Here indeed is geometry demonstrated in solid stone, counterpoint and harmony made visible (1). This is the last cathedral of first-class rank to be built as a whole in Gothic style, not merely in Spain but in the world, and to that extent it remains as the summation, the last word, of all that the mediaeval architects have to tell.

The plan (59) is laid out symmetrically and proportioned by rule. It has three aisles and external cellular chapels adopted from the Catalan scheme, a chevet of seven chapels surrounding an ambulatory, eastern arm of one square bay, a transept which does not project beyond the outer walls, and five bays of nave. If there is a fault, it is that all this is a trace too orderly, too much the outcome of hard work with scale and compasses, too little the child of fancy. Segovia has to a very high degree the national quality of appearing cubical, and each part of the church is as it were a separate box. This is particularly noticeable within, where each bay of vaulting is marked off by cross-arches rather too firmly from its neighbours, and horizontal bands of mouldings and enrichment at times become insistent. Some of these faults are lessened, if not entirely avoided, in the eastern arm (64), not begun until 1563 and by Rodrigo Gil, son of the original architect. What is especially noteworthy is that there had been a progressive improvement, in that Juan Gil had already eliminated some of the faults which appear in his earlier design for the new cathedral at Salamanca.

The great tower (1) of Segovia was struck by lightning in 1614 and afterwards altered. We do not know exactly what was done, except that its total height is said to have been lessened by 22 feet. The existing lantern is obviously part of the alterations carried out in 1620, but the tower proper seems to be homogeneous in design and it may be that what was taken down was a taller lantern of Gothic form. It is on record that the original tower was taller than the Giralda at Seville, the height being compared more than once

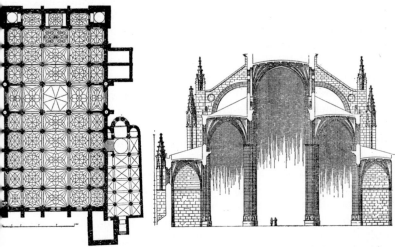

60, 61 Salamanca, 1152–c. 1200; and 1512– by Juan Gil de Hontañón

by a line brought thence. The design is very simple and consists
of stages of increasing height marked with sunk panels or windows
between narrow buttresses which increase the apparent scale of the
tower. Apart from the Renaissance lantern, there is a strong suggestion of English influence in massing and treatment, and Juan Gil
must at least have had some information on such towers as those of
Canterbury, Magdalen College, and Boston. His drawings for the
cathedral are preserved in the library off the cloisters, and are of
unusual interest in that scales are shown. Most Gothic drawings
lack a scale, but it is probably fanciful to suppose that this had any
esoteric meaning; more likely each master, or each building lodge,
adhered to certain regularly employed scales. For the essential
difference between the classical and mediaeval codes of proportion
lies in the fact that, whereas a single plan could serve for several
temples of different sizes by merely changing the module, each
Gothic design was separately related to actual human scale and the
real dimension was a vital part of the drawings.

From Segovia it is reasonable to move to Salamanca, to consider
first the new cathedral (60, 61) with its fundamentally similar design.
Though of nearly identical dimensions and closely similar forms, the
two churches make very different impressions. This is largely due
to the far richer external details at Salamanca, leaving less blank

walling exposed; in spite of the square east end, which makes so profound a contrast with the apsidal chevet of Segovia, the cubical composition at Salamanca is less aggressive because cloaked beneath enrichments. Groups of crocketed pinnacles make a braver show and the overall view for that reason more Gothic. The western portals too are a triumph of ingenious filigree carving and sculpture, however overloaded they may seem if examined closely. Internally (62, 65) there is more solemnity than at Segovia, partly due perhaps to the square east end which yields no softening curves, but largely to the heavy band of capitals encircling every pier and to the greater emphasis on horizontals elsewhere. The difference is, however, more subtle than this: the piers themselves, though superficially of the same type, with many moulded shafts rising from bases at different heights in a base of interpenetrating mouldings like wickerwork, have quite different values of light and shade. At Segovia the only shafts are small in proportion and the pier is made up of varied mouldings; at Salamanca the main members are round shafts of substantial size flanked by slender bowtels or separated by deep hollows, giving a far more solid and even heavy massing.

The effect of the new cathedral at Salamanca is then of splendour coupled with a grave decorum; precisely what was needed in the great church of the principal university of the Peninsula, and in a city larger than contemporary Oxford and Cambridge together. It was the enormous growth of the student population and the international fame of Salamanca as a centre of learning that had led to the building of this great pile to replace the far older Transitional cathedral, itself possessed of a grave dignity of its own. By a lucky accident the old church was not destroyed and still nestles under the wing of its giant younger sister. The transition in scale is perhaps more startling than the change of style; we are here once more close to the atmosphere of Jaca in a church whose total length is well under 200 feet.

The general character of this little cathedral (11) has already been discussed,* and it remains only to comment on a few of its special characteristics. The central cupola, as has been said, probably derives from Jerusalem, and the transmission was no doubt through returning pilgrims; but it was not from Jerusalem that they brought the method of superimposing an outer dome above an inner shell, or the many converging ribs which support the latter. The ribs,

* See p. 46.

62 SALAMANCA: New Cathedral. The Nave of 1512–38, by Juan Gil de
Hontañón, and choir of 1725–33 by Alberto Churriguera

69 arscovir: the Cloister of

65 SALAMANCA: New Cathedral. Looking
north-east in the crossing of 1538-60,
by Rodrigo Gil de Hontañón

64 SEGOVIA: looking east in the crossing of
1563-91, by Rodrigo Gil de Hontañón

66 ZAMORA: looking west from the Capilla Mayor,

67 CIUDAD RODRIGO: looking west in the church

like those earlier ones of the lantern at Jaca, are to be found nearer at hand in Moslem Spain, and may have been brought to Salamanca along the pilgrim road by way of Jaca and so to Zamora, the admitted original of this series of Gothic domes. Important not for its source but for its progeny is the circular moulded plinth on which the bases of the piers stand. These seem to have suggested the far later drums supporting the basket-work type of late-Gothic base, employed here in the new cathedral, at Segovia, Plasencia and elsewhere.

Interesting and important as the two cathedrals are, they are far from being the sole reasons for visiting Salamanca, one of the grandest of all the ancient cities of Spain and indeed of Europe. The mellow stateliness befitting an ancient seat of learning is enhanced by the happy accident of the local stone. It takes on a golden tone of the utmost splendour and quite unmatched elsewhere. But it is not only the stone which is golden in Salamanca, for its bread, the famous *pan candial*, has a crust of the same glorious colour as the stone, though luckily of a very different consistency. These colours on masonry seem to be due in part to living microorganisms, which probably differ from one district to another, and certainly grow only upon particular varieties of stone. Here is a problem in ecology which deserves detailed study. Used internally the stone of Salamanca does not turn to gold, but remains a warmed cream limestone of delicate tones but sturdy texture.

Between Salamanca and Portugal is the little town of Ciudad Rodrigo, accidentally famous for its sieges in the Peninsular War, in which the cathedral suffered marked damage. The church (67), another comparatively small building of the same general type as the old cathedral at Salamanca, is surprisingly different in detail. Salamanca was in progress from 1152 to 1189, Ciudad Rodrigo from 1166 to nearly 1230, when the vaults were finished. It is these vaults which are so unusual in Spain: octopartite and steeply domical, they are unquestionably derived from the west of France. Of the latest work, carried out in the first third of the thirteenth century, the most beautiful piece is the western doorway with its slender central mullion bearing a statue of the Virgin and on either side statues of the Apostles standing each upon a model of the Torre del Gallo of Salamanca, a testimonial to the fame which this latter must have achieved within a generation or so of its completion. This west front must at first have resembled that of San Vicente at

Ávila, the great portal being recessed between two towers linked by a tall arch. But here the towers were later cut down to chapels and a single central tower substituted in 1765 by Juan de Sagarvinaga, a Basque who had built the Sacristies at Salamanca (1755–59).

The stone of the cathedral is like fossilised mud of variegated colour, and looks as though lumps would fall out at a touch; but it is really solid and of sufficiently fine texture to be carved, as it is in the cloisters. These are of two widely differing dates, the south and west walks being Gothic, while those on the north and east are Plateresque. The structure of the earlier walks seems to be of the thirteenth century, but contains geometrical tracery inserted after 1319 by a master, Benito Sánchez, whose memorial tablet survives. The later master, Pedro Güemes, who completed the cloister in 1525–38 is also commemorated by a medallion portrait in high relief, together with that of the clerk of the works. The capitals of the church and the earlier part of the cloister are enriched with carvings of importance, while the choir stalls by Rodrigo Alemán are notorious for their impertinent and occasionally obscene grotesques. The sanctuary was rebuilt in 1538–50, it is thought by Rodrigo Gil de Hontañón, but although a pleasant work shows no signs of genius.

Leaving Ciudad Rodrigo, with its ancient mansions and its charming poplar-strown meadows, we must turn northwards to the last of the Leonese cathedrals, Zamora. Built upon a long ridge in a loop of the River Duero, the city is defended by ancient fortifications which gave it the name in ballad and romance of *la bien cercada*, the well-walled. Scattered through its long, narrow streets are some half-dozen Romanesque churches of great beauty, and at the southern end of the fortifications beside the old castle stands the cathedral. Zamora is the only Spanish cathedral city on the whole course of the Duero, a fact which gives it special importance when the vital role of this river is considered. All through the arid plains of Castile and Leon it runs, a source of agricultural riches and a boon to eyes tired of the glaring and barren landscapes of Spanish summer. Yet between Soria close to its source and Oporto at its mouth there is no centre of any size apart from this.

Few would now imagine that Zamora had been one of the key cities of the Peninsula in the wars with the Moors and between the Christian kingdoms; but that it was so in the twelfth century becomes more credible upon studying the cathedral (66). Though the same size as the old cathedral at Salamanca, Zamora appears more imposing because it is not overshadowed by a vastly greater successor, because of its commanding situation on the hilltop, and on account of its noble square tower, among the finest Romanesque towers in the country. The eastern part of the church was built in 1151–74, the nave finished in 1225, and the tower soon after 1236. More famous than the tower is the central lantern, the model for the Torre del Gallo at Salamanca and a singular specimen of structural ingenuity and the wide diffusion of art motives. Aesthetically it is less satisfactory, though the early pointed arcade which surrounds it and its corner turrets has a certain naïve charm. A curious point of chronology is that, while pointed arches are employed throughout the church, the windows at the top of the later tower are all round-headed.

The details are unusually delicate for the period and include finely moulded bases set on square plinths with a hollow splay of beautiful curvature, and ingenious though simple capitals which have little slots cut out beneath the abacus to give the idea of battlements, each cap representing a small castle. At the east end the sanctuary and its lateral chapels are a late rebuilding of 1496–1506, with good lierne vaulting of sharply moulded ribs. Here again an outstanding feature of the church is the set of choir-stalls begun in 1490 by Rodrigo Alemán, and the wrought-iron screens of the sanctuary are exceptionally good. But what most recalls the heroic past is the series of magnificent tapestries of the fifteenth and sixteenth centuries, among the most splendid in existence, now kept in the cathedral museum off the cloisters.

Going north again towards Astorga to pick up the pilgrimage road we cross once more the great tableland, intersected by rivers but dry and dusty, whitish-brown shading off to grey and purple in the west, where great ranges rise on the borders of Portugal and Galicia. By now we have seen all the cathedrals of Castile and Leon, the old united kingdoms from which the new Spains sprang. Exploring further we shall discover other families of buildings which in their turn would contribute to the later glories of Spanish architecture. But here is the heart of the matter, the bare wide meseta stretching from the Cantabrian cordillera to the Guadarrama, from the Sierra de Moncayo to the Montañas de León. What we have seen is not the whole, is not the greatest, but it is the basic, the fundamental, the essentially formative part of Spain and Spanish art.

CHAPTER THREE

Galicia and Asturias

THE passage from the central tableland of Spain to Asturias or to Galicia is a startling change. This is largely a matter of climate and vegetation but even more one of human atmosphere. Much as Galicia and Asturias differ from one another, they share in a relatively high rainfall and their landscapes are consequently un-Spanish. Asturias belongs to northern Europe, Galicia to the far-off western nations along with the Hebrides, Wales, Ireland and Portugal. Even though we know that the Atlantic Ocean is not the end of all things and that the world goes on across it and round about, the lands of sunset Europe are all tinged with a mournful shadow. These countries are at least half-way towards what men once called, between hope and fear, the Fortunate Isles. In one of his most brilliant and perceptive essays, Azorín captures the change in tempo and feeling that is experienced in leaving Madrid by the old and ramshackle Corunna express and waking up in the small hours at a wayside station to hear the clatter of wooden pattens on the platform and the murmur of strangely melodious words, later to see fine rain falling from an opalescent sky.

The truth is that in Galicia we have in a certain sense put the clock back and are visitors to a civilisation long gone and here alone poised between waking and asleep. Galicia is the last and least changed remnant of the ancient empire of Leon and has roots which stretch still further back to the days of Visigothic rule. For Galician is the closest living tongue to the language spoken at these former courts and driven out by the explosive vigour of Castilian, and to this distant corner there came as refugees many of those who were temperamentally unfitted for the hurly-burly of strenuous times. It is customary nowadays for Spaniards to speak of Galicia and its people with scorn, regarding it as a land of village idiots and menials, but we may seek a corrective in recalling that Alfonso the Wise, brother of that Eleanor of Castile who married our

68 Looking north-east in the crossing, 1075–1102, by Bernardo el Viejo and others

69 The exterior elevation of the Nave, 1088–1102, by Maestro Esteban

SANTIAGO DE COMPOSTELA

70 SANTIAGO DE COMPOSTELA: the western Towers of 1738–50, by Fernando Casas y Nóvoa, seen from the Cloister begun 1521–37 by Juan de Álava

Edward I, wrote his best poems in Galician, and that Rosalía de
Castro (1837–85) is probably the only European poetess of any
age that it would not be ridiculous to mention in the same breath
as Sappho.

It might be thought that the constant multitudes of pilgrims that
for hundreds upon hundreds of years flocked to the shrine of St.
James the Great would have effectively broken this ancient peace,
yet it is at Santiago de Compostela itself that we feel most strongly
the sensation of entering a world that is dead, or at least in a state
of trance like the Sleeping Beauty. During the daytime, it is true,
a swarm of shops and hawkers are there to catch the eye and purse
of the pilgrim and the tourist, but after dark the narrow arcaded
streets belong to a realm that has slowly sunk through the deep
abyss of past time, and the steady fine rain adds to the illusion that
these are palaces on the sea bed, many fathoms down.

The sources of the plan (10) and design of the eleventh-century
cathedral have already been discussed,* and the little that is known
of its architects. All the essentials of the interior as we see them
now were completed by 1200. The exterior is almost entirely
cloaked in the works of masters of a very different sort, brought
up in the most extravagant fantasies of the Baroque. It is not surprising that Santiago, the richest pilgrimage centre of Spain and
so a chief beneficiary of the wealth imported from her colonies in
the first two centuries after the discovery of America, should be
able to show more of this luxury art than any other cathedral of the
Peninsula. Though not extravagantly large in itself, Santiago's
cathedral is so placed among surrounding buildings of large scale
that the group as a whole appears immense. This impression is
heightened by the wide spread of the west front and its raised
position. Almost the whole of the outside (70) is transformed into
Baroque, the first important step being the building, on a mediaeval
base, of the belfry beside the south transept in 1676–80 by Domingo
de Andrade who had been working on the reredos of the high altar
since 1664. This set the tone for the rest, though the great western
towers and screen were not carried out until 1738–50, to the designs of Andrade's pupil, Fernando Casas y Nóvoa. The Baroque
inspiration still ruled when the north front was begun in 1758
under the local architects Lucas Ferro Caaveiro (pupil in his turn
of Casas y Nóvoa) and Clemente Fernández Sarela, who built the

* See pp. 39–41.

lower stage; but the rest was neoclassicised by Ventura Rodríguez after 1765, the Compostelan artists being dismissed, a singular example of the pressure of changing fashion.

The immense scale of the southern belfry, the Torre del Reloj, is set by its mediaeval base, made still more impressive by the addition of panelled pilasters, five on each face, which spring from corbels set in the plain face of the wall. This simple first stage is some two-and-a-half cubes in height, ending in a rich cornice surmounted by a balustrade broken out around four angle turrets and intervening frontispieces. Within these rises a second square stage pierced with large windows and again bearing a cornice and corner turrets, from which rises the octagonal lantern containing the bells. Casas y Nóvoa adopted the leading motives of this tower for his western pair but altered and on the whole improved the detail. His skill shows at its best, however, in the immense frontispiece or false front which he built between the towers and over the western portals. Seen from the west there is nothing mediaeval in this immense façade, but from other points of view one may see how thin a veneer is applied to the Romanesque towers which still survive (70), and how closely the whole composition is based upon the original structure. The most interesting result is that the front has a strongly dominant verticality marked by two orders of detached shafts in advance of the wall, by pilasters on the towers and by inverted consoles which support the lanterns.

The qualities of Compostelan architecture, Romanesque, Gothic and Renaissance, derive to a large extent from the local grey granite which especially contributed to the flat treatment of detail in the highly individual school of Galician Baroque architects. The wet climate too is conducive to a growth of lichens which fleck the grey with touches of green and gold and add to the already strong sensation of sunset shadows a pervasive melancholy. This is the architecture of evening, of pensive contemplation and reflections upon the world's change and slow decay. The sea is out of sight, but the west front of the cathedral seems to gaze out across the Atlantic towards the Isles of the Blest, as might a congregation of Celtic hermits in the golden age of Cornwall or Connemara. Had a Celtic nation ever produced a great architecture it would have comprised buildings such as this.

The original Romanesque treatment of the exterior was impressive (69). Inasmuch as the triforium gallery surrounded the

whole church, there was no clerestory, but two ranges of windows
in the outer walls. To give adequate abutment to the vaults within,
buttresses project between the bays, not as flat strips in the usual
manner of the time, but in a double order, and these two orders of
buttresses are linked together as a double order of semicircular
arches crowning the wall and framing the upper windows. A similar
treatment on a smaller scale can be seen on the still uncovered parts
of the western towers and was no doubt the source which suggested
to Andrade the application of vertical pilasters to the Torre del
Reloj. Internally the bay design is outstanding for its early period,
verticality being much emphasised by the deeply stilted arches and
the tall shafts which carry the cross ribs of the barrel-vault (68, 71),
while a string-course enriched with billets runs beneath the triforium in a plane behind these shafts and is sufficient to provide
a sense of continuity linking the bays.

The cloister (70), among the largest in Spain, is 146 feet square.
Begun in 1521, it was the outcome of an architectural competition
won by Juan de Álava, who directed the work until his death in
1537, after which it was continued by Rodrigo Gil de Hontañón
and others, and finished about 1590. The original design, as seen at
the north-west angle, is Gothic, with basketwork bases, no capitals,
finely grouped pinnacled buttresses and a rich perforated parapet.
During execution the arches became semicircular and classical
pedestals were substituted for the bases. But the result is successful
in spite of the occasional obtrusion of disharmonious detail. The
pattern of the buttresses is important as a documented work of
Juan de Álava, for it provides stylistic proof of the disputed extent
of his work at the very important new cathedral of Plasencia, as we
shall later see.

Santiago is the great centre of Galicia
and its former capital, but is far from
monopolising the artistic attractions
of the ancient kingdom. Lovers of
Gothic will find more to attract them at
Orense, a city with a special atmosphere
of its own. Orense is fortunate in the
quality of its light, quite different from
that of Santiago or anywhere else. Less
rainy than most parts of Galicia, moisture
here takes the form of a very fine

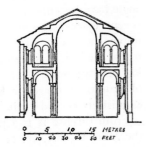

71 Santiago, 1075–1128,
by Bernardo

opalescent or pearly veil which is present even during bright sunshine. This produces a soft glow over the buildings of the town and the surrounding countryside; here, town and country interpenetrate to a degree unusual in Spain, and one might call Orense a garden city if that term had not acquired a special sense.

The cathedral's exterior is a mixture of many styles and entirely lacks aesthetic coherence. But within there is all the grace of the best Transitional Gothic (72). The plan and to some extent the arrangement of details are borrowed from Santiago, but they are completely transformed. The heavy triforium gallery is replaced by a normal clerestory above the main arcades, which are of stilted pointed arches of fine curvature, while the high vaults have plain cross-arches and moulded diagonal ribs, the latter springing from corbels placed beside the capitals which crown the vertical shafts bearing the cross-arches, a pleasing trick. The western entrance is a version of the Santiago Pórtico de la Gloria on a smaller scale; though lacking the majesty and much of the power of its prototype, the Orense Paraiso, as it is called, has a slim grace which is new. Of later works the most outstanding is the central lantern, internally rivalling that of Burgos in interest. It was built in 1499–1505 by Rodrigo de Badajoz.

In the angle between the nave and the north transept is the Capilla de San Juan Bautista, whose style suggests English influences, especially in its five-light window of reticulated tracery, some of whose supermullions rise in Perpendicular fashion to the crown of the arch (78). In the Cloister a Cathedral Museum is being installed to house the rich treasure which includes a magnificent processional cross and a series of Limoges enamels. The bays at the north-eastern angle have two fine wall-paintings of c. 1400, discovered during the recent works. The student of cloisters should not miss the other important one in Orense, now concealed within the barracks on top of the hill. It is readily accessible on application and of outstanding beauty; built c. 1308–32 for the Franciscan friary, it consists of groups of three or five bays of arcading on twin shafts with exquisitely carved capitals.

From Orense it is a picturesque journey through the gorges of the Miño to Tuy, set on a hill opposite to the Portuguese frontier town of Valença. The climatic change is very great, for Tuy lies at a low level and close to the sea. In spite of the river, the

72 ORENSE: the western portal of *c.* 1240

73 TUY: the Nave
of *c.* 1225

74 LUGO: the south
Ambulatory begun
in 1 3 0 8 b y
Juan Fernández

75　LUGO: the Transept of 1129–77, by Raimundo de Monforte

77 LUGO: the western Towers of 1769–84, by
Julián Sánchez Bort, seen from the Cloister of

76 MONDOÑEDO: the main front of 1705

surroundings look dried up and in this respect Tuy seems more Spanish than Galician. The cathedral occupies the top of the hill and is surrounded by narrow streets so that little can be seen of the exterior except for the unusual west front with its open porch (29) resembling in character though not in detail that of Montpellier Cathedral in France. The whole of the church is fortified and battlemented and it presumably must have been intended for defence in border warfare. The original work of the crossing and transept is Transitional and early Gothic, built between c. 1170 and 1225; the transept vaults were finished in 1239 and the west front reached by 1287. Meanwhile the very charming

78 Orense: window of Capilla de San Juan Bautista, c. 1468

cloister of pure Gothic was in progress in 1264, and though works on it are recorded in 1408 and 1464 it is clearly almost all of thirteenth-century date. The east end of the church was rebuilt with a square front in 1495–99, but the most striking alteration to its original appearance is the insertion of a series of strainer arches as at Vitoria, in this case built after the Lisbon earthquake of 1755.

It would seem that Tuy was intended at first to have a vaulted tribune abutting barrel vaults over the nave, as at Santiago, but in the course of erection the scheme was changed and a continuous band of blind arcading substituted for the triforium, while the vaults became ribbed cross-vaults (73). The transepts are aisled, as at Santiago, and this gives an air of consequence to the church in spite of its small size. The best feature is the western doorway with its outer porch, the latter of particularly effective proportions, with paired buttresses to the two piers and finely moulded arches, sharply pointed, resting on carved leaf capitals. The doorway within is single, with statues on columns at each side and a carved tympanum beneath a stilted pointed arch of seven orders.

Tuy is in the extreme south-west of Galicia; about the same distance from Santiago to the east is Lugo, a city and cathedral of far greater importance. Lugo is in the middle of a wide and high-lying countryside of heaths covered with gorse and ling, close to but not actually on the River Miño. The city is chiefly famous for its massive Roman wall built of slate, still making the complete circuit and with four gates and eighty towers, the finest in existence. The city has better claims to artistic fame in its mediaeval buildings and in the survival here of the tradition of guitar-playing. The cathedral (74–5) is closely imitated from Santiago in its nave but has short un-aisled transepts and a rebuilt Gothic chevet of c. 1308–30 by Juan Fernández, whose work is based on that of Burgos. The first architect was Raimundo de Monforte, who undertook the work in 1129, his contract stipulating that if he did not live to finish the church, it should continue under the direction of his son. It has been suggested that this son was the famous Maestro Mateo of Santiago; a nonsensical hypothesis, seeing that Mateo died in 1217, while Raimundo's son must have been of an age to direct building operations when his father's contract was drawn up in 1129.

As at Orense, there is here an aesthetic improvement upon the Romanesque design of Santiago: the nave is widened and is also a little higher, having a pointed vault; the short transepts make the design far more compact. Though rather too low, the triforium is much lightened. To the east of the north transept is a good tower, quite plain and unbuttressed, with pairs of two-light traceried windows near the top of its main stage. Above this rises the bell chamber with pairs of openings in which the bells hang, surmounted by a curious kind of truncated octagon with a balustrade. The belfry and its crown were added in 1577, clumsily enough. But not long before, perhaps about 1530, a very fine open porch had been added beneath, to the doorway of the north transept. This porch is precisely in the style of Juan de Álava's cloister at Santiago and may have been designed by the master when on one of his journeys to or from Compostela.

Lugo continued to suffer extensive additions and alterations. In 1726 an eastern Lady Chapel and a great cloister (77) were designed by Casas y Nóvoa, but both of these are excellent of their time. Less fortunate was the importation of the Frenchman Charles Lemaur who in 1764 classicised the *capilla mayor* and produced an execrable high altar in a style between wedding cake and gingerbread. Last and worst blow of all was the complete reconstruction of the west front to the designs of the uninspired engineer Sánchez Bort, who worked under some pressure from Ventura Rodríguez. This front was mostly built between 1769 and 1784, but the towers were still unfinished in 1830. Lugo is almost unique in being permitted the perpetual display of the exposed Host, an observance which brings many devotees and keeps the church open by day and night.

Lugo is on the main road and main line to Corunna and at the head of the side road that leads to the pretty village of Mondoñedo, with Galicia's last and least visited cathedral. The road climbs a high range, from which there is an amazing view of the little city almost immediately below. Though very small, the cathedral has an imposing front with towers placed outside the aisles and altered in 1705 into a Baroque composition with a central frontispiece (76). The design is extremely skilful, preserving the three Gothic arches which mark the nave and aisles, and the central portal and great rose. The two buttresses which projected between the arches are transformed into pilasters and the whole front is capped with a light cornice crowned with a balustrade broken forward round the towers and over the pilasters. The towers are brilliantly linked to the front beneath the cornice by means of a deep moulded course from which hang shaped aprons moulded back to the plain face of the wall.

Inside the west doors we face the *trascoro*, above whose altar is a standing figure of the Virgin and Child with six seraphim carved in wood; it is known as "la Ynglesa", being supposed to have been brought from Old St. Paul's at the Reformation. Above the *coro* on each side are richly carved Baroque organs. The vault is low but well built of large blocks and supported by cross-arches of square section and well-moulded diagonal ribs which here rest on nook shafts continuing down to the floor. The capitals are finely carved and bases well moulded, suggesting that first-class craftsmen were brought from a distance, while the master must have been adequately informed of architectural developments. For while the structural organisation is Galician, that is to say derived from Santiago, the piers have the circular plinths of the old cathedral at Salamanca and the wide west front with flanking towers is borrowed from Sigüenza, which even provides the model for the three shallow arches divided by buttresses. It is all but certain that Lampérez (who says that he had not seen Mondoñedo) is wrong in stating that there were no projecting transepts before the existing pair were built in 1778–97: the bays on each side of the crossing have always been true transepts, as high as the nave and sanctuary, and have attached piers at the angles of the projecting transepts, demanding a continuation. Such shallow transepts would again reflect the plan of Sigüenza. The east end had at first three parallel apses but those at the sides were cut through to make an ambulatory leading to the square east end which contains a range of four chapels, finished in 1603.

Mondoñedo lies on the direct route from Corunna to Oviedo, after a few miles passing the giant monastery of Lorenzana with its Baroque front. Though Galicia and Asturias both have a moist climate and thus resemble one another in their relatively rich vegetation, they are in other respects very different. Galicia is a country of the western seaboard, intersected by deep river valleys, with high heaths and ranges of hills between. Asturias on the other hand is a narrow strip of rolling country lying between the steep northern slope of the Cantabrian mountains and the coast of the Bay of Biscay. The soil is rich and also contains great mineral wealth, but the country is essentially a mountainous one and its inhabitants are famed for the typical obstinacy of a people of mountaineers. Historically, Asturian pride in this quality is founded upon the successful resistance of Pelayo to the Moors, but it has in recent years become symbolically attached, in a poem of Gerardo Diego, to the tower (79) of Oviedo Cathedral. In general, the Spanish cathedrals fared better than other churches during the Civil War of 1936–39, and even where mobs fired fittings and robbed the treasuries there was not usually deliberate damage to the structure. But at Oviedo the cathedral was twice the target of assault, in the miners' revolt of 1934 and again in the early part of the civil war proper. The steeple, pride of Asturias, was pounded by gunfire and most of the stained glass destroyed. The structural damage done has, after twenty years, been almost completely repaired.

Oviedo (81) is the only Spanish cathedral which incorporates substantial remains of pre-Romanesque work above ground, the Cámara Santa of the early ninth century. This was built by Tioda, the master who had completed the adjoining basilica by A.D. 802,

79   OVIEDO: the Narthex and Tower of 1508–12, by Pedro Bunyeres; the
Spire finished in 1556 by Juan de Cereceda

80 OVIEDO: looking east in the south aisle of the nave, 1487–97

as the Capilla de San Miguel, destined always to be the treasury of the most sacred relics. Apparently with the intention of preserving the sacred treasure from the effects of damp, the Cámara Santa itself stands upon a low subvault now known as the chapel of Santa Leocadia, with a simple semicircular barrel vault intersected by door and window openings. The relic chamber above consists of a vestibule, nave and sanctuary as if it were a small primitive church, but these are all of the same width. On this level only the sanctuary is original, the nave or antechamber having been rebuilt late in the eleventh century and provided late in the twelfth with splendid figures of the Apostles, standing two by two against the walls. Outside the Cámara Santa to the south stands a Romanesque tower of c. 1070–80, on a much earlier base. It is a fundamental design for the study of Spanish towers, already having the solid lower story surmounted by successive stages with one and two openings respectively, the lower stage being emphasised by setting the tall window beneath a much larger blind wall-arch, comparable to the arches along the sides of the nave at Compostela.

The next work in order of date is the earlier part of the cloister, begun about 1302, with bays of good Geometrical tracery imitated from Burgos but with marked improvements. The rest of the cloister belongs to the late fifteenth century and its Flamboyant traceries are of the same kind as those in the nave. The older church was completely rebuilt in the late Gothic period, beginning at the east end, where a chevet of three parallel apses was made, the sanctuary between 1388 and 1412 and the lateral chapels a few years later. There are likenesses to the old cathedral at Vitoria and other works in contemporary Navarrese style, and it seems certain that the architect must have come from that region. The transept was built in the latter part of the fifteenth century (in progress in 1475–79) under a master, Juan de Cándamo, who had been working at León Cathedral in 1454. Though it is said that the great tower had been started in 1431 by Pedro de la Tijera, it is difficult to connect this date with any part of the existing steeple, which seems at the base to be of one build with the western open porch or narthex of 1508–12, apparently designed by

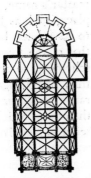

Lampérez: A. C. E. (Espasa-Calpe)

81   Oviedo, 1388–1512

139

Pedro Bunyeres. It is possible that some work had been done which was afterwards altered to conform in style to the rest of the main front.

It is the nave of Oviedo (*18, 80*) that stands out as something without parallel in Spanish architecture. Along with the transept and the later traceries of the cloister it is in pure Flamboyant style, even to its mouldings with their adjacent hollows meeting in a sharp edge. It is known to have been built in 1487–97, and appears to be the work of a Frenchman, probably from Normandy and evidently well acquainted with work in progress at Evreux. There is even a suggestion of the influence of English Perpendicular in the central mullions rising to the point of the triforium and clerestory arches. The bay design is good, but seems antiquated for Spain by reason of its fully developed triforium, almost as tall as the clerestory. An effective detail is the carrying up of shafts from the piers above their capitals to interpenetrate the hollows of the arch moulds, so adding to the vertical emphasis given by the tall wall-shafts which rise from base to springing of the high vault, and by the acute pitch of the cross-arches and domical ribbed vaults. These vaults are strongly suggestive of western France, where the old Aquitanian tradition of domical vaulting survived and was used with noble effect in such fifteenth-century churches as the abbey of Celles-sur-Belle.

Western France also suggests itself as the origin of the design of the tower, whose high-shouldered massing and relatively obtuse spire recall such steeples as those of Saintes and Marennes. The master's name, Bunyeres, may well be a corruption of some French place, such as Bagnères. At Oviedo the western narthex is known to have been built in 1508–12, and its detail agrees exactly with that of the tower. But it is curious that its otherwise symmetrical scheme is so arranged as to make the northern arch much lower than that beneath the tower, while on the contrary the lowest range of pinnacles on the northern buttresses is at a higher level than those which correspond to them on the south. These variations seem to negative the suggestion commonly made, that the cathedral was intended to have a pair of western towers. Bearing in mind the regional preference for a single steeple in Saintonge and the neighbouring parts of France, it seems more likely that this was the intention at Oviedo also. Certainly the decision was aesthetically justified, for a pair of western spires, without even the balance afforded by a low lantern, would have stultified their own effect. The lantern and spire are regrettably contaminated by the Renaissance and crude in their details, but in a distant view Oviedo's steeple is one of the very best of Spain.

Many pilgrims who undertook the journey to Compostela also visited Oviedo, renowned for the holiness of its relics, and the cave-sanctuary of Covadonga. This implied a route, in one direction or the other, along the northern coastal lands, which were to some extent opened up after the annexation of the Basque Provinces by Castile. Direct contacts between France or Navarre and Oviedo are thus explained, and there was probably always some direct transit by sea. Along the way there is no ancient cathedral but several churches of outstanding interest, among them the *colegiatas* of Santillana and Santander, the latter erected into a cathedral in 1752. Santillana is much visited for the sake of the extraordinary prehistoric paintings in the cave of Altamira and has itself been declared a national monument on account of the unaltered character of the streets and buildings. This has had the regrettable result of turning a living town into a museum specimen, but has succeeded in preserving an interesting body of buildings in good condition. Santillana, or Santa Juliana, was the ancient capital of that part of Asturias which fell to Castile, western Asturias with its capital of Oviedo being an integral part of the kingdom of Leon.

The church of Santillana had an immense jurisdiction stretching as far as Aguilar de Campóo beyond the mountains, and may fairly rank with the cathedrals. It seems to belong for the most part to the later twelfth century, though an inscription stating that it was not finished until 1287 may refer to the completion of the high vaults. There is a fine square tower above the crossing, concealing within a domed lantern on pendentives, and another grand belfry added to the west end, apparently built in imitation of the eastern lantern at a considerably later date. North of the church is a cloister of stocky coupled columns bearing richly carved capitals of the usual Romanesque type, rich in iconography.

At Santander the church resembles Santillana in general arrangement but is rather later in date. Owing to the levels of the site, it is set above a crypt which seems to have been built in the first quarter of the thirteenth century. This has three eastern apses and is four bays long. The church above, good early Gothic of arcade and clerestory only with well moulded piers and arches, was finished in 1310 but had a new sanctuary carried two bays further eastwards in the seventeenth century. Though not an especially distinguished work, Santander Cathedral is a light and airy building, recently well restored after the damage caused by the Great Fire of Santander in 1941. On the south side is a pleasant cloister of the fourteenth century, and on the north a curious open loggia giving access to the crypt beneath the outer range of chapels of the upper church.

CHAPTER FOUR

Catalonia and Valencia

SPAIN of the Middle Ages was linked to the outside world by two main currents. One, the crowd of pilgrims marching to Compostela, we have already explored in its course through Navarre, Castile, Leon and Galicia; the other was the tide of international trade that beat upon the Mediterranean shore, joining Barcelona, Valencia and Tarragona to the Balearic Isles, to France and Italy, to the shores of Africa and to the East. In sympathy with these two great influences from without there grew up two distinct codes of behaviour expressing two fundamental human outlooks, and about them crystallised two great kingdoms, Castile and Aragon. In the first, the Christian Faith was paramount, and next to belief, loyalty to the King and the principles of chivalry; Castile was, and is, a land of theological values. In Aragon, on the other hand, organised Christianity was prepared to accept a *modus vivendi* under which Moslems and Jews had for most practical purposes equal rights, and the King had to swear to abide by the liberties (*fueros*) of the realms over which he ruled, and to respect the independent authority of the *justiza* or chief justice, responsible for interpreting the law.

Superficially, this distinction would suggest that Castile was an aristocratic and Aragon a democratic country, but the truth was almost exactly the reverse. In Castile, a land of ancient free communities and quite devoid of slavery, there were no effective class distinctions and every man, rich or poor, regarded himself as a *caballero*, the mounted knight of a military society. Aragon, on the contrary, was a country of feudalism where only the nobles and the citizens of the great municipalities under charter enjoyed the privileges of the *fueros*, and there was a large unprivileged population of serfs. These differences in mediaeval organisation have permanently affected the tone and behaviour of the inhabitants of the two regions: Castile is notoriously conservative, the Levante (Catalonia and

Valencia) revolutionary in outlook; Castile lives off the land, the east of Spain by industry and trade.

The action of various influences is necessarily complex and over-simplification must be avoided, yet there is some truth in the generalised picture here given, which may be of value in understanding the different character of the eastern cathedrals from those already visited. Whereas the Castilian cathedral was an end in itself and (though there might be emulation between different sees) erected solely to the glory of God, the cathedral in the eastern kingdoms was closely bound up with the civic life of the great municipalities or at any rate became so as time went on. This was one of two great causes of the architectural likeness between their cathedrals and their civic halls and exchanges, the other being the influence exerted by the open preaching churches of the orders of friars. The ideal of the monastic, processional, church had much less force than in Castile, while even the cathedrals of the Mediterranean seaboard were affected by the results of the friars' movement to carry religion to the people, assembled in great congregations.

All this lay in the future when the first of the surviving cathedrals of Catalonia were built in the common Romanesque style of the eleventh and twelfth centuries. But there was one major factor that affected the style of Romanesque architecture in eastern Spain and not that of Castile: the importation of Lombard masons. The early buildings of Catalonia have a strongly Lombard flavour, and it is this more than any other single feature that differentiates them from the works of French derivation. But there is another, accidental, factor involved: the relatively early date of a number of the Catalan works which have survived. The combined effect of the remains of the eleventh century at Gerona, Vich, and the great monastery of Ripoll, is archaic in the extreme.

Political events repeatedly moved the frontier between France and Spain at the eastern end of the Pyrenees, but architecturally speaking the boundary runs to the north of the present French department of Pyrenées-Orientales, the ancient province of Rousillon, or in Spanish Rosellón. The present capital and see is at Perpignan, where the great church of 1324–1509, made cathedral in 1602, is a magnificent example of the Catalan cellular church, with a single span flanked by chapels between tall thin buttresses. There is a narrow transept, a wide apsidal sanctuary and two flanking apses. The openings of the cellular side-chapels are treated as an arcade, the clerestory wall above being small but pierced with round windows. Unfortunately the walls and vaults are largely covered with modern paintings which detract from the effect of majestic space given by the span of 60 feet.

Ars Hispaniae

82 Elne,
1042–68

The ancient cathedral of Rosellón was at Elne or Elna (*82*), nine miles south of Perpignan and twenty from the present frontier. Now a shrunken village, the city straggles round the hill on which the fortified church is built. Parts of the existing church are remains of that built in 1042–68. It has a heavy barrel-vault on cross-arches, curious rather than beautiful, and a massive western tower of stories bearing slightly recessed round-headed niches, with pairs of windows in the central niches of the top stages. The cloister on the north side is more than a century later in its earliest part; it consists of low arches in groups of three carried on paired shafts between square piers, both shafts and piers having elaborately carved capitals, some of which are grotesques of considerable character and skill in execution. The north and east sides, and the whole of the ribbed vaults, were added about 1300. Perhaps the most interesting thing at Elne is the foundation laid outside the east end of the old cathedral for the Gothic chevet of a new one in 1294 by the master Bartholomeus who came with his two sons from Perpignan, a valuable indication of the direction in which the artistic current was still flowing.

The first Spanish cathedral beyond the frontier is Gerona (*83*), splendidly sited above the River Oñar, and best seen from the railway as the train enters the city, the cathedral massing high over the church of San Feliú with its truncated spire. The nearer approach is somewhat disappointing, for the cathedral's bulk is so great as to dwarf the whole of its surroundings, and more especially the Baroque ornamental façade stuck to its enormous west wall like a set of stamps in an album. This was added in 1730–33 by the sculptor Pedro Costa of Vich, and is in itself a light and pleasing essay in movement and broken pediments. It is moreover well suited as a climax to the great staircase, an enterprise of civic planning on a scale fit for Rome and which has indeed been regarded by some observers as more beautiful than the famous staircase to the Trinità dei Monti.

The dusty whitish limestone front looks even bigger than it is, and is neither symmetrical nor coherent; but it has a certain elephantine dignity. The surprise of the front pales beside the shock of entry into the nave. Even the visitor who has studied plans, drawings and photographs has difficulty in taking in the physical possibility of what has been done. For, once the box-like *coro* is avoided and the east end seen, it is realised that the gigantic nave stands in relation to a full-sized normal cathedral as a hangar to an airship (*83, 84*). The sanctuary and its side-aisles fit within the cross-section and still leave a large spandrel partially filled with one great and two small rose-windows. Pushed out from the great central space are the lateral chapels which also continue around the ambulatory, giving the church a functional unity on plan which is not readily appreciated by the eye. Opinions still differ as widely on the aesthetic qualities of this huge vaulted space as they did at the conference of masters held in 1416 to decide whether it should proceed. It can hardly be denied that it has the effect of dwarfing the sanctuary, itself 82 feet high to the crown of the vault, or as high as Lincoln and higher than the nave of Canterbury.

The east end appears as an imitation of the classical Gothic chevet brought from northern France, but it has been greatly altered in the process. The precise steps by which the design reached Gerona are obscure, in spite of the very detailed researches on the spot of M. Pierre Lavedan and others. It used to be thought that both Barcelona (begun in 1298) and Gerona (endowed in 1292 but not actually started until 1312) were modified copies of the cathedral at Nar-

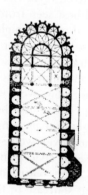

83, 84 Gerona, 1312–, by Enrique and
others; nave 1416–, by Guillermo Bofill

bonne, but M. Lavedan has shown that this thesis is untenable for
the simple reason that nothing more than the ambulatory chapels,
if so much, of Narbonne had been completed even by 1309. But
this does not rule out study of the drawings for Narbonne as an
important step in the progress of designing both the Catalan cathedrals, and from what we know of the processes of mediaeval design
such a study must have taken place. The triangular problem is further complicated by the intervention of several different masters in
the work of each chevet: at Narbonne Jean Deschamps from
1286–95, Dominique Favran until 1309, followed by his son
Jacques Favran until after completion of the choir in 1332; at
Gerona master Enrique, of unknown origin though often mistakenly
said to come from Narbonne, from the start in 1312 until his death
in 1320, when he was succeeded by Jacques Favran from Narbonne,
who in turn gave place in 1330 to Guillem de Cors who had completed the chevet by 1347; and at Barcelona an unknown master
(possibly the King's mason, Beltrán Riquer) who began the work,
followed by Jaime Fabre brought from Palma de Mallorca in 1317
and who was still in office in 1339.

Leaving aside detailed consideration of Narbonne, M. Lavedan
has shown that at Barcelona there is a change of detail between the
work of the ambulatory and its chapels on the one hand, and the
square bay east of the transept on the other, and that the eastern
work appears to be the later of the two, contrary to usual practice;
while at Gerona the ambulatory and chapels seem to be the first
work, evidently designed by Enrique, and the square bays to the
west a second stage under Jacques Favran. If this reading of the
evidence is correct it implies that the eastern chapels at Gerona are
earlier in build than those at Barcelona even if later in design. What
seems to emerge from the amount of coming and going of masters
and the simultaneous execution of great works is that there was
almost constant revision of the plans as a result of discussions or
deliberate imitation. Without the drawings prepared at each stage,
such as those which actually survive for Cologne, Strasburg and
Vienna, it must always remain impossible to apportion with certainty the shares of each architect or local school in the finished
works.

Possibly even more mysterious than the exact chronology is the
disputed identity of Jacques Favran with Jaime Fabre. The two
names appear in various forms, Latin, French and Catalan, but are

in fact identical both as to Christian and to surname (*Faber*; in English, James Smith). The two men appear as exact or almost exact contemporaries and as architects of two cathedrals of the same general character and only sixty miles apart. On the other hand there is nothing whatever in the documents to prove identity, and against it are the certainties that while Jacques Favran was from Narbonne and son of the cathedral master there, Jaime Fabre's previous connections are with the island of Majorca. The analogy of the contemporary eighteenth-century architects with the much less common name of Thomas Ivory, of Norwich (1709–79) and Dublin (1720–86), warns us against placing much reliance on the mere coincidence of names, and the weight of evidence is in favour of two distinct men.

It is worth while at this point pursuing Jacques Favran further, for he may have had a decisive influence in proposing the single span of the Gerona nave. Specifically named as the Master of St. Just at Narbonne, he was party to a deed of 12 July 1324 by which he ceded all his rights in a house in Perpignan to a silversmith there. In April of that year the works of the great church of Perpignan had begun and the coincidence is a strange one: M. Lavedan discards it on the ground that if Favran were just come to Perpignan to direct the works of the church, he would not be disposing of his house there. To this there are two possible answers: that a cession of rights to a silversmith was very probably a mortgage and that the transaction really records Favran's purchase of a property in Perpignan; alternatively, that he had been resident for a time in order to direct the setting out of the church and the start of operations, after which he sold his house as in future he would give only occasional visits of supervision. In any case it is all but certain that Favran was indeed the architect of St. Jean at Perpignan, with its enormous nave vault abutted by the side chapels.

The idea of applying the solution of a single span, already well known on a modest scale in Catalonia, is then probably to be set to the credit of Jacques Favran who, doubtless well acquainted with the enormous nave vault of Toulouse (1210–13), was engaged in building one almost as wide. That of Gerona should surpass both, and also that projected at Albi. It took a hundred years for so daring a project to wear down opposition, and there seems to have been more than one false start. In 1386 the chapter obtained technical advice but apparently continued with the rival design of three aisles. Finally their master Guillem Bofill, appointed in 1415, raised the question of the single span once more and succeeded in getting it reopened. One of the most remarkable architectural conferences ever held was the outcome.

The minutes of evidence given at the conference may be read in Street's book. They are of considerable technical interest on account of the utterly contradictory views expressed on the subject of safety, both in regard to the proposed single span and to the possibility of joining further arches to the work already existing. Bofill's own views, which won the day, are of special value because he asserts that the foundations already laid would be more than sufficient for the abutments "since they have a third more of breadth than is required"; clear proof that there was at the time a definite system of proportion followed in the building of abutments for great spans. Since such a system cannot have been derived from the mathematical theory of structures, quite unknown for several centuries to come, it indicates the existence of a body of traditional rules, possibly built up by means of experiment with models.

It seems likely that, once definitely in progress, the single-span nave of Gerona must have enjoyed a wide fame, for the same un- usual idea is found in project at Roslin Chapel near Edinburgh, begun in 1447 in a style showing many links with Spain and Portugal. Contemporary works in the sanctuary and side aisles of St. Giles, Edinburgh, including clustered piers of distinctively Catalan- Aragonese style, suggest that more than one Iberian master must have reached Scotland or else that a number of Scottish masons had spent their wander years in the Peninsula.

Gerona possesses an early tower on the north side, built in 1038– 1117, and a Romanesque cloister of c. 1180–1210. The cloister is of the same character as that at Elne, rich in carvings of Biblical type and in strange grotesques; the tower is more interesting archi- tecturally, for it has a singular system of decorative treatment. What we have, for it may have been intended to carry it still higher, is divided into six stages of blind recesses, each capped by a series of small rounded-headed arches. The lowest stage has ten of these, the next eight, and the remaining stories two groups of four each, with a central pilaster. Each of these four upper stages has a further sunk panel in each half of the face, either single or double-headed. There are two very small round-headed windows in the fifth stage, but no larger windows comparable to those at the top of the contemporary tower of Vich, which suggests that at least one more story was intended.

The marvellous silver altarpiece and canopy of the fourteenth century must be mentioned in passing; though slightly damaged in the civil war they have now been restored. A more serious work of destruction was wrought in the south porch, where ten of the twelve terracotta Apostles made in 1458 by Antón Claperós of Barcelona have disappeared. The porch itself was begun in 1394 by Guillén Morey, brother of the designer of the great porch at Palma, but the Gerona work was never finished and is covered by a shapeless box pierced with an elliptical arch. One more external feature deserves attention: the unique flying-buttresses of the chevet, practically horizontal struts between the springing of the vault and the blunt unpinnacled heads of the buttress standards. It is possible that this unusual arrangement was produced by the raising of the aisles high above the surrounding chapels so that there was not room vertically for a raking flyer of the usual kind. But it is one more proof of the adventurous ingenuity displayed by the building lodge of Gerona. ✓

Barcelona has been for nearly a thousand years the capital of the western Mediterranean, holding a position comparable only to those of Venice and of London. Its great and continuing prosperity has made it a mark for the venomous darts of envy and its inhabitants are maligned in Spain as uncivil and uncultured. There is even less truth in this than in the similar gibes levelled at the Galicians, and Barcelona may comfort herself with the well-deserved tribute of Cervantes, Castilian of Castilians, who through the mouth of Don Quixote called the city "treasury of courtesy, shelter of strangers, hospital of the poor, home of the brave, avenger of the wronged, pleasant exchange of firm friendships and in site and beauty unique". It is indeed the extraordinary physical beauty of the surroundings and the harmonious way in which the town, ancient and modern, has been contrived to fit them, that give to Barcelona its charm.

On top of a hill in the midst of the old city is the cathedral (85–7), hedged in on three sides by narrow streets but with an ample space on the north-west, opposite to the main front, unusually pleasing for a work of neo-Gothic and in fact based upon the surviving design of 1408. The central spire of openwork springs from the fifteenth-century lantern at the west end of the nave, and is flanked at each side of the wide front by two smaller spires well subordinated in

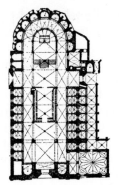  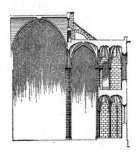

85, 86, 87   Barcelona, 1298–1430; cloister, 1382–1448,
by Bernard Roca

scale. The great central portal and the vertical lines of the buttresses make an effective composition which is skilfully floodlit at
night, and also lit internally behind the stained-glass windows. At
the opposite end is the original chevet, deeply embedded in its circuit
of buttresses, solid up to the top of the high ambulatory and thence
with flyers striking between the round windows, a series of eyes,
of the clerestory. The best way to enter is through the cloisters, a
delightful oasis surrounded by noble arcades and with a pool occupied by white geese. The east walk (really south-east) leads to the
south transept door, within which we pause in what gives the
impression of pitch darkness.

Barcelona Cathedral is in fact very dark, but after the eyes have
become accustomed to the gloom the architecture takes on the
velvety glow of a deep brown pansy, here and there punctuated by
touches of exquisite jewelled colour from the stained glass. The
windows are small, placed high, and glazed in deep colours, and
there seems to be little doubt that the effect was intentional. It
might be thought that such an artificial night would conceal crude
details, but the work is of extremely fine design and execution,
producing soft gradations of tone. Beneath the high altar, which is
raised high above the general floor level, is a crypt entered from the
west by an open flight of stairs: a *confessio* of the Early Christian type.
This is lit from the ambulatory by small windows of four miniature
Gothic orders, built as if they were model doorways. Around the
apse the chapels preserve all their old altarpieces and fittings, as
does the whole church. Saved from the destruction of 1931 to

1939 it is an incomparable treasury of mediaeval art and probably gives a closer impression than any other in Europe of the state of a great church in the Middle Ages.

The complex early history of the cathedral's fabric has been touched on in connection with Gerona, and is hardly relevant to appreciation of the great beauties of the design. Whoever it was who first determined the unusual compound of southern and northern styles, mingling the cellular nave of Catalonia with the triforium of metropolitan France, was a genius of high rank. The rest of the work, however different in details, follows from the example set in the early years of the fourteenth century. After 1365 the nave was carried westwards by Bernard Roca, who also began the cloister in 1382 and built the pair of transeptal bell-towers between 1385 and 1389. By 1408 a design for the west front had already been produced by the French master Carlí, but the chapels inside it and the western lantern were not built until 1418–30, under Bartomeu Gual (*17*). The western screen which he carried across has spandrels filled with tracery in a manner which seems very close to English fashion of the time, as seen for example in Henry V's Chantry at Westminster Abbey, and the idea of a western transept carrying an octagonal lantern looks curiously like a conflation of the two transepts of Ely.

From Barcelona it is an easy day trip to Vich and the great early monastery of Ripoll, which lies on the same main lines of railway and road leading towards Toulouse. Vich is a town of greyish-yellow stone, beaten by the sun in an open valley. The outstanding feature of the cathedral (*88, 91*) is its tall Romanesque tower, built between 1038 and 1180, decorated in a similar manner to that of Gerona and likewise of six stories, but with windows of substantial size in the sixth. Above this is a seventh stage of uneven masonry with large openings supporting a roof, evidently a late addition. Apart from this tower the only visible part of the work begun in 1038 is the

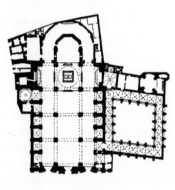

Junyent

88 Vich, 1780–1803, by José Morató; cloister, 1324–1400, by Ramón Despuig

crypt (92), discovered during the reconstruction of the cathedral after its sacking in the civil war. This crypt has an apsidal east end and two rows of pillars carrying a groined vault with cross-arches. Of the mediaeval church, largely rebuilt late in the twelfth century, nothing remains, though the rebuilt stones of the lower cloister belong to this period. The upper cloister of 1324–1400 designed by Ramón Despuig, and re-erected on a new site in response to public outcry in 1806, is one of the richest in Spain. Its geometrical traceries are almost all of different patterns, displaying the utmost ingenuity and grace.

The present church is almost entirely of the years 1780–1803, a complete design in severely neo-classical style by José Morató (22). Its square piers are formed of four Corinthian pilasters bearing their entablature, above which stand cubical dies carrying the domical vaults. The proportions are good and the church has a cool dignity which provides a foil for the giant paintings of José María Sert, produced in the last five years of his life to replace his previous series burnt in 1936. Painted mainly in a sienna grizzale, with occasional deep red draperies, the biblical scenes appear in full relief as if carved on the walls. Full of dynamic power, Sert's paintings make the best of what might otherwise seem a dull and heavy building. Of the Gothic cathedral there are no structural remains, but there survives from it the superb polychrome alabaster retable (90) of the high altar, now placed in the ambulatory. It was made by Pedro Oller in 1420–27 and is one of the most remarkable survivals of its kind. Oller carried out other works of sculpture at Poblet and in Barcelona Cathedral and cloisters.

Ripoll, though never a cathedral, deserves to be visited as in some sense the Catalan counterpart of the Romanesque Santiago de Compostela. The church as it now exists is largely a restoration undertaken in 1888, but based on extensive remains and views and descriptions of its state before the exclaustration of the monks in 1835. The heavy barrel-vaulted nave with double aisles of square piers supporting low round arches is a reconstruction of the original work of 1020–32 (of which a few arches remain) and demonstrates the grand scale and proportions which could be attained in a crude age of very limited technical and artistic capacity. The plan, with a T-shaped transept at the end of a long nave and with a central apse flanked by three smaller apses on each side, is an earlier version of what we shall find at La Seo de Urgel. On the south is a good

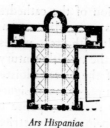

Ars Hispaniae

89 La Seo de Urgel,
c. 1131–82

Romanesque cloister begun in 1172 with a Gothic upper story finished in 1383. But the great glory of Ripoll is its western portal of 1160–68, one of the triumphs of twelfth-century sculpture.

La Seo de Urgel lies high in the upper valleys, almost on the boundary of Andorra, the independent mountain community one of whose suzerains the bishop is, jointly with the head of the French state. But unlike much of the Spanish Pyrenees, the valley around Urgel is green and smiling, and the town is still delightfully unspoilt. The cathedral (*89*) is built of a hard limestone containing fossils, with something of the appearance of solidified mud, and taking on a rich orange-brown patina like the stone of Palencia and that formerly quarried in the Isle of Wight. In the west front and other parts bands of a close-grained purple stone have been introduced for contrast. In recent years a number of excrescences of late date have been carefully removed, so that it is now possible to obtain an idea of the aesthetic intentions of the original designers.

Begun about 1131, the church is known to have been vaulted in 1175–82 by Raimundus the Lombard. It is evident that he or some other Lombard must have been concerned from the start. The plan has the elongated T-transept seen at Ripoll, here with only two apses on each side of the large central apse, but with large square towers at the transept ends. The central apse is crowned with an external gallery, and above its roof a round window admits light through the gable of the short square sanctuary which precedes the apse. Immediately behind this, at the centre of the transept, is a crossing with the start of four pendentives, above which the space is irregularly drawn in to an elliptical dome. The transeptal towers were never completed, but have the vertical strip buttresses or pilasters and small-scale arcading found elsewhere in Catalonia. What is unusual is that the towers are built quite blind and with immensely thick walls, as if for defence. The west front (5) also exploits the motive of two widely spaced towers on each side of a central mass. Here the mass is the west wall of the church, following the section of nave and aisles with their low-pitched sloping roofs. On the apex of the gable is perched a curious little open-work turret

90 VICH: the carved retablo of 1420–27 by Pedro Oller

92 The Crypt,
begun in
1038

VICH

of two stages, apparently intended as a look-out. The two lateral towers, not marked off from the front in any way below the aisle roofs, are built outside the aisles and shortly above the roofs are brought in with broaches to become short octagonal turrets which look as though they had been meant to be covered with spires.

The interior is dark but impressive by its fine proportions. The barrel-vaulted nave is lit by twin windows on the north side, and there are also round-headed windows placed high in the aisles. In the west front there are three doors, those of the aisles each surmounted by a single window while the larger central portal stands beneath a carved string-course. Above are two ranges of windows in the west wall, the lower consisting of a wide window between two narrower lights, each of a single recessed order; then an enriched string-course and in the gable a single narrow light between two round bull's-eyes, all in a frame of attached shafts and rampant arcades on corbels beneath an elaborate crowning cornice.

From Barcelona it is also easy to visit Palma in Majorca, the one island cathedral of Spain proper, for the churches at Ciudadela on Minorca and at Ibiza were only raised to episcopal rank in modern times. On several occasions Majorca has constituted a separate kingdom, under Saracens or Christians, and Palma has never lost the atmosphere of a capital city, a feeling which to the present day is more marked here than at Burgos, Toledo or even Valladolid. Only Seville among Spain's provincial cities can vie with Palma in aristocratic spirit, only Barcelona in the forceful impact made by the continuity of commercial and artistic life, stretching from remote times down to and beyond the present day.

The cathedral of Palma (93) has a finer site than any Spanish cathedral except Lérida and Segovia, and is architecturally far more significant as a work of deliberate composition than either of these. It ranks as one of the very few European cathedrals of the Middle Ages whose exterior comes near to an aesthetic equality with the interior, and it is furthermore most fortunate in having escaped becoming the centre of indiscriminate and hugger-mugger building of various dates. I have earlier said something of the purposeful design of Palma,* but it may be permissible to dwell upon one of the existing wonders of the world. In the first place, it has not only a magnificent site but that site is immediately upon the sea, so that the traveller by ship can see from the horizon this amazing palace

* See p. 52.

of enchantment hovering in the morning mists or shining brilliantly in the Mediterranean sun. And as the ship approaches, the superb measure of its bulk begins to be appreciated and then the controlled punctuation of greater and lesser buttresses, the built-up massing of the eastern chapels, the cliff-like west end (*15*). Lastly, at the centre of balance, the wonderful gateway of the great porch, the Mirador, staring into the sun's eye at noon.

When the detail of the seaward, or southern, face of the cathedral is studied it produces an astonishing effect of military architecture. So much so, that it is tempting to suppose that the architect was that Master Pere Salvá who in 1309–14 was building the extraordinary castle of Bellver on a neighbouring hill. The buttresses, standing in their ranks, appear as ranges of palisades composed of the blades of broadswords set upright. But they are by no means a mere range of evenly spaced supports. The bay containing the great porch is broader than the rest, and is marked by a wider and taller window than those of other bays, both in the triforium level and in the clerestory of the high nave, and these windows carry a greater emphasis in that the palisade of the lower buttresses is here broken open by the portal. East of the entrance are four bays, three to west; and each of these bays is divided into three by the lower buttresses.

Lampérez: Arq. Crist. Esp. (Espasa-Calpe)

93, 94   Palma de Mallorca, *c.* 1306–1601

But not equally divided, for the distance between the pair of buttresses, flanking each chapel window, is more than that between either of them and the great buttress next to it. The emphasis is strongly vertical, but all is held together by a series of horizontal string-courses, five in number, slashing across the lower buttress, while four more (and a fifth hardly seen behind the pinnacles of those beneath) divide the tall counterforts of the high buttresses themselves and mark them out from the plain triforium and clerestory walling behind. There is no regular increase in the width of the bands marked out by these courses, but those above are much wider than those below, decreasing the effect of pressure towards the skyline.

Seen from the land side the effect is only less striking, for here is the massive tower preserved from an earlier period than when the church was laid out, and on a different alignment. The belfry consists of eleven stages divided by corbelled cornices into three groups of four, four and three; and above the topmost stage a larger cornice with bartizan turrets and the beginning of an octagonal lantern, left unfinished. In the upper of the tower's three main sections the three stages increase upwards in height and have each three windows on each face. In spite of the obvious fact that the tower was built before the present design of the cathedral had been reached, these horizontal stages divided by string-courses bring the tower into close relation with the church, and may perhaps have suggested the method of horizontal emphasis to the later architect.

If the outside is impressive, the church within is breathtaking in beauty (94–5). The whole is one vast volume of space, englobed and fragmented by the walls and pillars. So well are the proportions related to human scale that the huge size can be fully appreciated and the exquisite gradations by which the whole is divided and subdivided. In almost every respect there is an antithesis, so marked as to seem intentional, to what we have seen at Barcelona. Barcelona preserves the French chevet and the antiquated triforium; Palma rejects them. Barcelona has soft pillars of many and subtly moulded members; Palma has plain octagonal piers. Most of all, Palma is luminous where Barcelona is but darkness made visible. This is the most extraordinary feature of Palma, for all the other cathedrals of the Levante are exceptionally dark, from Transitional Tarragona to the fifteenth-century nave of Gerona, while at Palma it is as though walls and vault had been made solid in order the better to display the qualities of light where it is admitted. In so many ways exceptional, it is curious to find that Palma is none the less typically and even extremely Spanish in the cubical impression which it makes externally and internally. This not only leaps to the eye from its ground plan and section, but is a dominant factor in the building's impression, a geometrical ratio endowed with power. And indeed it is a singular power that the material fabric of Palma has: a greater quantity of space is enclosed with a smaller amount of supports than anywhere else in the whole chapter of the mediaeval search for structural perfection. Here at Palma, if anywhere, the mason's dream of the conquest of the skies by the right cutting and setting of stone upon stone was fulfilled.

The old parish church of Ciudadela in Minorca became the cathedral only in 1798. It is a good example of the Catalan church of a single span and with cellular side-chapels, built probably in the first half of the fourteenth century. The smaller island of Ibiza also has its cathedral, again an earlier church raised to diocesan status in 1782. Externally its position and mass against the skyline are a fine sight, with the slender tower marking the top of the peak on which the old city of Ibiza is built. Inside it is a disappointment, for in 1712–28 it was classicised in a dull and utterly tasteless way, leaving nothing of interest but the thirteenth-century sacristy with its fine entrance. It seems likely that the mediaeval church still survives beneath the later veneer, and it is to be hoped that it may one day stand revealed.

Returning to the mainland, another excursion may be made from Barcelona to the churches of Manresa and Solsona, the one reputed a cathedral by popular consent and the other an early church made cathedral in 1593. Manresa well deserves its name of La Seo, for within the group of greater churches of the Catalan type it is both impressive and original in design. As seen from the valley of the Cardoner, here followed by the main line to Lérida, it bulks grandly above a rocky outcrop, overtopped by its slender square tower, pierced with tall lancets. Like Palma, Manresa can be appreciated for its exterior, though there is here a less self-conscious arrangement of bays and buttresses. Inside, the bays are of two stages only, with octagonal piers on tall plinths below, and above the capitals clustered wall-shafts supporting the vaults from a springing at the base of tall clerestory windows. The surrounding aisle is unique in that it is pierced through the buttresses which form the usual range

95   PALMA DE MALLORCA: the Nave of 1368–1406, by Jaime Mates
and Guillermo Oliveras

96 The Belfry of 1391–1416, by Guillem Solivella and Carli

97 The interior, looking east, 1203–78, by Pedro Decumbo

of cellular chapels around the whole church including the apse. The design was made by Berenguer de Montagut of Barcelona in 1322, but completion was delayed for more than two hundred years.

Solsona, which I have not seen, is the converse of Manresa; far from being an integral work of art, it consists of major remains of three different periods. The three parallel apses belong to the Romanesque church of 1161–63, curiously surviving behind the apse of a single-span church of the fourteenth-fifteenth century which was placed within the old walls and destroyed the original arcades. On the south is the Romanesque tower, capped with a late belfry and balustrade, while the west and side fronts are Baroque additions, the latter probably designed by Francisco Pons in 1780. The main front, still unaffected by neoclassical ideas, may well be fifty years earlier in date. The cathedral contains the notable late Romanesque sculpture of the seated Virgin and Child known as the Virgen de la Claustra, and important paintings and carvings have recently been gathered into the Diocesan Museum.

Tarragona, proudly seated on its rocky hill, is now a little city compared to Barcelona, but its cathedral disputes with Toledo primacy over Spain. When the present cathedral (98) was begun, about 1171, the metropolitan province extended from the Pyrenees to Alicante and from Bilbao to the Balearic Isles, and the cathedral is accordingly laid out on a grand scale. Although for the most part built with pointed arches, it remains true to Romanesque construction and massing and looks both heavy and dark. Though built on the highest point of the town on the site that had been covered by the temple of Jupiter and later by a mosque, it is too deeply embedded in surrounding buildings and too much altered at various dates to have much importance for its external composition. The great apse is all the same a noble work of defensive art, not unlike that of Ávila, and from the south-east this groups well with the far later belfry that overtops it on the south. From within the cloisters too it is possible to feel something of the aims of the successive masters who added to the eastern apse the high blind walls of the sanctuary and transept and the octagonal lantern. The cloister itself is one of the noblest in Spain, early Gothic with fine ribbed vaulting, but with round arches and oculi piercing the wall beneath its pointed main arches. Begun in the last five or six years of the twelfth century it must have been finished unusually quickly. The carved capitals form one of the most accomplished groups of their kind.

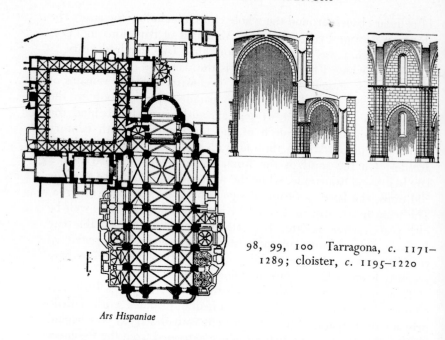

98, 99, 100 Tarragona, c. 1171–
1289; cloister, c. 1195–1220

Ars Hispaniae

The Transitional bays of the nave were begun in 1230 under a
cleric, Fray Bernardo, who died in 1256, but whether he was the
architect or simply the administrative chief is not known; in 1266
died Master Raymond de Milian, who had vaulted the eastern nave.
At any rate the direction of the design was soon to fall into quite
other hands, for the two western bays and the west front, built
between 1272 and 1289, were directed by a Norman master, Bartolomé, who was the sculptor of nine of the statues of the Apostles
which flank the great west door. The west front is a curious
mixture of two styles: to right and left are the end walls of the
aisles, each with a Romanesque round-arched doorway of rather
small scale and, much higher up, a circular window moulded in
many orders. These must remain from the work done in the first
period of building, which probably carried the outer walls entirely
round the church. Between these, and making no stylistic concession
to them other than a certain solidity, is the front of the high nave,
begun in 1278 and finished twenty years later, apart from a few of
its statues added in 1375 by Jaime Castayls. Architecturally it
never was finished, for its gable and buttresses are left uncapped.

Here is a most interesting design by a northerner faced with the fresh problems of a southern climate and a building of proportions quite different from those he knew. The nave of Tarragona is very wide but of moderate height and, like all Spanish buildings of its time, intended to have a roof of low pitch. These squat proportions gave no scope for a design of the usual French pattern, but this was adopted to the extent of designing a gabled termination which must, even if completed, have remained a false front. Such vertical emphasis as was possible is secured by the pairs of sturdy buttresses at each angle and their projecting lower stages, beneath very tall solid pinnacles. Similar pinnacles were to have crowned the tops of the main buttresses, but only a part of one exists. Not counting the gable, only two stages were possible in a front this shape, the doorway below and a great rose above, and the success of the composition is due to the great skill with which the relative proportions and mouldings of the two have been adjusted.

The rose, as Mr. Bevan has pointed out, is one of the many versions of that in the south transept of Notre-Dame in Paris, possibly the most copied single design of the whole Middle Ages. But at Tarragona it is transformed into something radically new by placing the tracery within a moulded circle instead of on the outer face of a plane of tracery carried over blind spandrels within a square. The translation into terms of moulding is carried down into the great porch, which at Tarragona has no sculpture round the arch, the traceried wall arcading surmounted by the range of statues ending on the line of the springing. The tympanum has an ingeniously contrived window above a sculptured panel arranged in the form of a low segmental arch which harmonises perfectly with the enclosing upper arcs of the portal. This porch is the ancestor of a whole line of those built during the later mediaeval period in eastern Spain, including the Mirador at Palma, the unfinished south doorway of Gerona, and others of less importance.

The interior (12), in spite of its heavy and archaic design, has a grandeur and majesty unparalleled by any other Spanish church of its time, and the effect achieved is due largely to the sharp contrast between the broad expanses of unbroken masonry and the solid piers, on the one hand, and on the other the exquisitely precise and crisp carving of the capitals, a point long ago remarked by Street. These capitals have an almost Byzantine flavour in their deeply pierced acanthus leaves, and the scrolls and interlaces of the abaci. The total effect is heightened by the later additions of central lantern, finely carried on squinches above the crossing, and the tall pinnacles of the great altarpiece in the sanctuary of 1426–34, the work of the famous Pere Johan of Vallfogona, who worked also in Barcelona and Saragossa between 1416 and 1444. The stalls begun by Francisco Gomar in 1478 have prodigal displays of detailed carving in oak, but the strong horizontality of their canopy contrasts with their otherwise completely Gothic spirit. Of later works the chapel of Santa Tecla in the south nave aisle deserves attention, for it is one of the few examples in Spain of French gaiety of the mid-eighteenth century, sharply distinguished from Baroque on the one hand and the solemn neoclassicism of the French Court of Spain on the other. The chapel was rebuilt in 1760–75 by José Prats, while its sculptures are by Carlos Sala.

Tarragona is the best centre from which to visit the great Cistercian monastery of Santes Creus, one of the burial-places of the kings of Aragon. It can be mentioned here only for the double interest of its cloister, where there appears the earliest curvilinear tracery in Spain, made in 1331–41 by a master who is recorded to have been English, though his name appears in the unlikely form of Reinard de Fonoyll. In another direction,

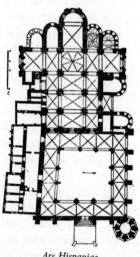

Ars Hispaniae

101 Lérida (old cathedral), 1203–78, by Pedro Decumbo

on the way to Lérida, is the other royal pantheon and likewise Cistercian abbey of Poblet. Both Santes Creus and Poblet are fantastic survivals, monasteries which contain royal palaces and even villages in addition to the church and claustral buildings proper, and both are among the most important remains of church architecture of the twelfth century. Beyond Poblet the way to Lérida crosses a watershed and gradually descends through immense plains, the Llanos de Urgel.

Lérida is visible from a great distance, standing up as an acropolis above the bank of the River Segre. It is surrounded by the modern town on the lower ground, a parched and dusty centre of baking heat in summer. The climb to the top of the great crag on which the fortress and the old cathedral (101) are set is arduous, but well rewarded by the view as well as by the artistic treat offered by the cathedral. Occupied as a barracks for 250 years this outstanding church has at last been cleared of intrusive walls and floors and is in process of a careful restoration of the most appropriate kind. Important as the church was, archaeologically speaking, throughout, it was virtually impossible to get access to it, and even then was aesthetically inappreciable. Now it is a complete and rediscovered gem of untouched Transitional and Gothic art, as remarkable an addition to the catalogue of the world's great buildings as was a few years ago the Tinell, the great hall of the royal palace in Barcelona.

The main front of the church hides behind the great cloister, which serves as an atrium or forecourt, but the cloister is entered through a splendid porch, the Puerta de los Apóstoles of the end of the fourteenth century. To the right, at the south-west angle of the cloister, rises the octagonal belfry (96) begun about 1350 by Jaime Castayls who made monuments at Poblet, and statues for the front of Tarragona in 1375; and finished in 1416 with the lantern designed by the French master Carlí, also described as Carlos Galter of Rouen, whom we have already met as designer of the west front at Barcelona. To the west the cloister, apart from its central porch, presents a heavy face marked by massive buttresses, but on the south, overlooking the escarpment and the immense view over the plain, a great traceried window fills the whole of the space between each pair of buttresses. Long blocked, these lovely windows are in process of restoration and admit brilliant shafts of patterned light to the spacious walks. Beyond the cloister on the south side is the south door of the nave, a round-arched Romanesque work sheltered behind an outer portico made in 1386–1400 by two foreigners, Bartolomé of Brussels and Esteban de Gostant, who seem also to have built the elegant little Capilla de los Requesens alongside.

It is evident that Lérida, begun in 1203 by Pedro Decumbo or Dercumba, was closely modelled upon Tarragona, of whose church this is a reduced copy. But Lérida remains less altered than its exemplar and is now more capable of full appreciation from a wide range of viewpoints. Its taller lantern groups nobly with the turret on the south transept and with the belfry, above the happily graded apses of the eastern chapels. Internally, though the smaller scale is noticeable, the more compact plan increases the effect of the central space and the illusion of height (97). Here, as at Tarragona, the beauty of the effect comes from the contrast between the simplicity of the structure and the fine quality of its carved enrichment. Also of great importance are the remains of wall-paintings of c. 1300 in the sanctuary, exquisite line-drawings of scenes from the New Testament.

The cloister is one of the most unusual and puzzling works in Spain. Placed as a western atrium, it is in any case an anomaly in the Gothic period, and its huge scale finds no parallel. These features are valuable proofs of individuality on the part of the master who planned it, presumably Pedro de Pennafreita the first, who died in 1286 after working on the vaults and lantern of the church from 1278. It has been held by some authorities, and most recently by Don Leopoldo Torres Balbás, that the work did not start until 1310 under Pennafreita's namesake and successor; but it is impossible to credit, even at the ultra-conservative Lérida, a survival of Romanesque carving and mouldings well into the fourteenth century. Moreover, the work is demonstrably of two builds of quite distinct style: the first comprising at least the east and part of the north vaulted walks with their piers and arches bearing zig-zags, a work surprisingly belated even if put at c. 1280–1300; and the second consisting of the internal buttresses added after the vaults had already forced the piers out of plumb, as well as the magnificent traceries of fully developed Geometrical work, inserted under the older arches. The south and west walks belong entirely to the later build of c. 1310–50, but the traceries appear in all cases to be very substantially later insertions in the openings, though they themselves display a considerable chronological development.

In the lower town is the new cathedral, designed in 1760 by Pedro Mártir Cermeño who in 1753 had designed the church of San Miguel del Puerto at Barcelona, and built between 1764 and 1790 under the general supervision of the royal architect Francisco Sabatini and more immediately under that of José Prats, whom we have already met as the designer of the chapel of Santa Tecla at Tarragona. The church is chiefly important as the only new cathedral designed as such in the second half of the eighteenth century, and as the source of Morató's design for the rebuilt cathedral at Vich. Externally Lérida is a poor and dull work of blind walls and an unimpressive front, a low portico of three archways of equal height between towers consisting only of small open turrets. The low-pitched gable stands behind these, pierced by a single circular window. The interior is surprisingly pleasant, more suave and less vigorous than its child at Vich, and with good lighting from windows placed in the clerestory of the side-aisles, the section being that of a hall-church flanked by cellular side-chapels beyond the aisles, on the traditional Catalan pattern. All the fittings were destroyed when the church was sacked and fired in 1936, but the structural damage has been repaired.

Following the coastal plain from Tarragona towards Valencia, the Ebro was formerly crossed at Tortosa. The new coastal road has by-passed it with mixed results: Tortosa runs less risk of losing its quiet charm, but is visited by few, and its exquisite cathedral remains almost unknown. This is due largely to Street's neglect and to the late date of the work having rendered it un-fashionable among the more recent antiquaries who have concen-trated attention upon the Romanesque, early Gothic and Renais-sance periods. Yet Tortosa is that rarity, a complete major church of High Gothic style and first-class quality. In saying complete, one must except the west front designed by Martín de Abaria in 1625, a weighty Baroque work of little fantasy, not built until 1705–57 and left without its intended towers. I have already described the successive stages by which building began*: the preparation in 1345 of a plan by Antonio Guasch, rejected in favour of one by Benito Dalguayre in the next year, and the laying of the first stone in 1347. Dalguayre's plan (*102*) is remarkable for its combination of important features from the practice of France and Catalonia, and its almost unique system of apsidal chapels which, instead of being separated from one another by intervening walls, are structurally an outer ambulatory of square bays separated by triangular wedges of vault.

Externally the arrangement of the double range of flying but-tresses crowned with little towers and the embattled parapets sug-gest a fortress, though the original elevation by Benito Basques of Montblanch has a more florid treatment. Internally there is a reminiscence of Barcelona with the triforium omitted. The piers of the central apse are linked by pierced stone screens of delicate curvilinear tracery (*103*) and there is unusual subtlety in the placing

* See p. 43.

of the capitals of the arcades, of the high vault and of the aisle vaults at three different levels on the moulded piers. Only the chevet belongs to the first build (–1441), while the nave was continued very slowly and finished only in 1568, and the high vault of the last bay not set until 1708. We know little but the names of the continuators, but the masters of the original work who succeeded to Dalguayre were Andrés Juliá, also master of the Valencia chapter-house and tower; Paschasio de Xulbe (–1428); and the latter's son Juan (–1452), both of whom were brought to the Gerona conference of 1416. The uniformity of style throughout is unusual, though the bases of the western bays (105) differ from those of the work consecrated in 1438. Both the earlier and later works contain some four-centred arches, analogous to those built later at Astorga and more closely to some fifteenth-century work in England, a surprising and so far unexplained coincidence. On the south side of the church is the delightful little cloister, of small architectural significance it is true, but of clear, simple design and refined charm.

From Tortosa the road to Valencia passes down the coast by the foothills of the mountain ranges which hem in the Maestrazgo, and through Castellón de la Plana, nominally the see of an old diocese whose cathedral remains at Segorbe, twenty miles inland from the ancient town and castle of Sagunto. Segorbe is a dusty little town, heavily damaged during the civil war, and very little of interest or importance remains at its cathedral apart from the fifteenth-century cloisters of considerable charm, with an upper story of continuous openings of small scale, probably of the early sixteenth century. The church of a single span was built by Juan de Burgos in 1483–1534, but greatly altered about 1600 and again, by Mauro Minguet and Juan Bautista Gascó, in 1791–95.

Valencia is the third city of Spain, ranking in importance after Madrid and Barcelona, but it cannot be said that its cathedral (106) as a whole corresponds to its rank. This is by no means entirely due to the lamentably cold classical transformation of the interior in 1774–79 by Antonio Gilabert and Lorenzo Martínez, for damage caused by the mob in 1936 has

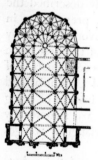

Tormo: Levante
(Espasa-Calpe)

102 Tortosa, 1346–, by Benito Dalguayre; west front, 1625–1757 by Martín de Abaria

103 TORTOSA: the Ambulatory begun in 1347, by Benito Dalguayre

105 TORTOSA: the Nave, begun in 1441

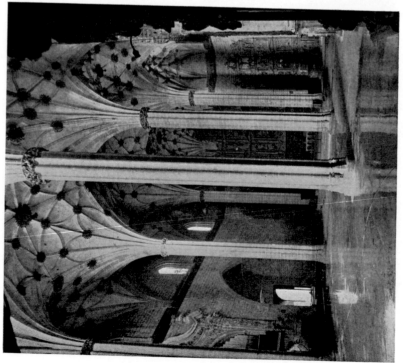

104 BARBASTRO: the church of 1500–33, by Juan de Segura
and Baltasar de Barazábal

revealed enough of the mediaeval building to show that its squat proportions are original. Outside it is only isolated features that can be seen: the tall Miguelete or belfry, the central lantern, the Baroque west front and those of the transepts. These works are all of different dates and must be considered separately. The earliest is the south door, called the Puerta del Palau, a round-arched portal entirely Romanesque in character though with traces of mudéjar and of the coming Gothic Transition, a strange design to have been carried out after the known date of 1262 for the start of the works. This becomes even less explicable considering that the first work included the setting out of a fully developed Gothic chevet of five bays and eight chapels, there being thus two chapels to each of the three apsidal bays and consequently no central chapel. Even more curious is the very close resemblance to the doorways of Lérida, produced in

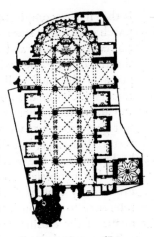

after Tormo: Levante (Espasa-Calpe)

106 Valencia, 1262–c. 1356, by Arnaldus Vitalis and others; west tower, 1381–1429, by Andrés Juliá and others

the first half of the century and by a school of masons notoriously conservative. Street was possibly very close to the true explanation when he remarked on the likeness of many details to Italian work of the period. It has constantly been stated that the two first masters whose names are recorded, Arnaldus Vitalis in 1267 and Nicolas de Autona in 1303, were a Catalan and a Burgundian respectively. But there is no reason why the first should not be Arnaldo Vitale rather than Arnau Vital, while it is a good deal more likely that "Autona" is a misreading of Ancona than a corruption of Autun. The scheme of the church, with its low vault and very wide arcades (107), is very close to that of Italian churches such as Santa Maria Novella at Florence, while the extraordinary resemblance of the Puerta del Palau to the work at Lérida may be due, as tradition has it, to the bringing of seven hundred maidens from Lérida as wives for the colonists at the reconquest of 1238.

The north doorway or Puerta de los Apóstoles seems to belong to the first third of the fourteenth century, though all that is certain is that it was completed by 1354. This is a rich and entirely Gothic porch containing statuary around the arches of all its three orders, a carved tympanum and a gallery of blind tracery above and behind the traceried gablet which crowns the arch. Set back behind this plane is the end wall of the transept, with a great rose whose tracery includes the double equilateral triangle or Solomon's Seal, and above it another traceried gablet against vertical panelling. The soft grey stone has weathered terribly, and much had already to be restored in 1432, but the design is still beautiful and forms a worthy background to the weekly judgments of the Water Tribunal, held here for centuries on Thursday at noon. The design is clearly inspired by that of the main front of Tarragona, but with further reference to the south transept of Notre-Dame and French developments of the closing years of the thirteenth century.

The central lantern, with its two great stages of elaborately traceried windows filled with sheets of alabaster instead of glass, is a mysterious work. While the large piers of the crossing indicate that a *cimborio* was intended from the start, the date of what exists has been much disputed, being placed by Lampérez at the beginning of the fifteenth century, by Lavedan a century earlier, by Tormo "many years" before 1380 when there is evidence that a lantern was in existence. Substantial works, possibly of repair only, were carried out on it in 1430 by Martín Llobet. The elaborate geometrical traceries much resemble those of the cloister at Vich,

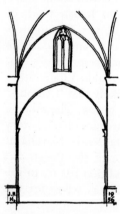

107 Valencia: Gothic bay design

known to have been begun in 1324 and completed in 1400, and it seems reasonable to suppose that the building of so ambitious a lantern may well have covered a substantial period of years. A date of *c.* 1330–60 does not appear to contradict any of the available evidence. Aesthetically, the alabaster windows are regrettable, for they give the tower a blind appearance sadly out of keeping with the delicate fantasy of its detail and its excellent outline.

Last of the external features, the Miguelete and the adjacent main entrance (26) claim attention, a strangely associated pair. The tall octagonal tower, of four stages divided by narrow string-courses and with its angles marked by thin buttresses, is absolutely plain except in the top stage, where each side is broken by a lancet window crowned with a gablet set against blind tracery. Work seems to have begun in 1381 and ended in 1429, the first architect being Andrés Juliá from Tortosa and the last, responsible for the ornamental crown, Pedro Balaguer who was sent to Lérida and Narbonne in 1414 to study other towers for the purpose. He was already famous for his noble city gateway of 1392–98, the Puerta de Serranos. The finest of all octagonal towers of the Catalan type, the Miguelete forms a singular foil for the curious Baroque façade which adjoins. This was begun in 1703 by the German Konrad Rudolf, and finished by 1713, but its upper stage and enriched frontispiece are the work of Francisco Vergara the elder, who had worked under Rudolf. This is a work of much charm, though unduly compressed to fit the narrow space available.

The Miguelete is reached through a passage with a curious ribless vault of a type also found in Bohemia and Poland, and here apparently due to Francisco Baldomar, who in 1437–62 built much larger vaults of the same type in the church of Santo Domingo in Valencia. The interior of the cathedral has little to recommend it, and apart from the ascent of the Miguelete need be entered only for access to the former chapter-house, now the chapel of the Holy Grail, built at the order of Bishop Vidal de Blanes (1356–69) by Andrés Juliá or Juliano. Square on plan, it is covered with an octagonal vault, the corners being filled with triangular vaulting almost identical with that of the rather earlier chapter-house of Pamplona. It is a splendid room, one of the noblest of its kind, and a fit shrine for the extraordinary relic which it contains. Since the possession of the legendary Grail by Valencia Cathedral is a fact far from widely known, I will here recapitulate the main facts of its known history. The cup itself is of oriental cornelian, dark red with greenish lights, and undoubtedly of Roman date; a base, stem, knop and handles were added at an early date, probably in the ninth century. Said by tradition to have been used by the Popes down to Sixtus II and to have been sent by St. Lawrence his deacon in A.D. 258 to Huesca, his birthplace, for safety during the persecution of Valerian, and later removed to San Juan de la Peña in 713 at the time of the Moorish invasion, it is matter of history that the cup was at San Juan de la Peña in the thirteenth century, was removed to Saragossa in 1399 by King Martin, in 1424 taken to Valencia by Alfonso V

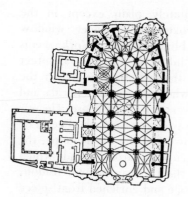

Lampérez: *Arq. Crist. Esp.* (Espasa-Calpe)

108 Murcia, 1394–1465; tower, 1521–, by Jacopo and Francesco l'Indaco; west front, 1737–54, by Jaime Bort y Melía

and given to the cathedral in 1437. In 1936 it was removed only three hours before the cathedral was sacked by the mob and hidden until 1939, after the victory of the Nationalist forces. Regardless of the question whether this is, or could be, the Cup of the Last Supper, it seems likely enough that during its sojourn in the mountain fastness of San Juan de la Peña its fame gave rise to the grail legends of the Middle Ages.

On the way to Murcia and just before crossing the frontier between the Aragonese and Castilian realms is the small town of Orihuela with a church made cathedral in 1564. Built *c.* 1305–55 it is a pretty little *colegiata* of no great distinction, and much altered at later periods, notably by the daring removal (*c.* 1500) of two piers to make a grand transept and by the addition of a row of square chapels at the east end, late in the sixteenth century. The transept vault has curious spirally twisted ribs and the north transept a Renaissance portal of *c.* 1540 attributed to Jerónimo Quijano.

Murcia has belonged to Castile ever since the Reconquest, but its architectural affinities are with the Levante rather than with Andalusia or New Castile, and it is therefore convenient to deal with it at this point. Set, like Valencia, in the midst of a fertile irrigated plain, the city is the focal point of a great area and its narrow streets are constantly filled with activity. In the middle of the business district and surrounded by thoroughfares stands the cathedral (*108*) closely beset by buildings on all sides except the west, where the view of the main front and tower offers one of the most sumptuous of all Baroque compositions (*20*). The front, built in 1737–54, is the masterpiece of Jaime Bort y Meliá, brought from Cuenca and sometimes said to have been a foreigner, but from his names apparently Valencian or Catalan by origin. Less imposing than the towered front of Santiago, so nearly contemporary, that of Murcia has a greater ease and frivolity, suited to its southern setting. It is sculptural rather than architectural in its effects, and Bort's fame was based upon his work as a sculptor. The central section succeeds in its ample proportions where the comparable attempt of Rudolf at Valencia fails, and is besides supported by the buttressing masses forming fronts to the side aisles and, beyond them and at a lower level still, the lateral chapels. The design has the immediate effectiveness of good stage scenery, and as such it must be regarded. It is seen at its superb best by night, when floodlit from the fountain in the foreground sending up a perpetual golden rain beyond which the towering masonry glows softly against the dark.

The tower is both earlier and later than the front. Begun in 1521 by the Florentine brothers Jacopo and Francesco l'Indaco, it had reached the top of its first stage by 1525, shortly before Jacopo's death. The second stage, similar in general character, was built under Jerónimo Quijano from 1526 to 1545, and there the work stayed for more than two centuries. At last, about 1765, Juan de Gea took in hand the completion, but it was not ended until 1792 after the routine interference by the ubiquitous Ventura Rodríguez. The design, however, in spite of a certain amount of amendment by the eighteenth-century architects, fortunately remained in its essentials that laid down by Quijano, who had produced drawings for the whole work. Strange as it may seem, the composition formed by a Baroque front and a tower begun in the Florentine Renaissance and ended by the severest academician of neoclassicism is entirely satisfactory and exemplifies that asymmetrical symmetry so often seen in the grouping of domed mosque and minaret.

The cathedral was begun towards the end of the fourteenth century, the plan (108) having affinities with Tortosa in the circuit wall surrounding the ambulatory, and with Valencia in the even number of its chevet chapels, two corresponding to each bay of the internal apse. But in spite of the low proportions of the interior there are reminiscences of Castilian style and the ridge-ribs of the vaults suggest a link with Burgos. For the south the church is well lit, the walls being whitewashed and the piers and shafts picked out in cream. Corresponding to the original build is the outer doorway of the south transept, the Puerta de los Apóstoles, built about 1440 by the master mason Alonso Gil, a well-designed work beneath an ogee label moulding under a traceried frontal flanked by pilaster buttresses. At the west end two bays of the original design were converted by Bort into a single square bay supporting a cupola; the idea is presumably derived from the western lantern at Barcelona. Of considerably greater interest is the ten-sided Capilla de los Vélez, substituted in 1495–1507 for two of the chapels on the south-east of the ambulatory. Manifestly imitated from the Capilla de Santiago at Toledo and that of the Constable at Burgos, both then of recent construction, this is a coarser but none the less striking conception, close in some respects to the Portuguese Manoeline style. Internally it has straight-sided reticulated traceries of almost English appearance, similar to the window in the Capilla de San Juan at Orense. The vault (24) is a splendid star-polygon with double tiercerons and series of curving liernes forming a ten-petalled flower at the crown. The chapel has been attributed to the cathedral master mason, Juan de León, who is also credited with the Plateresque portal of the north transept; but the private builders of the chapel may have employed their own architect. The outside is carved with a great chain of twisted links held up by stone rings, a fantasy coming near to the Manoeline extravagances at Batalha.

CHAPTER FIVE

Aragon

THE eastern seaboard of Spain, which has just been traversed, belonged in the Middle Ages to the Crown of Aragon; through marriage in the case of Catalonia, and by conquest so far as concerned the Balearic Isles and Valencia. Behind this coastal region lay Aragon itself, a very different country speaking a different language, Castilian. Aragon consists very largely of highlands: the Pyrenees and their foothills on the north, and the mountainous areas towards west and south through which ran the boundaries of Castile and Valencia. Across the middle lay the fertile plain of the Ebro, a connecting link between Castile, the Basque country and Navarre above, and southern Catalonia below. At the centre of this valley lies Saragossa, the capital. In contradistinction to Castile, a nation of Christian culture with no toleration for Moslems and little for Jews, Aragon remained until the end of the fifteenth century a polyglot land of three religions and a mingled cultural outlook. The Moslems of Aragon, the Mudéjares as they came to be called, were particularly skilled in the architecture of brick, plaster and glazed tiles, and buildings of this character became typical of the countryside. So distinct is this flavour that the comparatively small area of Aragon proper must be treated as a separate region.

Upper Aragon, that is to say Aragon along the line of the Pyrenees, had three early cathedrals: Jaca, Roda de Isábena, and Huesca. With Jaca, whose story is so closely linked to Navarre, we have already dealt. Roda, a see from 957 to 1149, still has the much altered church of 1063–67, of three aisles and three bays, with three parallel eastern apses, a church so simple that it barely enters the category of cathedral architecture. To the north is a twelfth-century cloister of plain design, probably built after Roda had ceased to be a cathedral. Some thirty miles to the south-west lies another former cathedral, Barbastro (*104*). But in this case the church did not hold cathedral rank when it was built in 1500–1533, by Baltasar de Barazábal to the design of Juan de Segura, being a see only from 1571 to 1851. The church in this case too, singularly enough, is of three aisles and three bays, with an additional narrow bay at the west and three parallel apses at the east; there are three lateral chapels on each side, showing the influence of the Catalan type of plan. Architecturally Barbastro is of interest as an extremely pure specimen of the Aragonese type at the end of the Gothic period, a hall-church with all its aisles of equal height, tall slender pillars of clustered mouldings and complex lierne vaults. It has also the special interest that these vaults approach very closely to the English fan-vault in their form, and even more noticeably in appearance. Geometrically, however, they do not conform to the definition of having ribs of equal spacing and equal curvature.

Thirty miles west of Barbastro and in the midst of rolling country covered in the spring with immense fields of wheat lies Huesca, a small brisk town of steep streets. The church was begun in or soon after 1273 and much of the plan belongs to this period, together with the project of a great triple portal in the west front, based on French models (30). As it is now, this front is singular rather than beautiful, for it includes work of three different and incompatible periods. At the base is the central doorway, a splendid work of seven orders filled with statuary and carving, flanked by splayed projections and, on the south side, remains of a lateral doorway to the aisle, now blocked. On the north a sixteenth-century chapel projects, destroying the corresponding doorway. Above the great doorway and truncating its pierced gablet runs a brick gallery in typically Aragonese mudéjar style, pierced with windows of shapeless heads, not pointed but appearing slightly ovoid rather than semicircular. This is covered with a tile roof, sloping up to the east and brought forward on heavy wooden cantilevers to form a shade of deep projection over the central porch. Above this again, and seeming to grow up through the tile roof on a line set back from the portal, is the upper stage of the main west front, a square-topped wall with corner turrets of buttressed form and two intermediate buttresses flanking a small rose. The stage is divided horizontally into two parts by a richly carved string-course, above which the face is heavily incrusted with Isabelline ornament including flanking two-light blind niches with triple-cusped tracery. The slender corner turrets and the intermediate buttresses are treated as clustered columns with bases, at different levels, of basket-work interpenetrating mouldings. They are carried up for some distance above the top of the front, but now have no pinnacles. This ornamental frontispiece is very closely paralleled by the design, on a smaller scale, of the retable of the high altar within, though here it is the outer turrets that are carried higher and are of greater importance; in the altarpiece it is the inner pair.

To the left of the front is a massive square tower above which rises an octagonal belfry; the tower was being built by 1302 and was still in progress in 1327. In the corresponding position at the south-west angle is an octagonal turret now almost buried in the mudéjar work of the gallery and tiled roof. Work on the tower's pinnacles is mentioned in a document of 1422 when Pedro Jalopa, whom we have already met at Palencia, was master of the works, but no pin-nacles now exist. The development of the church is complicated in spite of the apparent simplicity of its plan, an exact square divided into six rows of six squares in each direction, a double row from west to east representing the central nave and single rows the side-aisles and the cellular chapels beyond them. A double row on the east side of the square gives the plan of the transept, beyond which are the central apse and four smaller apses. In the original plan the side-chapels of the nave did not exist and only the aisles were vaulted. On the other hand the sturdy triple wall-shafts were clearly intended to carry vaulting, badly as the present vaults fit them. In the central apse and the transept these shafts are finished off with figured capitals bearing polygonal moulded abaci, while in the nave the carving is almost entirely reduced to foliage and the abaci are round. Evidently the original work went on very slowly, and may only have reached a temporary completion with wooden ceiling to the nave by 1411, when attention was turned to the cloisters, finished by 1459.

It is the late work at Huesca that is of outstanding interest. Besides the upper part of the west front it includes the whole of the high vaults and the flying-buttresses added to support them, and the flanking chapels on each side of the nave aisles. This im-portant new programme was decided upon after long consultations with a number of Navarrese and Basque masters to one of whom, Juan de Olózaga, the work was entrusted in 1497 after his proposals had been demonstrated by marking them out in a field outside the city with pegs and string. The vaulting (116) is of very beautiful design and execution in star patterns, three of the bays of the nave having, unusually, stars of six points with no diagonal ribs. The arch to the central apse (*117*) is of double-cusped pendants, similar to contemporary English work in, for example, Bishop Alcock's chapel at Ely; the motive is apparently of Flemish origin. The main phase of alterations was probably over by 1509, when Olózaga undertook the work of the chapels, which he finished in 1515. Shortly afterwards the great altarpiece was designed, and its carvings made between 1520 and 1534 by Damián Forment.

From Huesca to Saragossa is only some fifty miles, but the change in scenery and feeling is marked, from the foothills of a mountain range to the flat plains on each side of Spain's greatest river. The capital of Aragon is entered over the grand stone bridge of 1401, with the two cathedrals visible on either hand. To the right or westwards is the extraordinary pile of El Pilar, with its two towers and many cupolas, while to the left is the tall steeple of the older church, La Seo. For Saragossa is the only Spanish city where, as in Dublin, two cathedrals share the see between them. Of La Seo the only external features of aesthetic importance are the mudéjar east wall of the chapel known as La Parroquieta and of the great apse, made of panelled brickwork with inlays of glazed tiles in the second half of the fourteenth century, possibly by craftsmen brought from Seville; and the Baroque north front and tower. The mudéjar brickwork has fascinating pattern and colour, but altogether lacks architectural composition. The tower, built of brick in 1682–90 to a design sent from Rome by Giovanni Battista Contini, is most unusual, of four main stages surmounted by a singular bulbous roof of the regional type. The succession of square and octagonal stories too reflects the influence of the mudéjar brick towers and perhaps in turn suggested some of the motives employed nearly a century later by Beratúa at La Calzada. The front, by Julián de Yarza, is of much less interest, and gives no idea of the character of the church within.

Internally, La Seo is a hall-church of five aisles and side-chapels, with the central nave slightly higher than the aisles, but without clerestory lighting (*110*). It has reached its present state by many accretions to the original church, of which fragments remain in the central and northern apses, begun in 1189. This was enlarged between 1316 and 1412, but of this work hardly anything remains visible. In the opening years of the fifteenth century the church was crowned by the building of the first lantern for Pope Benedict XIII, "Papa Luna", who employed a committee of mudéjar architects, Juce de Galí, Ibraim de Pina, Mahoma Rami and Musa el Calvo ("the bald"). Their work was not sound and led to consultations in 1417 with the masters Corla (Carlí?) and Isembart, the latter coming from work at Daroca and probably the vault-builder found at Palencia in 1424–29 and Seville in 1434. The old *cimborio* was propped up until 1501, by which time further substantial extensions to the church were in progress. Two outer aisles were added to the existing three soon after 1490, and in 1498 preliminary steps were taken for the rebuilding of the lantern. This time architects were brought from Toledo, Barcelona, Huesca and Valencia, and on their advice the old work was taken down. It was rebuilt by 1520 under Juan Botero, and is one of the finest of its class. The vault is of the same plan as that of the fourteenth-century kitchen at Durham, both deriving from Saracenic sources. Externally the Saragossa lantern is a buttressed brick octagon through the roof of which appears a smaller octagon with its angles set towards the sides of that below; the treatment is very simple and hardly suggests the internal richness of detail. Finally, between 1546 and 1559 Charles de Mendivi added two more bays at the west end of the church, beyond the *trascoro*, and at the same time unified the treatment of the whole interior (*111*). The total

npérez: Arq. Crist. Esq. (Espasa-Calpe)

109, 110 Saragossa (La Seo), 1119–, 1316–1412, and 1546–59, by Charles de Mendivi; tower, 1682–90, by Giov. B. Contini

effect as we see it is therefore very late Gothic, some of the carved capitals including Renaissance detail, but the vaults with their wooden filigree pendant bosses belong entirely to the Middle Ages.

El Pilar, on the bank of the broad muddy stream of the Ebro, is a church of a very different sort (23). It gives a general impression of un-European exoticism, with its orange-brown brick and coloured tile roofs in patterns. But its plan is almost identical with that of Juan de Herrera at Valladolid, though here the fronts are on the long sides. Of the four corner towers only two have been finished, in modern times. The building was originally begun in 1677 to plans by Francisco de Herrera the younger, and was intended to be in a Baroque treatment. What we now see is, however, largely the outcome of extensive alterations made by Ventura Rodríguez in 1753–66, when all the subsidiary cupolas were added. It can hardly be pretended that El Pilar is a satisfying work, but it is one of the largest cathedrals in Spain and possesses a certain degree of solid magnificence to be expected in such a famous shrine and centre of pilgrimage.

Tarazona is fifty miles west-north-west of Saragossa in the lower ranges of the Sierra de Moncayo, a picturesque mountain town perched upon a steep rocky hill. The cathedral stands on flat ground at the base of the hill and, though of only middling size, is impressive by reason of its piled-up central lantern (113), a far more complex and architectonic version of that at La Seo in Saragossa. Designed by the same master, Juan Botero, it is a later work, built mainly between 1543 and 1545. The buttresses of the main stage have two series of pinnacles with pillared openwork caps, and above this rise two further stages instead of one. In the latter half of the sixteenth century the main parts of the church reached their present form, the brick gallery of the *capilla mayor* being finished in 1560 and the south-west tower in 1588. The classical cavern of a porch to the north transept, forming the main entrance, is perhaps still later. Earlier work on the tower had been done at the end of the fifteenth century by Alí el Darocano, a mudéjar master also responsible for the gallery and battlements which crown the nave. Whether he can have been the author of the late Gothic vaults inserted in the nave about the same time is less clear.

Internally the cathedral is difficult to appreciate on account of its mixture of periods and the changes of plan which seem to have taken place in each. The chevet and ambulatory were originally

111 SARAGOSSA: La Seo. The interior as reconstructed in 1546–59 by Charles de Mendivi

112 The interior of 1152–1235, with the pulpit by Maestre Pedro, 1506, in the nave, begun *c.* 1362

113 The Chevet and the Lantern of 1543–58, by Juan Botero

TARAZONA

built between 1152 and 1235 in a north French style, the continuous triforium of small arches being closely based on that of Chartres. In 1361 the church was seriously damaged at the invasion of Aragon by Peter the Cruel of Castile, and the square chapels of the apse, the western piers of the crossing, and the nave arcades seem to belong to a rebuilding begun soon after this (112). The walls of the nave show very marked distortion, presumably due to pressure from the vaults, though the flying buttresses outside look substantial enough. The most intriguing part of the whole cathedral is the cloister, built in 1504–29 and unique in style. Structurally it is late Gothic and built of brick, the buttressed piers towards the garth having sunk patterns of partly Gothic and partly mudéjar style. But the pointed arches between them are filled with an elaborate screenwork in which are openings filled in turn with thin sheets of stone pierced in filigree patterns. Singular as this mixture of styles and motives may appear, the result is charming.

Teruel is at the extreme southern end of Aragon, near the coastal ranges which divide the old kingdom from Valencia. Rather more than a hundred miles south of Tarazona, the way to it lies through the heart of the most Moorish section of Spain, the group of river valleys centred around Calatayud, whence the road and railway to Valencia climb through the orchards of the fertile valley of the Jiloca past the extraordinary sight of the empty walls of Daroca with their hundred towers, not less remarkable than those of Ávila. Teruel lies beyond the watershed and beside the Guadalaviar, in a strange country of whitish dusty hills, and looks as much a Moorish as a Christian city. It is not a mediaeval see, and the ancient cathedral, no longer with that rank, is twenty miles to the west at Albarracín, an apsidal church rebuilt about 1531 and still keeping its excellent stellar vaults of that time, but otherwise hidden beneath a severely classical lining of the eighteenth century. Teruel, though it became cathedral only in 1577, dates from 1248–78, but has suffered many alterations. The first church consisted only of the central nave of the present building, with the tower at the west end begun in 1257. This church was covered with a splendidly painted wooden ceiling, of Moorish artesonado character but with Gothic paintings of figures in many of its panels. In 1538 the bay in front of the sanctuary was reconstructed and transepts thrown out in brick to abut an octagonal lantern of Saragossan type, designed by Martín de Montalbán.

After the erection of the church into a cathedral it was decided to enlarge it, and between 1596 and 1614 side-aisles were thrown out. A square ambulatory behind the *capilla mayor* was made in 1658, so that the building acquired a rectangular form, now much obscured by alterations and additions. Externally the western tower with its seventeenth-century crown and the lantern of patterned brick form a good composition, none the less successful for its accidental character. Montalbán's lantern, though less ambitious than that of Tarazona, improves upon its model at Saragossa and has internally an excellent vault. Like most of the buildings of Teruel, the cathedral was seriously damaged during the civil war, but has been carefully restored with on the whole pleasing results. In the process of repair the plaster vaults of the late seventeenth century were removed to expose the magnificent *artesonado* ceiling of the nave and the Gothic ribs of the vaulted sanctuary.

CHAPTER SIX

New Castile and Extremadura

ONCE the Reconquest had passed the line of the Guadarrama range, its velocity increased by leaps and bounds. First an enormous area down to the Sierra Morena was taken in, during the twelfth century, leaving Andalusia (apart from the kingdom of Granada) for the first half of the thirteenth. As we have seen, the magnitude of the victory gave to the kingdom of Castile a great new world to people and to reconvert. Toledo remained until the end of the sixteenth century a city with a large Arabic-speaking population, but elsewhere it was not Castile's policy to leave large bodies of Moors settled within the realm, and there is very little sign of the employment of mudéjar craftsmen as compared with Aragon. Occasionally there might be a reversal of policy, as when Peter the Cruel deliberately favoured his Moslem and Jewish subjects, playing them off against the Christians, but this did not have much effect upon church building, though it goes far to explain King Peter's consistently bad reputation with historians.

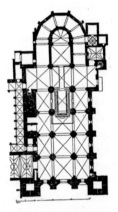

114 Sigüenza, c. 1155–1300; cloister 1503–08, by Alonso de Vozmediano

New Castile is a dry and dusty land, a plateau like Old Castile, but much less watered and with enormous expanses of rolling wasteland and open plains. None the less it is still a part of northern Spain when compared to Andalusia, and with the notable exception of Toledo (the city, not the cathedral) it has a similar human atmosphere to much of the adjacent country on the other side of the ranges. There is, for instance, no great difference of feeling at

Sigüenza from what we have known at Osma. Even at its head-waters the little River Henares is flanked by poplars and between the pale barren hills are rich farmlands. The city of Sigüenza climbs a rocky hill to the castle on the top, a Castilian counterpart of Tarazona, and here too the cathedral was built upon the lower ground.

The diocese was founded in 1124, and it is to be presumed that work on the cathedral (*114*) began soon afterward, but the first reference to the building is in 1156, and a consecration took place in 1169, probably of the east end, then built with five parallel apses of which the central alone has survived. Building continued through the thirteenth century and sexpartite vaults were introduced, usually considered the earliest in Spain. The nave seems not to have begun until 1192, but it is probable that it had been designed and set out earlier than this, in the time of Bishop Cerebrun of Poitiers, for not only is the character of the nave Poitevin, but the west front in particular, with its tall arches and the towers outside the aisles and standing forward from the west wall, is directly based upon Poitiers Cathedral. In addition to these western towers a slender tower was built in 1300 against the south-east angle of the south transept.

Sigüenza is one of the very few Spanish cathedrals whose outward effect is as great as, or even greater than, that within. Approaching from the west, that is to say from Madrid, the breadth of the front and the stern castellated appearance of the towers, as well as the large scale of the building in relation to the city, are the dominant effects (*115*). Opening up the north flank the transept with its great rose comes into view, and the low square lantern which has been added in the recent restoration of civil war destruction. This is one of the best examples of bold reconstruction of a lost feature in modern times and deserves high praise for the success with which it completes the grouped composition that was undoubtedly intended by the original architects. Another fine view is from the south-east, where the central apse builds up finely to the lantern and south-eastern tower. One peculiarity of the western towers, as seen from any oblique angle, is that they always look as if they were of different sizes. In fact they are planned symmetrically but each has a stair turret attached at the inner angle of its eastern face, and the two inner walls are flush, not marking the turret, which makes the further tower as seen from western viewpoints, the nearer

115 SIGÜENZA: view from north-west

117   The Sanctuary, begun in 1273 and vaulted in 1497–1509

116   The Nave vault, 1497–1509

119　The Transept, 1155–69, raised in c. 1226

118　The Cloister of 1503–8, by Alonso
de Vozmediano

SIGÜENZA

120 SEVILLE: detail of the Retablo Mayor begun in 1482, showing model of the city in c. 1510, crowned by the cathedral and Giralda.

when viewed from the east, look bigger owing to its longer diagonal dimension.

It is hard to obtain any adequate general impressions of the interior, so much altered is it by the insertion of doorways and altarpieces of later periods. The transept is the least encumbered part and now that it is adequately lighted by the restored lantern has a grand effect. The eastern crossing piers lose some of their stateliness by being divided into two stages by a complete circuit of Corinthianesque capitals, with enriched abacus, and fresh bases for the upper series of shafts. The south-western pier reduces this awkward arrangement to a mere series of annulet mouldings, while the north-west pier is a round drum, like the pair of nave piers west of the crossing. M. Élie Lambert, who has studied the structure in detail, in part explains these strange inconsistencies of design as the successive works of several building campaigns. The Romanesque lower stage of the eastern crossing piers belongs to an early project, the church with five parallel apses; to the same period belong the outer walls of the nave (themselves carried out in two stages) and the four western nave piers. Later the whole church was raised by a stage, building on top of the existing capitals both in the sanctuary and nave; and later still the south-west crossing pier was rebuilt, at some time well on in the thirteenth century. This explanation is certainly correct in principle, but M. Lambert is not entirely convincing in his correlation of the separate works with the known dates of the cathedral, as he is unprepared to admit that the scheme with five apses and the Romanesque capitals can be earlier than the first work at Tarragona, certainly begun after 1171.

This is to treat the history of Spanish architecture as though it were an integral part of that of France. It would indeed be unthinkable *in France* that there should be so great a discrepancy in date between two works of the same style. But it has to be remembered that in Spain in the twelfth and early thirteenth centuries there was no steady internal development of style, but an incoherent succession of individual borrowings, at times of actual craftsmen, at others of drawings or general ideas only. In these conditions there can be a very large differential time-lag between works as far apart as Tarragona and Sigüenza, especially when it is borne in mind that between them there lay in the middle of the twelfth century a no-man's land in which pockets of Moors were holding out against the Reconquest, and further that relations between Castile and Aragon were often as strained as those between England and Scotland in mediaeval times.

The hypotheses advanced by M. Lambert are forced upon him by his antecedent thesis of an architecture proceeding by "schools" such as the "Cistercian Hispano-Languedocian" school to which he attributes the work at Tarragona and Sigüenza. But we now know that even in the twelfth century much architectural progress was made by individual designers adopting eclectically from various admired buildings features which they wished to incorporate in their own work. Only by discarding this artificial attachment to the internal development in Spain of a given school can the whole of the structural and documentary evidence be reconciled. In this way we arrive at a solution perfectly in keeping with the dates of the respective works judged by the standard of France. The crucial dates are those of 1156, when the second bishop, Pierre de Leucate from Languedoc, died leaving funds for the completion of the chevet chapels and the transept; 1168, when Leucate's successor, Cerebrun from Poitiers, was translated to Toledo; and 1169, when a consecration including at least a part of the south transept took place. The plan of the nave and west front are quite certainly derived from Poitiers, while the scheme of the original east end with its parallel apses and low arcades comes with equal certainty from Languedoc.

The Languedocian design must therefore belong to the episcopate of Pierre de Leucate, and was probably already far advanced when he died in 1156; from the likeness of the eastern crossing piers to the responds of the nave aisles it must be assumed that the first two bays west of the crossing (as far as the break in the work noted by M. Lambert) were also built at this time. The two western bays with the west front and the beginning of the towers, all carried out together and by a gang of masons different (as shown by their marks) from those who worked in the east nave, were then carried out under the Poitevin bishop, Cerebrun, who will also have applied his predecessor's funds to completing the eastern arm and transept sufficiently for consecration to take place. There seems then to have been a concentration of activity upon the subsidiary buildings, for a chapter-house was described as new in 1181 and the cloisters and their dependencies were built after 1168 and finished by 1192. In 1198 it was reckoned that at least fifteen more seasons of work would be needed to complete the church, and this we must remember referred to the low church of a single stage. Then it was decided to raise the whole church a stage higher, and this was undoubtedly the work in progress in 1226, as M. Lambert has shown conclusively by comparison with the details dateable to 1223 at the neighbouring abbey of Santa María de Huerta. The building of the entire south-west pier of the crossing, and of the upper stages of the rest of the nave piers, with the high vaults, all belong to the middle and later part of the thirteenth century. Further works or repairs were in hand in 1335, and to somewhere about that period belongs the middle part of the south-west tower. Further works, not now to be identified, were going on about 1425-30, and between 1468 and 1495 the vaults of the crossing and sanctuary were rebuilt. The cloister was rebuilt in 1503-08 by Alonso de Vozmediano, the chapter-house in 1527 by Francisco Baeza, and a sacristy erected in high Renaissance style in 1532-34 by Alonso de Covarrubias. During the sixteenth century the north-west tower was at last carried up, and then or soon after the south-west tower completed. A great change was made by the building of an ambulatory in 1567-1606, ostensibly in conformity with the old work but really in an extremely dry classical manner. Thus the cathedral reached the state which it retained until our own time, apart from the addition of a neo-classical south porch in 1797 by Luis Bernasconi.

I have thought it worth while to particularise the stages of development at Sigüenza, for it is one of the most fundamental buildings in Spain of its original epoch. It possesses noteworthy beauties of several periods, among them the late cloisters which are not only of good design but of special interest for the remarkable approximation of their tracery to English Perpendicular work, to such an extent that only close examination reveals the essentially Flamboyant character of the detail. Of the post-Gothic buildings the finest is the Sacristy, a strange reversion to Romanesque proportions and construction with its round barrel-vault supported on cross-arches. But the thing which all visitors see and remember, when they have perhaps forgotten even the appearance of the cathedral itself, is the tomb of Don Martín Vázquez de Arce in the Capilla de Santa Catalina, off the south transept. The figure of the young *doncel*, reclining at his ease and calmly reading his book, is too famous for detailed description. But it is worth considering the date and the style of this monument, so definitely of the Middle Ages, and carved at the very moment when the romances of a dying chivalry were first getting into print. It might be the story of *Palmerin of England* that Don Martín holds between his hands, or the famous *Tirant lo Blanch*, whose author incorporated descriptions of England from first-hand knowledge, though dying in 1486 Martín could have had in his life only a manuscript of these. And though it could not be Malory's *Morte d'Arthur*, in its glowing pages he would have found himself spiritually at home. The tomb was made in or soon after 1491, just at the moment of Christian Spain's final victory over the Moors of Granada and the discovery of America. All this Don Martín was not to know, nor the profound changes of other kinds about to befall the world in which he lived. We, with our backward vision over so much that might have dimmed the keen ideals which moved this youth to die fighting "the enemies of our holy faith" as his epitaph has it, may feel that he was happy in the moment of his death.

Going from Sigüenza to Madrid we pass Alcalá de Henares, the great university city, with its collegiate church known as La Magistral. This has a kind of cathedral rank, for the title of the see is Madrid-Alcalá. Very severely damaged in the civil war, the structure is in course of repair and is worth a visit as one of the few complete large churches of the Isabelline period. It was built in 1497–1509 by Pedro Gumiel, known as *el honrado* because his jobs never exceeded his estimates; the works began with the west end and continued towards the apse. The building has a certain astringency of style, exaggerated now by the loss of its fittings and of the splendid tomb of Cardinal Cisneros to which it served as a shrine. It gives the impression of being a conservative reaction against modernism, going back to the aisled plan with ambulatory and that in imitation of Toledo, with three rectangular bays between four triangles. The sanctuary and the crossing form two square bays and there is a nave of five oblong bays with a plain west front, flat-topped and between simple buttresses, the only concession to enrichment being an ornamental overdoor and architrave.

Madrid is a cathedral city more by courtesy than in any historical sense, but it possesses two cathedrals. The older is the *colegiata* of San Isidro el Real, built to designs of Fray Francisco Bautista in 1622–64 as the church of the Jesuits. Though counted as an example of early Baroque by some it is in fact a grim monument of the severest

121 TOLEDO: the Transparente of 1732, by Narciso Tomé

122 The Sanctuary of c. 119
1208, perhaps by Ricar
of Burgos

123 The Ambulatory, alter
in 1448–90 by Hanequ
de Egas

CUENCA

classicism, closer to the style of Juan de Herrera than to its own contemporaries. Its cold grey stone contributes to this effect and startlingly suggests the portals of a prison on the pavement of the fine old Calle de Toledo. Internally all its glories have departed since it was sacked in 1936, but the structural damage has been put right. The new cathedral of Nuestra Señora de la Almudena, begun in 1880 to designs by the Marqués Francisco de Cubas, is much more impressive in spite of its unfinished state. The crypt is an essay in the most solid Romanesque, while above are columns and parts of arcades of neo-Gothic, and work is now in progress on a wide-spreading front flanked by tall towers in the Renaissance tradition of Madrid. There is a faintly ridiculous side to this historical pageantry of painstaking copies of the national styles adopted in succession for the various sections of the work but at least Madrid, the artificial capital of an artificial grouping of kingdoms, is being provided with an artificial epitome of all the cathedrals of Spain.

South of Sigüenza there are only two ancient cathedrals in the whole of New Castile: Cuenca and Toledo. Long left unvisited owing to its isolation, Cuenca now lies on the main line of railway from Madrid to Valencia and deserves to be seen for its wild beauty and unspoilt charm, a city set on a hill surrounded by deep chasms and in the midst of a vast rolling countryside covered with rosemary, whence thousands of hives of bees derive most of the honey of Spain. The cathedral (122), high on the slope of the hill, is one of the most controversial of Spanish buildings. On account of the difficulty of communication, Cuenca was left on one side by Street, so that we lack the sound common sense which he brought to so many buildings of complex history. On the one hand is the view of Lampérez, endorsed by Émile Bertaux, that the design is Anglo-Norman, and this was supported with more detailed arguments by Miss G. G. King. Against this stands the flat denial of M. Élie Lambert, who finds nothing of either English or Norman character but would trace certain features which Cuenca shares with Norman and with English work to a common Franco-Burgundian source. In this conflict Mr. Bevan contents himself with summarising the main arguments on each side.

As in the case of Sigüenza the mistake, and it applies to both sides, is in supposing that because a building was erected as early as the twelfth century its architect must have been ignorant of everything except the traditions of one local school in which he had been brought up: that the whole work is to be fitted into the strait-jacket implied by such terms as Burgundian, Angevin, Languedocian and the like. What is quite as common is to find that a church derives its plan largely from one school, its structure from another and individual features or details from sources extraneous to both. Thus it is at Cuenca. M. Lambert demonstrates a genuinely close resemblance of plan to Saint-Yved at Braine in all main proportions, but even so there is no evidence that Cuenca ever possessed the one unusual characteristic of having its lateral chapels placed obliquely; and their arrangement seems to have been that normal in almost all Spanish work of the time. In structure, Cuenca has sexpartite vaults, certainly French but not derived from Saint-Yved; in the eastern arm it has a clerestory but no triforium, in the nave a clerestory with an internal unglazed tracery of triforium character for which a parallel (not a very close one) exists at Saint-Seine-l'Abbaye, northwest of Dijon. But the use of this device of the "transparency" is comparatively late and probably invented by Pierre de Montreuil for the nave of Saint-Denis started in 1231, though it occurs near the same date in the triforium of the chevet at Troyes. This then, occurring as it does only in the nave at Cuenca, merely shows that the designer was working with a knowledge of the latest advances of style in the period c. 1230–55, during which the Cuenca nave must have been built.

Obviously certain features do suggest an Anglo-Norman origin, and the problem is to identify them and to show whether or not the resemblance is accidental. The first item is the square lantern tower (124) above the crossing, unbuttressed with plain angles, and with a range of lancet windows. It is not merely a question here of the possession of a central tower, but of the particular architectural form adopted. And there is no question that this form is indeed Anglo-Norman, being found in the Romanesque period at Winchester and St.-Gervais at Falaise, and in Gothic times at the Abbaye-aux-Dames, Caen, Wells Cathedral and Old St. Pauls, in the last case with added buttresses. Scottish central towers, notably at Glasgow, follow the same model. Trondhjem Cathedral in Norway, always under predominantly English influence, also has a central tower of this form, and with a triforium arcade internally of four bays in each face, as Winchester had at a much earlier date, Winchester has three windows in the upper stage where Falaise (with Cuenca) has four; but Cuenca internally is in three bays each of two lancets or lights on each stage, while Wells has three bays in the lower level and three pairs of tall lancets above. As regards the tower at least, Cuenca certainly owes something to the Anglo-Norman region.

124 Cuenca: central tower, c. 1210–50

Internally there is only one important feature which at first sight gives a strongly English impression: the sanctuary piers with a circular core surrounded by slender shafts, encircled at half-height by moulded annulets and standing on circular bases (123). These are of an exquisite elegance, comparable to that of the similar pillars at Lincoln.* M. Lambert refuses to accept either an English or a Norman origin and claims that they are derived from the alternate nave piers of Laon which do indeed have clustered shafts round a cylindrical column, and moulded annulets. But bases and capitals at Laon are in square offsets and the whole effect is a heavy and clumsy one, utterly unlike that of Cuenca or of the Norman examples on which M. Lambert admits these features of Laon were based. This difference in feeling must be held to rule out any possibility of direct imitation of Laon, while it tells strongly in favour of a more direct link with the Norman sources. To sum up, Cuenca is not of immediately English inspiration, but at least two major features of its design come from the Anglo-Norman region, and most probably from Normandy.

As regards date, there is no reason (pace M. Lambert) to question the general belief that Cuenca was begun at the east end a few years before 1200 and was able to be consecrated in 1208 at the latest; and that the nave was built thereafter and finished by c. 1250 The main later alteration consisted in breaking down the lateral apses and building a great double ambulatory, beginning about 1448 and ended before 1496. This was probably designed by the Toledo master, Hanequín de Egas from Brussels. In 1664 or thereabouts there was a great rebuilding of the west front in an uninteresting and rather slight Baroque, but this was demolished after the fall of the tower in 1902. In spite of the double disaster which has over-

* The extremely close similarity of the piers in the chapter-house at Las Huelgas, also with circular bases, but lacking annulets, strongly suggests that Cuenca is an earlier work of the Anglo-Angevin master Ricardo.

taken the main front, Cuenca Cathedral remains a wonderfully complete and homogeneous monument, and one which can be appreciated as a whole, especially inside. It has a clarity of detail and a fine finish, for example in the members of mouldings, rather unusual in Spain and giving it a jewel-like quality the more to be appreciated in the almost savage beauty of its natural setting.

Toledo, the metropolitan see of the primate of Spain, has a character unlike that of any other Spanish city. To a far greater degree than even the towns of Andalusia it has retained a flavour of the Orient in its narrow lanes and steep hills. It is a surprise not to hear the muezzin still calling to prayer from strategically placed minarets, and no straining of the imagination is needed to picture the co-existence of Moors and Spaniards referred to by Cervantes as still a commonplace of his own time. Toledo was the one great exception in Castile to the general rule of expulsion or at best disfavour to the conquered. It was not until 1580 that the use of the Arabic language was forbidden and even then an exception was made in favour of church services, showing that there was still an important section of the population whose mother tongue was not Spanish. At the Reconquest in 1085, Alfonso VI had promised

125, 126, 127 Toledo, 1226–c. 1400, by Martín and others; cloister, 1389–1425, by Rodrigo Alfonso

absolute equality of treatment to the three religions, and though his French archbishop Bernard shamefully dishonoured this undertaking by a persecution of the Moslems and the Jews, Toledo on the whole remained the one great centre of tolerance in Castile until the end of the fifteenth century.

The bad habit of attempting to visit Toledo in a single day from Madrid has been inculcated in recent years, and does serious injustice to one of the most richly endowed centres of Europe in historical and artistic treasures. The cathedral (125-7) alone deserves the serious attention of several hours to do justice to its fabric and to its treasures. To an extent unusual even for Spain the building contains important works of many periods, covering every century from the thirteenth to the eighteenth. The first stone was laid in 1226 and the ambulatory and its chapels were built in the next twelve years by the first master, Martín the Stonemason, who may still have been living in 1269. Work continued westwards with some changes of design, apparently introduced by Petrus Petri (? Pedro Pérez), who was master for a long period before his death in 1291. His work includes the crossing and part of the nave aisles. The nave continued slowly for another century, and between 1389 and about 1425 the cloisters were built to the design of Rodrigo Alfonso who was also building the charterhouse of El Paular. The lower parts of the west front (131) with its towers and three porches were built by Juan Alfonso from the monastery of Guadalupe, perhaps Rodrigo's brother. The north-west tower was carried up in 1425-40 by Álvar Martínez, but the spire was added by Hanequín de Egas from Brussels in 1448-52. Egas later built the great south doorway or Puerta de los Leones, from 1452 to 1465, and died about 1471. In 1493 the high vaults were at last finished. The choir stalls were in progress from 1495 to 1543 and the *retablo mayor* made in 1502-04. Enrique de Egas was concerned with the building of the Mozarabic Chapel in the south tower from 1504 to 1519, and in 1531-34 the Capilla de los Reyes Nuevos off the north-eastern ambulatory was made by Alonso de Covarrubias. The upper part of the west front was begun in 1606 by Juan Bautista Monegro, while the cupola of the Capilla Mozárabe beside it was designed by Jorge Manuel Theotocopuli, son of El Greco, and built in 1626-31. Last of all the major changes in the structure was the insertion of the Transparente (121) behind the high altar, a masterpiece of the most extravagant Churrigueresque, finished by Narciso Tomé in 1732.

Even in this somewhat lengthy recital a great many architectural works of substantial importance have been omitted, but it can be seen that Toledo is far from being an integral work of art to be accepted as a unit. It must be examined piecemeal, though with profound admiration for the skill of the successive artists who have nevertheless achieved a sum total on the whole harmonious. The outside is so closely hemmed in by the narrow streets of the old city that only a few sections can be viewed adequately, among them fortunately the west front. Here, as at Oviedo, is a great steeple left apparently with intention unbalanced; or rather, balanced by a mass of different shape, namely the cupola designed by El Greco's son. The front seems at first to have been planned for a pair of towers in advance, as at Sigüenza. This plan may go back to a very early stage of the works, even though it was not fulfilled until the fifteenth century. The great porches are not very successful examples of their kind, even considering the late date, but the tower in its proportions and composition must be reckoned a masterpiece. Much of the credit has to be given to the Brussels master who completed it with its unique crown and spire, one of the finest of Gothic conceptions, each stage growing from the one below and the spire through all.

Hanequín was not quite so successful in the Puerta de los Leones, the south portal, which is a somewhat chilly design though carried out with rich architectural and sculptural detail. Its inner face, towards the church, is more ingenious but regrettably altered in Renaissance times so that it cannot be properly appreciated. Nor can much be seen of the narrowly squeezed north front, the Puerta del Reloj, built at the beginning of the fourteenth century at the bottom of a steep lane, though its portal has some good sculpture. It is only inside the church that it is possible to assess the intentions of the designer, and there, better than in most Spanish cathedrals, can be seen a unity of composition which must go back to the original plans and sections, in spite of the changes in detail which mark the succession of several masters.

It was shown by Lampérez that, although the derivation of the plan and a substantial part of the construction were from France, the actual method of setting-out, the proportions, and important features such as the curious triforium of the sanctuary, were undeniably Spanish. Moreover Toledo is the best instance, save the much later Seville, of the Spanish preoccupation with area and with a cubical volume of space. These qualities are infused throughout the whole of the interior, marking it out as distinctly Spanish as the height of Beauvais shows that it is French, or the length of Winchester that it is English. Toledo is in this sense a type cathedral, exemplifying almost all of the traits which are most characteristic of the national architecture. And if it fails it is perhaps by being too much a type to be entirely itself. But Toledo is one of the truly impressive buildings of Europe, not least because of the substantial amount of mediaeval glass still in its windows, though the earliest of this dates only from 1418 and much of it belongs to the decadence of Gothic glass-painting and some to the Renaissance.

The mediaeval diocese of Toledo was immense and included not only the area of the modern diocese of Madrid-Alcalá but also that of the pseudo-diocese or priorate of the Military Orders whose church at Ciudad Real has cathedral rank. This possesses comparatively slight interest, and what there is is limited to the interior (135), for the late tower was heavily restored in the nineteenth century. But it deserves to be compared with Coria for its single span, though here with an apsidal east end begun about 1490 and covered with a good vault with pendant bosses. The remaining vaults, which have patterns of increasing complexity, were set between 1514 and 1580, together with two lateral chapels which form a kind of false transept. These last works were finished by Antonio Fernández.

Of far greater importance are the three cathedrals of Extremadura: Badajoz, Coria and Plasencia. These have been consistently neglected owing to their remoteness from the centres of modern life, though the province to which they belong has a great variety of natural beauty and wonderful riches in unspoilt towns and villages of ancient building. The countryside falls into two distinct parts, to the south the rich fertile valley of the Guadiana, now heavily irrigated, with almost equally fertile hills beyond it; and to the north the hillier country of the modern province of Cáceres, climbing up to the heights of the Sierra de Gata. Linking the two is a rolling plateau of savannah, wide natural meadows dotted with holm oaks and little pools and marshes where the pensive black-and-white figure of a stork lends an air of almost prehistoric remoteness.

The cathedral of the lower lands is Badajoz, beneath the picturesque frontier fortress which crowns a steep hill beside the Guadiana just before it reaches Portugal. Externally the church has little but its strange figured crenellations and its simple four-square tower, largely due to a campaign of work ended in 1419, but with a sixteenth-century belfry surmounted by a still more curious parapet of vases on pedestals. The inside (*132–3*) is whitewashed with the marked-out imitation masonry so general in Spain, and here relieved by a gilt cornice which runs round the main walls at the springing of the high vaults. The stone is a granite and this is responsible for the very plain forms of mouldings and enrichment, but these are suitable to the small scale of the building and of considerable beauty. In particular, the bases of the eastern piers are finely organised, with a neat transformation from the curving mouldings to the polygonal bases beneath (*128*).

The plan of the original cathedral, built between 1232 and 1284, is extremely simple and regular. The eastern arm, now rebuilt as a square sanctuary flanked by square aisles set back one bay on each side of a presbytery covered with a saucer-dome of *c.* 1600, probably had three parallel apses beyond the presbytery. West of this is an unaisled transept and a nave of five bays. An unusual feature is the almost equal width of nave and aisles, all bays of vaulting approaching to squares on plan. A marked change in the profiles of capitals and bases west of the transept suggests that there was a definite break between completion of the eastern arm and crossing, and the building of the nave, but the general design remains unchanged throughout. The bay design is extremely simple, amounting to an arcade beneath lunettes in which there are now small rectangular clerestory windows, apparently modern insertions, though Lampérez speaks of small blocked windows in this position.

Coria is nearly a hundred miles north of Badajoz, a tiny mediaeval city on a steep hill immediately above the River Alagón. Its cathedral, on the brow of the hill, has something of the aspect of a fortress with small windows placed high and a substantial tower with cupola and lantern added in 1756–60 during repairs after the Lisbon earthquake. The lower stages of this tower are Plateresque, and include a notable spiral staircase with open centre in an octagonal turret with fluted sides, but the belfry replaces two stages which fell in the earthquake. In its present form it closely resembles that of Ciudad Rodrigo by Juan de Sagarvinaga, but has three openings on each of its faces instead of two. In detail as well as in composition, particularly in the proportions of the lantern crowning the cupola, Coria's tower is the finer of the two, which may both be by the same architect. To west of the tower is the main north porch of the church, a good late Gothic portal in moulded orders separated by bands of carved foliage and flanked by well-composed spirelike buttresses. On the south front toothing was left for the construction of a similar entrance which was never carried out. That on the north was not completed in its original style, and may have suffered in the earthquake, as it now presents two superimposed stages of blank openings and a top stage with a single window perhaps of mid-sixteenth-century date.

J.H.H. 1956

128 Badajoz: base of eastern piers

This north porch appears on plan as a transept, and inside it would seem that it was originally built as one, together with the opposite southern arm. Now the openings are walled off at a low level with archways converting them into mere porches, above which are galleries containing the organs. The sequence of events at Coria is puzzling, for between 1473 and 1570 a large number of documented works were projected or carried out, some of which may relate to the older church which disappeared about that time. The building of the second chapel (or bay) from the entrance done by Francisco Moro of Plasencia in 1473–81 may thus have been within the church of three aisles which certainly preceded the present rectangle of a single span. But the fresh undertaking of 1496, when Martín de Solórzano and his brother Bartolomé were called from Palencia to build the *capilla mayor*, the two *colaterales* (? transepts) and all their vaults, the work to follow the model of Santo Tomás in Ávila, seems almost beyond a doubt to be the beginning of the existing work. Santo Tomás in Ávila which had just been built in 1482–93 had a single span, a short transept and vaults of very similar character to that spanning the narrow bay between the transepts at Coria. Alms were collected for the work in 1496 and 1498, but a dispute arose in 1502 when fresh designs for the vaults were submitted by Bartolomé de Pelayos, Martín de Solorzano and Juan de Ruesga. The design of Pelayos was accepted and he continued the work for three years until his death, when he was succeeded by Sebastián Lasarte. Fresh trouble broke out, and after 1506 building seems to have been suspended. Thirty years later the building was in danger and various masters were consulted, among them Rodrigo Gil de Hontañón, as a result of which Pedro de Ibarra (probably son of the great Juan de Álava) was entrusted with the completion of the church, which he continued to direct until his death in 1570. To the time of Ibarra probably belong all the Plateresque details, including the lower part of the tower and the west front, as well as the alteration of the transepts into porches and perhaps the vaulting of the nave bays.

Coria, with its single span of 55 feet, represents the logical conclusion of cathedral development during the Middle Ages. The church has at last become entirely a surrounding shell or shrine about the sanctuary and the choir, and nothing more (129, 134). Likewise the east wall has become a broad flat surface against which can be placed a magnificent altarpiece of the largest compatible scale instead of revealing the beauties of an apse pierced by windows. Here the retablo that now exists was designed by Juan and Diego de Villanueva and made in 1745–49. It is a splendid Baroque work untouched by neoclassicism, finely composed about a great central niche containing a carving of the Assumption. The way in which the broken cornices and pediments are made to conform to the lines of the Gothic vault is most successful and a lesson in harmonising two distinct styles. The effect of the church is also enhanced by the colour of its stone, an orange-brown granite with black specks, which looks a soft brown at a short distance. The shafts and vaulting ribs are coloured a blue-grey with distemper.

The contents of Coria Cathedral are only second in importance to the fabric, and include a magnificent series of carved stalls, some made in 1489 and the rest, closely copied from the earlier set, by Martín de Ayala in 1514. Meanwhile, in 1508, the wrought-iron screen for the *coro* had been ordered from Hugón de Santa Ursula of Burgo de Osma, a noted smith, and in 1512 the Plateresque sculptures of the *trascoro* were being made by Miguel de Villarreal. On the north side is a small square cloister with plain ribbed vaulting, apparently considerably older

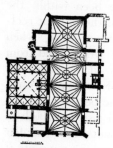

Lampérez: A.C.E.
(Espasa-Calpe)

129 Coria, 1496–1570, by Martín de Solórzano and Pedro de Ibarra

than the church though perhaps dating only from the fifteenth century. Its arches are unfortunately walled up. On its east side is an unusual balcony overlooking the main entrance to the cathedral, and surrounded with Plateresque enrichments of the same kind as those on the lower part of the tower.

From Coria to Plasencia is a road journey through rolling country with few trees, bare and open, yet in the spring covered with sheets of flowers. Like Coria, Plasencia stands on a bluff rising sharply from the bank of the river, here the Jerte. To the north-east are the perpetually snow clad peaks of the Sierra de Gredos, while all around lies a vast saucer of completely open countryside. Rising

after Lampérez

130 Plasencia, c. 1320–1400, by Diego Díaz, and 1498–1578, by Enrique de Egas and Juan de Álava

enormous over the roofs of the ancient city is the bulk of the new cathedral, beside which the remains of the old cathedral are completely dwarfed. For here the new project, instead of being laid out to one side as at Salamanca, was to swallow up the whole of the old structure, starting at the east end. In the outcome, half of each church was left, sanctuary and transept of the new, nave and cloister of the old (130). From the first glimpse Plasencia is seen to be one of the quite exceptional works of art which so rarely take on life. Truncated fragment as the new cathedral remains, and consequently difficult to appreciate at its full value, there can be no question of its superlative quality.

The building history of both cathedrals is obscure in its details, though there are a considerable number of definite dates and names available. Of the surviving structures the earliest seems to be the west front of the old cathedral with a Romanesque doorway of five simply moulded orders and in the gable a large rose. To the north-east of the other buildings stands a massive detached belfry, now absorbed into the buttresses of the new work. It was probably begun in the thirteenth century and finished in the first half of the fourteenth, by which time the nave which now survives was in progress and perhaps also the north and east walks of the cloister. But not later than c. 1250 a remarkable chapter-house had been built by Maestro Remondo, square on plan but vaulted as an octagon with radial ribs and covered by a roof imitated from that of the Torre del Gallo at Salamanca. The nave, begun *c.* 1320 by Diego Díaz and carried on through the century, was directed by Juan Francés, "the Frenchman", in 1389. Though it now suffers from coats of whitewash on the walls and greywash on the piers, in a scaling condition and about to be cleaned as the adjacent cloister has already been, the impression is a gracious one, and it is hard to understand the depreciation it has met from the few writers who have deigned to mention it. The design is taken from that of Badajoz, whose piers are almost reproduced, though the details are substantially later. Also derived from Badajoz are the nearly equal widths of nave and aisles, and the low bay design. At Plasencia it is the vaults which are of the greatest interest, domical bays with diagonals and tiercerons with ridge-ribs, finely carved bosses and, strange feature paralleled in Benito Sánchez's cloister at Ciudad Rodrigo, carved figures appearing one in each compartment of the web. The proportions are extremely good and an effect of height is produced by the unbroken wall shafts; one can be thankful that so much of the old work was spared even while regretting the incompletion of the new.

To the south lie the cloisters, small but charming and with a pretty patio containing a good sixteenth-century carved fountain in late Gothic style. The north and east walks are strangely archaic, and the work may have adhered to a design produced in the thirteenth century. But work is said to have been begun in 1416 by a Moor named Asoyte; a statement which can only refer to the west and south walks, known to have been finished in 1438, but which show no Saracenic characteristics. The master under whom they were completed was Juan Martín, and it may be that Asoyte carried out some work now lost. The east walk is cut into by the south transept of the new work, but is not completely blocked by it. The chance interruption of the programme at this precise point was fortunate, for otherwise both chapter-house and cloister might have been destroyed without any worthy substitute being put in their place.

Outside the north aisle of the old nave is a second aisle, communicating with the original aisle by openings cut in its wall. This second aisle is in fact a part of the north aisle of the new cathedral, with its side-chapels, but vaulted over at a low level pending com-

131 TOLEDO: the west front, 1418–44, by Álvar Martinez, and Tower,
c. 1400–18, by Juan Alfonso, with lantern and spire of 1448–52, by
Hanequín de Egas

132   Looking north-west in the crossing

133   Looking north-east from the south aisle

135 · CIUDAD REAL: interior, 1490–1514: retablo
by Giraldo de Merlo, 1616

134 CORIA: interior by Martín and Bartolomé de Solórzano and others, 1496–1506; retablo 1745–49

136 PLASENCIA: the Sanctuary of 1513–22, by Enrique de Egas,
Francisco de Colonia, and Juan de Álava

pletion of the high parts of the work. The character of this aisle was misunderstood by Lampérez, who marks only its outline on his plan, calling it an *atrio vestibulo Greco-Romano* in spite of its series of Gothic bases to the responds of each bay. It has some importance as it proves that the new plan provided for at least five bays west of the crossing, and for chapels between the great buttresses, on the Catalan cellular scheme. At the east end of this aisle is a door in the partition wall dividing the old and new works, the only direct communication between the two cathedrals.

On passing through this door the immediate effect of the lofty vaulting, perfect proportions and lovely colouring is breathtaking. There can be few architectural experiences so thrilling for purely aesthetic reasons (37, 136). Here is an unfinished work, a mutilated torso on which the head miraculously remains though the limbs are broken off; among the world's masterpieces it shares in a peculiar manner with Mozart's Requiem a tantalising compound of genuine and pastiche. Imagination can go so far in reconstructing what is lost, but no further; and in this case the worst of all is our inability to see the exquisite beauties of the part that we have from an adequate distance, as we should have been able to do in walking eastwards up the nave aisles. I have spoken of the colouring of the work: it is a most unusual soft but warm greyish-brown which can only be described in terms of watercolour, weak sepia with a touch of burnt umber and a trace of madder brown. The texture is close and hard without appearing rough.

The mere size is large enough to be impressive but entirely related to human scale. The span of the central nave, and of the apsidal sanctuary, is 56½ feet, nearly four feet wider than that of Seville, and it measures 116 feet internally across the transept. Its scale is consequently appreciably larger than that of Westminster, Lincoln or Rheims, and in overall width (for here the transept is not wider than the nave) rather exceeds Notre-Dame de Paris, Chartres, Amiens and York. We are in what would have been one of the world's greatest buildings, in scale if not in size. The height is great by English standards though not by French, but appears greater than usual in Spain because of the compactness of the plan, the whole of which, except for the cellular chapels, is raised to the same level as the vault of the sanctuary. Furthermore, the vaults are knit together by convolutions of curving ribs which flow from the sanctuary into the crossing and nave and, with the curves of the free mouldings which sweep out from the great piers, give the illusion of the whole being one vast canopy floating in air.

The skill shown in proportioning every part to the total unity is so brilliant that it can rarely if ever have been surpassed. The bases of the piers and responds are the most complex of their kind, with mouldings interpenetrating like wickerwork; yet the composition of the whole provides just sufficient visual support for the pier, neither raising the pedestal too high nor dropping it flatly too close to the floor. So wonderfully endowed a genius deserves recognition, and fortunately his name is known: Juan de Álava. For it was unquestionably he who completed the *capilla mayor* and was ordered to build the crossing to the same height; and it is in the work of the crossing with its superb detached piers that the work reaches its highest pitch. Yet it seems that we cannot give Álava the sole and exclusive credit, for he was building on the foundations of other men. The story is complicated and not all of its details are yet clear. It was in 1497 that Rodrigo Alemán, the famous carver, was engaged to produce new choir-stalls for Plasencia, and it was stipulated that his work was to be done under the supervision of Enrique Egas, the royal master mason and chief architect; when the cathedral laid the foundations for its new chevet in the following year there can be little doubt that it was Egas who acted as their architect, and this is confirmed by the resemblances of plan and general disposition to his known work of the Capilla Real at Granada, built between 1504 and 1517. Just how much was done in and after 1498 is unknown, but the works came to a stop for several years. In 1513 a fresh start was made, but presumably on the existing foundations, and Francisco de Colonia was appointed master; Juan de Álava was soon after joined with him in the direction on the ground of Colonia's "little knowledge", and was made sole master to the exclusion of Colonia by 1521, the year before the completion of the *capilla mayor*. From 1521 to his death in 1537 Álava alone was responsible. At his death confusion seems to have reigned: Alonso de Covarrubias came and signed drawings but did not return; in the next year Diego Siloé came and prepared drawings which may have been those for the south front, and Rodrigo Gil gave advice. In 1544 he was appointed *maestro mayor* and for several years the work progressed according to his drawings; in 1548 Fernán Ruiz from Cordova came to advise. Then after thirty more years of inconclusive work it was decided to call a halt and in 1578 the Sacrament was translated to the new high altar.

What was done took eighty years, and if energy and money had been available no doubt all the rest could have been accomplished before another century had elapsed. But the impetus was gone, and we have only to compare the uninspired Renaissance fronts and north aisle with the stupendous Gothic achievement that had gone before to rest thankful that no more was done. The old nave and the old chapter-house and cloister were spared; and even better, we have no internal clash produced by either a series of classical bays or an attempt to improve upon Álava's detail. Such is Plasencia. We have here the authentic last words of Spanish Gothic design: going back to the ancient plan of parallel apses, as at Astorga, adopting the principle of the hall-church with nave and aisles of the same height; building chapels between the mighty buttresses, as in Catalonia; surpassing the previous attempts of Castile in the inter-penetration of mouldings, the proportions of detail, the sweep of vault-ribs and the interlacing of patterns which should have an aesthetic, if no structural purpose. And appropriately all this was accomplished by a man from that centre of the Spanish realms at last reunited, the upper basin of the Ebro on the borders of the Castilian Rioja and the Basque country: Juan de Álava.

CHAPTER SEVEN

Andalusia

A WHOLE world of romanticism is represented by the single word Andalusia in the ears of the non-Spaniard. It is not quite the same thing in Spain itself: the romance and gaiety are conveyed, the attractions of southern beauties, courtyards of myrtles and palms waving their fronds in sub-tropical heat by the Mediterranean. But there are at least two other emotions aroused in the Spaniard by the mention of Andalusia: an admiration, perhaps as near to real envy as he can compass, of the fertility of the rich valleys and plains; and a good-humoured condescension at times coming near to scorn for the typical southerner. To the Castilian the Andaluz is a loquacious windbag, steadily pouring out a stream of highly coloured exaggerations in an abominable and often unintelligible patois; a terrible boaster and a confirmed idler. The Castilian will tell the stranger that he has not seen Spain until he has been to Andalusia, but it will be one of the last places he thinks of visiting himself. And it is precisely because Andalusia is consequently almost a foreign country to the northerner, as Scotland is to the ordinary Englishman, that its songs and dances have such a monopoly of interest throughout the rest of the country. There is besides a deeper reason for this attitude towards the South: during the early centuries of chivalry to which every northern Spaniard looks back with a faintly wistful pride, Andalusia was in fact a foreign country, the land of the Moors, justly famous for its culture and learning, but famed also for craftiness and the practice of the black arts. The Reconquest has not stripped Andalusia of this exotic appeal.

Viewed with the cooler imagination of an impartial observer, Andalusia is not, as a country, very different from the rest of Spain. In it there are, as elsewhere, enormous variations in landscape and its human content is noted for a lack of homogeneity. This is due

7 MÁLAGA: the
Sanctuary of
1549–80, by
Diego de Vergara

38 CADIZ: the New
Cathedral of
1722–1832, from
the south-east

140   JAÉN: the interior of 1634–54, by

139   GUADIX: the interior of 1549–74, by
Diego de Siloé and Juan de Arredondo, altered

in part no doubt to a strong survival of Moorish blood, which included everything Asiatic and African from the true Arab to the Berber and from the Circassian to the negro. But it is quite as much a consequence of the planting of the South with colonists brought from every part of Christian Spain. It is tempting to consider whether the superficial friendliness and easy chatter of the Andalusian may not be a habit that arose from this very fact of many strangers, with matter of interest to communicate to one another, being forced to live together in the same society. It might certainly explain Andalusian boastfulness and love for the exaggerated story, where every man seeks to outdo his neighbour, and also the strange mangling of the language, elsewhere a first charge on the national consciousness.

When we come to consider Andalusian cathedrals, there is another reason for their difference from those of all the rest of Spain. Taken as a group, they are of exceptionally late date, and only one of them, Seville, has any remaining work earlier than the sixteenth century. Of the remaining seven four, Almería, Granada, Guadix and Málaga, could not be founded until after the victory of 1492. They represent then a different epoch and a changed outlook from the majority of the buildings we have already seen. Rather appropriately, in view of the Andalusian's habit of exaggeration, their leading feature is a preoccupation with size: most of them are in an absolute and not merely a relative sense very large buildings. In this there is a reflection of the ideas of grandeur that sprang from the success of the Reconquest and, later, from the union of the warring kingdoms and the acquisition of colonial wealth.

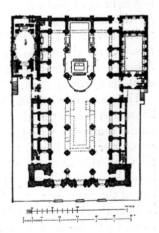

A broad belt of country separates the cathedrals of Andalusia from all the rest of Spain; it is over a hundred miles from Murcia to Almería or Guadix, nearly a hundred and fifty from Toledo to Jaén. It is through Jaén that the transition is best made, not only because the city is on the main road from Madrid to Granada,

141   Jaén, 1512–1688, by Enrique Egas, Andrés de Vandaelvira and others

but because its atmosphere is intermediate between the two physical and temperamental climates. Jaén was for 250 years the great bulwark of Christian Spain over against Granada, "guard and defence of the realms of Castile" as its motto reads. Because of this the impression it gives is mainly Castilian. Its inhabitants are reserved and self-reliant rather than talkative and lazy. Set proudly among the mountains, peopled largely by the descendants of the picked knights of Castile who for long were stationed here, there is at Jaén an echo of such northern cities as Oviedo and Pamplona. Only rarely does any fragment of architecture suggest that we are in the deep South.

The cathedral (*141*) strikes a different note. Almost entirely a work of the Renaissance, it might be one of the great cathedrals of Spanish America, and the impression is heightened by the high mountain ranges which hem it in. From the Cross which stands on a rocky peak to the north-west, close to the ancient castle of Santa Catalina, a marvellous bird's-eye view is obtained of the city, dominated by the noble bulk of the cathedral. From here the whole can be seen, as if it were a model of itself, displaying its proportions and the massing of its towers and dome. At close quarters all the four sides are impressive, not least the plain east wall with its solid buttresses, the lower part of it remaining from the Gothic church begun in 1512 and with an excellent band of Isabelline enrichment. At the north-east corner is the lower building of the Sagrario, added between 1764 and 1801 to designs by Ventura Rodríguez. Apart from these two exceptions the building is essentially that designed by Andrés de Vandaelvira in 1534, and directed by him until his death in 1579.

The parts carried out by Vandaelvira himself are the Chapterhouse and Sacristy at the south-east angle, and the range of chapels on the south side with the transept front. These set the style for the remainder, which was to take over a century to finish. For more than half this time the works remained almost at a standstill, but between 1634 and 1654 the chevet, with the transept and eastern half of the nave, was completed by Juan de Aranda who in 1626–28 had been making the marble high altar of Cordova, and the central dome by Pedro de Portillo in the next six years. Finally, Eufrasio López de Rojas was appointed architect and between 1667 and his death in 1684 completed the west nave and the greater part of the front, whose towers were finished in 1688. Last of all, the remaining vaults and the *coro* were brought to an end in 1726 by José Gallego of Salamanca. Except in the west front, where López de Rojas introduced a little Baroque feeling in his interpretation of the old designs, the whole is essentially what was proposed by Vandaelvira and can be regarded as that rarity, a cathedral of homogeneous style.

The cool creamy stone gives an atmosphere of great freshness to the church and especially to the inside, though it is perhaps too brilliantly lit (*140*). The scheme is that of a hall-church, with side aisles as tall as the nave, a transept of very slight projection, and low lateral chapels between the buttresses. From the substantial remains of the east wall, it seems likely that this scheme was that intended for the Gothic church designed after 1492, probably by Enrique Egas, and which was partly built between 1512 and 1519 by Pedro López from Seville. As at Valladolid, the Renaissance designer was prepared to accept the outlines already laid down by his mediaeval predecessor. For this reason the cathedral has still something of the feeling aimed at by the great hall-churches built while Gothic was the ruling style, and there are faint reminiscences of Plasencia in the tall and slender piers composed of four half-columns against a square core, treated as a Corinthian order with fluted and reeded shafts. Vistas of space run in every direction and, to a degree most unusual in Renaissance work, are directed upwards to the dome and the domical vaults, puffed up like sails by a following wind.

Jaén succeeds by the exquisite proportions of its structure and detail, just as Plasencia succeeds in another style. And this suggests an important truth to be kept in mind in the consideration of all art: that it is the quality of inspiration that counts, and not size, nor costly materials, nor the elusive and changing phantom called style. There is another point brought out by the simultaneous study of the histories of Plasencia and Jaén, both so unusually successful in their diverse manners. This is the initial responsibility at both of the great architect Enrique de Egas, the genius responsible also for the Capilla Real at Granada and the plans of the cathedrals there and at Málaga, and for the Hospital Real at Santiago. But we shall see that at Granada and Málaga even the splendid impetus of a plan by Egas could be wasted by failure to make good use of its qualities. This is the reverse of the medal: even given the best of plans by a genius, a master lacking the right quality of inspiration will be unable to produce satisfying elevations and details for the building.

Jaén is one of the fortunate examples where two men of the highest genius have followed one another at the same site. It would be difficult to name any church built in Renaissance style, other than Wren's St. Paul's, which can be felt as the equal of Jaén in quality. More should be heard of Andrés de Vandaelvira, who also designed the so-called cathedral at Baeza (1567–93) and other buildings there and at Úbeda.

The entry into Andalusia proper, that kingdom of Granada which preserved a part of Spain for Islam for two centuries and a half after Seville had fallen, lies through the Sierra de Lucena to the south of Jaén. But for our purposes it is better to take the more circuitous route of the railway and visit Guadix first. Guadix is a forgotten little city near the bottom of a valley in the midst of dry stony mountains pitted with still inhabited caves. It takes the place of the Roman *Acci*, claimed as the first Christian see in the Peninsula, set up in the second century. Its successor (*139*) is a modest enough building in a strange mixture of Gothic, Renaissance and Baroque. From a distance it is the tower of c. 1550–1600, partly of brick, that claims attention, but its design is poor. On a nearer approach the Baroque west (really east) front deserves much closer study. The aisles being almost of equal height with the nave, and there being no towers, the façade is structurally a flat wall broken only by the three doorways and by round windows lighting the aisles. This was ingeniously diversified by attaching four triangular prisms, with hollowed sides, the two central flanking an ornamental frontispiece and having three orders, while those at the sides have only two. Treated with broken entablatures, niches, panelling and festoons this becomes an unusual instance of Baroque motion, which is accentuated towards the top, where parapet and pinnacles take on a pie crust character.

Internally the church is less interesting. Its plan, derived from that of Málaga Cathedral, was drawn by Diego de Siloé in 1549, and the apse with ambulatory and chapels was carried on until 1574 under Juan de Arredondo. It is not now certain what the design of this was, nor how much of it remains, for in the eighteenth century a major transformation was carried out, together with the completion of the nave and front. But it would seem from the singular quasi-Gothic vaults, sometimes supported on pointed arches and ribs of more or less Gothic section, that most of the church must have been built in a decadent mixture of styles during Arredondo's

142, 143, 144
G r a n a d a ,
1521–, by En-
rique   Egas,
Diego de Siloé
and   others ;
Capilla   Real,
1504–21,   by
Enrique Egas
(beyond south
    transept)

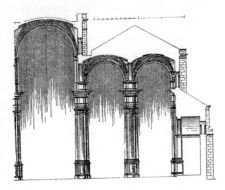

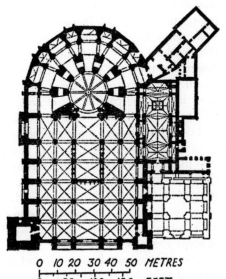

0 10 20 30 40 50 METRES

0   50   100 150 FEET

term of office. The Baroque veneers and additions date from between 1710 and 1796. The proportions are good and the warm cream of the stone is pleasing, but there is little religious atmosphere.

This criticism can be levelled with more force against the gigantic cathedral of Granada. It is inherent in the aesthetic faults of the building, but unfortunately is emphasised by the commercialisation of its rather dubious attractions, a fee of six pesetas being charged beyond the five pesetas which admit the tourist to the really beautiful Capilla Real alongside. Though not quite so large as Seville, the church is enormous, and in its plan (144) a magnificent summing up of the great factors of Spanish style: five aisles, external cellular chapels, an ambulatory bounded by a circuit wall. But it also has a new feature introduced by Diego de Siloé, the evil genius of the work, a tall dome on stilts for sanctuary instead of an apse. This idea, brilliant in itself, is rendered ungainly in execution, as is the

227

whole church. The bay design (142) is based on two superimposed orders, the lower of Corinthian piers somewhat resembling those of Jaén but less elegantly detailed and with an elongated entablature matched by a correspondingly deep band around the outer walls, the upper of heavy box-like pilasters with tall awkward pedestals. Above this rise the arches of the high vaults supporting in turn domical vaults bearing ridiculous imitations of Gothic patterns. To make matters still worse, the whole of the interior is covered with a dead white limewash which seems to increase its already marked physical chill.

The original designs were made in 1521 and work began under Enrique de Egas two years later. After five seasons Egas resigned or was dismissed and Diego de Siloé took his place, continuing as master until his death in 1563, by which time the domical sanctuary was complete. The transept vaults were not closed until 1640 and the last bay of the nave finished only in 1703. Meanwhile Siloé's design for the west front had been discarded and a new one produced by the painter Alonso Cano in 1667 (27). This is by far the most interesting part of the church, a piece of architecture related only to the much later Galician works of the extreme Baroque which practically abolished the classical orders. Cano's front at Granada is, as might be expected, a study in light and shade drawn with firm sweeps of the brush and of a telling simplicity which is in fact an elaborate scheme of subtle proportions between the dominant and subordinate parts. If the front has a fault it lies in its somewhat hard and static quality, a strangely frozen otherworldliness which seems out of place in its setting, and curiously foreshadows characteristics of some modern architecture.

Granada Cathedral must be reckoned one of the world's architectural tragedies, one of the saddest of wasted opportunities. It is far otherwise with the Capilla Real which nestles beside it and now forms an integral part of its structure, linked by the great door of the south transept, originally the main portal of the Capilla Real. The chapel, founded as the tomb chapel of the Catholic sovereigns in 1504, was designed in 1506 by Enrique de Egas and was finished by 1521. It is an exquisite building of pure Gothic with notable lacework vaulting of the finest detail. The whole is of admirable proportions and on a much smaller scale foreshadows some of the effects of the new cathedral at Plasencia. Far less florid than the earlier burial place built for Ferdinand and Isabella, San Juan de los Reyes in Toledo by Juan Guas, the Capilla Real is outstanding for its restraint and poise.

From Granada it would be natural to visit the two coastal cathedrals of Almería and Málaga, but I have been to neither, and give here only a brief description of each for the sake of completeness. Almería is slightly the earlier, designed after destruction of the former church in an earthquake in 1522. It was begun soon after and, being of small size, was completed by 1573, though the tower continued until the early years of the next century and there is a large classical cloister surrounded with a wall and corner towers which suggest a fortress. Apart from these defensive works, perhaps directed against the Barbary pirates, the exterior has little of interest. Inside the church is very late Gothic with some Renaissance details and elaborate late vaulting with curving liernes.

The cathedral of Málaga (137) is much larger, falling not far short of Granada in its dimensions. Its bays are substantially larger, for it has only three aisles instead of five, flanked as usual by cellular chapels. The west front has towers outside the aisles and in advance, as at Toledo, while the transept fronts are flanked by large cylindrical drum towers as if they were the entrances of a castle. The unusual feature of the design is its combination of the hall-church with an ambulatory. Thus the sanctuary is entirely surrounded by high aisles from which it borrows light, a most singular feature to find in Spain, though paralleled in central Europe in Gothic times. Indeed the plan of Málaga, though it has obvious resemblances to that of Murcia, seems to derive in its structural implications from the hall-choirs of Zwettl and Schwäbisch-Gmünd built in the mid-fourteenth century.

Plans for Málaga were made by Pedro López and Enrique Egas but were superseded in favour of one by Diego de Siloé, according to which work was begun in 1528. In 1549 fresh drawings were prepared by Diego de Vergara, and it seems that most of the eastern arm reached completion under him by 1564. The transept was vaulted in 1570 and the sanctuary ten years later, while work came to a halt in 1588. The western nave and the great towers were not begun until 1719, and were directed by José Bada for many years; they were at length left unfinished in 1783. The whole of the external design is heavy in the extreme and its feeling was only too faithfully followed by Bada, who did succeed in adding a few Baroque touches in the shape of broken pediments. But his tower is a solemn and lifeless succession of stages, each encased in a lanky Corinthian or Composite order. Internally the orders are treated in a similar way to those of Granada though with greater imagination, while the vaults are saucer domes on pendentives, and made hideous by ribs and relief designs of the German strapwork kind.

It would be inappropriate here to give a detailed description of the Great Mosque of Cordova, still by a freak of history known as La Mezquita to the Christian population whose cathedral it now is. All that concerns us is the implantation of a Christian church, as a fresh part of the structure, into the vast pillared aisles of the mosque. The decision to undertake the work was made in 1521, it started in 1523 and the sanctuary and transepts were complete by 1560, two years after the death of the architect, Fernán Ruiz the elder. His son of the same name continued the church, building the walls of the *coro*, which was vaulted in 1598 by his successor, Juan Oliva. All this, except the *coro* vault, had been done in a style substantially Gothic, but exotic and overloaded with ornament. The oval dome over the crossing was built in 1599–1600 by Diego de Praves, in completely Renaissance style and unusually well proportioned. The best feature of the church is the transept, so organised as to embrace in its walls three bays of Moorish arcading on each side. In this way there is free circulation between the central church and the whole of the surrounding structure. Ruiz the younger also designed the great tower on the north side of the courtyard, cloaking the old minaret with Renaissance balustrades and increasing its height. The work went on from 1593 to 1617, but was altered later to strengthen the base, and the lantern was added in 1664.

From the calm of Cordova to the hectic activity of Seville is little more than eighty miles, yet the two cities represent two entirely different facets of Andalusian life in spite of many superficial resemblances in their architecture and the charming little court-yards filled with flowers common to the houses of both. Cordova in its easy-going way has been content with the Mosque built by its predecessors, with the relatively slight addition of the new cathedral swallowed up in the midst of it. Seville on the contrary, and at a much earlier date, determined to destroy its mosque and to build in its place a church, in the words of one of the Chapter "so great and of such a kind that those who see it finished shall think we were mad". This typically Andalusian sally was spoken at a meeting on 8 July 1401, when various designs had already been

145 CADIZ: interior, looking south-east, of the church begun in 1722 by Vicente Acero

146 SEVILLE: looking north-west in the Nave of 1402–32,
perhaps by Charles Galter (Carlí)

under consideration for some years. The official minute of the decision taken was that "a new church shall be made so good that there shall be none its equal". The first stone was laid in 1402 at the south-west corner and thirty years later half the church was built, though its high vaults had not been set. The old Capilla Real at the east end could not be demolished until royal permission had been given in 1435, by which time the transept had been reached. Apart from the new Capilla Real, not built until 1551–75, the eastern half of the

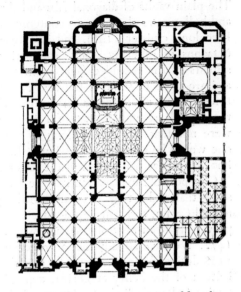

147 Seville, 1402–67, possibly by Charles Galter of Rouen

church was completed by 1506, when the central lantern was finished. After only five years it fell, and its rebuilding gave the occasion for the heavily enriched work of the surrounding bays, designed by Juan Gil de Hontañón. What the old lantern and the Giralda in its Moorish form were like can be seen from a detailed carving in the *retablo mayor* (120).

Though we have no certain information as to the architect who made the original designs, he may have been the Alonso Martínez who appears as master mason of the cathedral in the 1390's. Whoever produced the plans (147) and details was not only a genius, but astonishingly well informed. The five aisles are of course taken from Toledo, but not the disposition of the bays, which are made half as wide again and square in the aisles. Only five of these bays make up the nave, the two eastern taking the *coro* and leaving an ample space of three bays at the west end. The front, unlike those of most Spanish cathedrals, has no towers and there is no suggestion that it was ever intended to build any. The cellular chapels beyond the aisles point to Catalonia, and it is at Barcelona (87) that we find a cross-section that could have inspired this at Seville (148).

233

The plain vaults of diagonal ribs and the piers of many small shafts and hollows are also close to contemporary works there such as the Barcelona cloister (*146*). But the bases with their hollow-sided octagons of differing scales, supporting not only shafts but also salients of the moulded face, seem to have no parallels in Spain and are close to some of the best French and English work of the time. A trick of carrying a vertical moulding up into the vault above the capitals resembles that of a much later date at Oviedo. If it were not that the bases belong to the first years of the building one would be tempted to attribute them to one of the Frenchmen known to have had charge of the latter stages.

One possible explanation may be offered. The cathedral records show that at least by 1439 and until 1454 the master mason was named Carlín, and that he was succeeded by Juan Normán who had previously been his assistant, and whose term of office lasted until 1472. We have already met a French master named Carlí, who in 1408 designed the west front of Barcelona and in 1416 finished the lantern of the belfry at Lérida, appearing also under the name of Carlos Galter de Ruán (of Rouen). Is it possible that this man was identical with the architect of Seville? The plans must have been prepared by the time that the first stone was laid in 1402, but may have been made after the decision of the Chapter taken in July 1401. If, as is all but certain, 1454 is the date of Carlín's death, he could

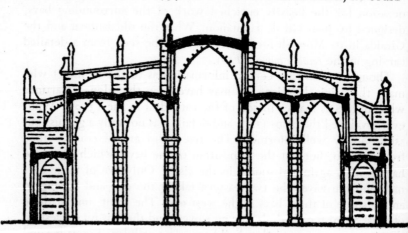

Lampérez: Arq. Crist. Esp. (Espasa-Calpe)

148   Seville, 1402–67

have designed Seville at the age of twenty-one and died at seventy-four. That such a career is by no means impossible is proved by the modern instance of Liverpool Cathedral, designed by Sir Giles Scott in 1901 when he was twenty-one, and still in progress under his direction fifty-five years later. Master Mateo was in charge at Santiago at least forty-nine years; Robert Stowell died in 1505, fifty-three years after he had been appointed master mason of Windsor Castle; Sir Christopher Wren did not die until fifty-five years after preparing his first design for St. Paul's; Michelangelo not for fifty-nine years after being called to Rome by Pope Julius II. Alternatively Carlín may have been son and successor of Carlí. Against these hypotheses it may be advanced that in 1434, five years before the first recorded mention of Carlín, there is a mention of payments to a certain master Ysambret for his contract with the Chapter for the new work, for his travelling expenses and for the days he spent in Seville. From this it is evident that Ysambret (Isambart) was a stranger and a contractor, but the latter fact is against his being the *maestro mayor* responsible for the design. From his rare name we may conclude that he was very likely identical with the Isabrante who was finishing vaults at Palencia Cathedral in 1424 and perhaps with the Isembart who was one of the masters consulted in connection with the *cimborio* at Saragossa in 1417; and further that he was almost certainly a Frenchman.

As a training-ground for the future architect of Seville, Rouen fits extremely well, for not only do we there find bases which can be regarded as prototypes of those at Seville, but there was in the last years of the fourteenth century a burst of building activity under the great mason Jean de Bayeux, simultaneously master of the works of the city of Rouen, of the cathedral and of the abbey of St. Ouen. Few other cities of France, in this time of depression due to the wars with England, offered such opportunities. As a working hypothesis it is then permissible to suggest that the architect of Seville, whether Carlos Galter or no, may have served his apprenticeship in Rouen where he would learn by heart those details which he would never afterwards forget, and during his wanderyears came to Spain and acquired a knowledge of both Barcelona and Toledo. It is to be accepted that his successor Juan, surnamed "Norman", at any rate came from Normandy, and this may account for the English usage of a longitudinal ridge-rib in the high vaults begun in 1467. Or this might be derived through the usage of the school of Burgos, for in

1496 the works were viewed by master "Ximón", almost certainly Simón de Colonia, and in the incomplete state of the records there is no reason why this should have been his first visit.

The aesthetic effect of Seville is hard to define. Outside it is impressive mainly for its great size and to a certain degree for its ornate fronts, largely modern. But the interior is the thing, and is certainly among the most notable in the world. Limiting comparison to the European cathedrals in Gothic style, the serious competitors can be reduced to Bourges, Lincoln and Cologne, from which Seville might be said to win on points. Among the Spanish cathedrals only Palma and León combine the four essentials of unity of style, elegance of proportions, substantial scale and, most difficult to define, the quality of power which gives life to a building. In this last elusive factor León is somewhat wanting, as it is in scale; over Palma, Seville scores in its greater size and complexity of parts, giving it a sense of mystery which Palma cannot possess. In quality the new cathedral of Plasencia was able to outdo Seville but lacks unity of style even in what was accomplished.

Yet even in giving the palm to Seville there must be some qualification of the very high praise awarded. As compared with Barcelona there is an awkwardness in the relations of the clerestory to the high vault, the main springing being placed on a level with the heavy suite of horizontal mouldings beneath the clerestory balustrades, a regrettable return to the common form of a much earlier period. A worse error is the carrying of a moulding round the vaulting shafts at the level of the arcade capitals, producing an unnecessary punctuation. The many and rather small shafts and mouldings of the great piers are slightly indistinct in their tonal values, no member having an adequate dominance. The stained-glass windows, and in this respect Seville ranks next to León, admit too much light and are in many cases of a date too late to join perfectly in the harmony of the composition. But when all has been said, Seville Cathedral remains the highest overall achievement of Gothic Europe, and possibly of European culture of all times.

After Seville almost any other great church would be an anticlimax, and certainly any Gothic church. Did geography permit, it would have been refreshing to turn from Seville to Compostela and contrast the finished product with the daring forerunner from an age of barbarism in process of becoming civilised. In fact, our farewell to the Spanish cathedral must be at Cadiz, beside the Atlantic waves towards which Santiago gazes from afar. Cadiz has two cathedrals, or rather two churches, each bearing the name. The old cathedral, now the parish church of La Santa Cruz, became the see only in 1624, on its removal from Algeciras, but had been built in 1602 on the site of an earlier church destroyed by the English raid of 1596. It is a simple Roman Doric building with a small dome, internally whitewashed. Pleasant in its proportions, it would be quite insignificant as architecture apart from its massive tower, more suggestive of a castle keep than a church.

The New Cathedral (*149*) is one of the largest churches in Spain and

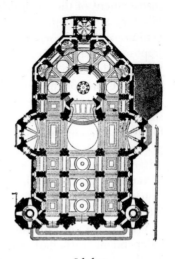

Schubert

149   Cadiz, 1720–1832, by Vicente Acero

the only complete cathedral of Baroque style among them. Designed by Vicente Acero in 1720, it was started two years later, but the church was not finished for 110 years, while the towers were completed only in 1853. The plan is eclectic, with polygonal ambulatory and alternate heart-shaped and square chapels surrounding a rotunda sanctuary of the Granada type surmounted by a cupola, a large dome over the crossing, transepts with apsidal ends, three bays of nave and a wide west front with circular towers beyond the aisles. The front, though its design was altered by Manuel Machuca in 1789, is fundamentally Acero's, as can be seen by comparison with his front at Guadix. Here too is the same Churrigueresque preoccupation with motion and the flowing line. Unfortunately Machuca's academic upper stage has robbed us of what might have been a most notable Baroque frontispiece comparable with that of Murcia. The original build was carried out in a fine brown stone of admirable texture, while the later additions are in a cold white stone like marble; the contrast is regrettable, though of historic interest to the antiquary. Internally Acero's blending of curving surfaces and obliquely placed masses is most successful, and nave and central dome have an admirable spatial effect (*145*). In the nave too the management of the Corinthian order, with an upper stage of double pilasters at 45 degrees acting as wall-shafts for the vaults, is ingenious and an enormous improvement upon the bungling superimposed orders of Granada and Málaga. The heavy horizontal emphasis of the main entablature is however a blot upon the otherwise excellent lines of the central space. A worse mistake is made in the ambulatory, where the arches above the openings of the heart-shaped chapels, placed on the angles of a half-octagon, are made to follow the re-entrant angle with broken-backed effect. There is no decorative scheme and the impression of the interior is at present a miserable one as it is a scaling whitish-grey with unsightly patches of varying tone. Well cleaned and possibly with the judicious addition of a little gold-leaf, this could be one of the grandest church interiors in Spain.

With Cadiz not only our topographical tour but the history of an independent cathedral architecture in Spain comes to an end. Neither the academic revivals of a Renaissance at Lérida and Vich, nor the exhumations of an equally academic copy of mediaeval styles in the more recent cathedrals of new erection, can be considered living continuators of this great tradition. We have to go outside the ranks of the cathedrals to Gaudí's church of the Holy Family at Barcelona to rediscover the thread of purpose which we have in our wanderings followed for so long.

Epilogue

BEFORE setting out on our tour of the Spanish cathedrals we reviewed briefly the history of Spanish church architecture, and are now free to look back upon the scene. In the panoramic landscape which includes the whole development of a major art-form in a great country we may discern a number of outstanding features: major peaks and landmarks that form the crises of the long and complex narrative. In some cases these are the peaks formed by notable masterpieces such as Santiago, León or Seville; elsewhere the total value may be less noticeable but the intrinsic interest no less, for the light which it throws upon the origins of design and forms of construction.

Spain, like mediaeval England, is a country possessing to a very high degree an intensely national culture, with the power of attracting and assimilating many and diverse influences from abroad. But whereas England at an early date realised a cultural and political unity, and received foreign influences from a few sources and at dates well spaced out, Spain was torn by the conflicting interests of two great religions and of half-a-dozen states, while foreigners and alien currents of art from many quarters were constantly and often simultaneously seeking admission. The process is necessarily a somewhat bewildering one, and it is the more surprising that the outcome should have been an art so highly national and one which achieved so nearly perfect a balance between its diverse constituent parts.

Since our study has been of a series of Christian churches, it is natural that it should have yielded relatively few examples of motives from Islamic sources. But at the very beginning stands the ribbed lantern of Jaca, of undoubtedly Moorish origin, and possibly the vital link which was to lead to the structural system of Gothic architecture. Even though the precise date of this feature remains uncertain, that of its Saracenic forerunners is not. The ribbed vault, even if not as a form of structure, and the pointed arch both existed in southern lands before they became integral parts of the heritage

239

of the North. Not only is Lethaby's thesis of the fundamental unity of Saracenic and Gothic art thereby strengthened, but another shrewd blow is struck at the doctrine of a mechanical evolution of structure which has for so long obsessed students of architectural development to the exclusion of an adequate consideration of other factors in design. The evidence of Spain favours a nice balance at all times between the structural considerations which must needs concern the builder, and the factors of appearance and use which are all that normally interest the client.

Not only the pointed arch and the ribbed vault but the use of cusping, the application of geometrical patterns to surfaces and the design of window tracery all appear to owe their very origin or their importance to the example of Saracenic usage, viewed largely though not exclusively through the medium of Spain. It cannot be too often nor too strongly emphasised that the culture of Cordova and Seville from the eighth to the twelfth centuries was on a substantially higher plane than that of any other part of Europe. It is a naïve and insular assumption that seeks to find in each country the roots of its own particular form of civilisation and its own forms of art. Culture and art are carried hither and thither, always by human individuals, in utter disregard of the artificial frontiers of states and in spite of the tendency of each such state to fit itself out with a cultural suit of clothes made after its own desire. Of this dual and paradoxical flow and interchange there is no better instance than Spain.

From within the orbit of Christendom Spain received important contributions at all periods. In the twelfth century came the remarkable domed lanterns of Zamora and Salamanca from the Crusader kingdom of Jerusalem; Catalan art was already very largely Lombardic; the early Romanesque architecture of the rest of the country was mainly brought from Burgundy and from southern France, especially by the pilgrims' road to Compostela. Different regions of France continued up to the Renaissance to supply the greatest part of the external influences which repeatedly brought fresh ideas to Spain, but the role of Burgundy and of the Royal Domain has perhaps been somewhat exaggerated. Spanish architecture from the late twelfth to the sixteenth centuries was more easily affected by those western regions of France where English political influence was paramount: for on the whole the story of western Europe in that period is of two opposed camps, in one of which England and

Spain were generally drawn together to counterbalance the growing power of Paris. Dynastic alliances and ease of geographical access saw to it that more or less constant advantage was taken of this in the architectural field.

The first pure Gothic, disencumbered of the heavy trappings of Romanesque, appeared at Cuenca and at Burgos and in both cases the introduction seems to be directly traceable to the coming of the Anglo-Angevin master Richard or Ricardo, brought by Eleanour, the English queen of Alfonso VIII of Castile. The English alliance continued through the thirteenth century, and the use of ridge-ribs at Burgos and elsewhere, and later the adoption of star-patterned vaulting throughout the peninsula, must be set down to English influence. Later, it is of the greatest significance to find that by far the earliest curvilinear tracery in Spain and the first grotesque carvings (babewynes) were brought to Spain in 1331 by a mason of English origin. Even though these may have had little direct influence, they underline the fact that the French adoption of the ogee curve and its development into the Flamboyant style depended upon English sources.*

Both in Castile and in the Aragonese-Catalonian realm many of the alien masters came from the extreme parts of France : Normandy, Brittany and Picardy; while a later wave of artists, largely carvers, came from Flanders even before that country was dynastically linked to Spain. Apart from the early names of Fruchel at Ávila, Martin at Toledo and Henricus at Burgos, all no doubt of French origin, there are at least two French architects of the highest rank who came to Spain in the fifteenth century, Charles Galter from Rouen about 1400 and Juan Guas of Lyon† about 1450, besides the French designers of Oviedo and Pamplona. Among the Flemings the greatest were Hanequín de Egas, from Brussels, and Jusquín of Utrecht, while a Netherlandish ancestry is probable in the case of Andrés de Vandaelvira. Germany sent the two notable masters Hans of Cologne and Gil de Siloé.

Within Spain itself it is noticeable that a number of the outstand-

---

* The generally admitted fact that the appearance of a complete style based on the use of ogee curves is later in France than in England is not necessarily incompatible with the isolated use of ogees in France at a much earlier date. The subject cannot here be discussed in detail, but it must be stressed that Dr. Pevsner's claim that a small pair of ogee arches in the south porch of St. Urbain at Troyes are "the earliest of all surviving ogee arches" will not stand.

† Or of St.-Pol-de-Léon, Brittany.

ing designers of the later periods came from the Basque Country and the neighbouring parts of north-eastern Spain: Juan de Álava, the Solórzanos, the Rasines and the family of Gil de Hontañón. Towards the end of the Gothic period Aragon came to depend almost entirely on Basque and Navarrese masters, as it had formerly done upon Moslems and Mudéjares. In view of the absence of cathedrals and other major buildings from the mediaeval Basque Country, this fact is another remarkable testimony to the importance of this region of Spain in providing a fund of dynamic vitality.

It must not be overlooked that Spain gave as well as received. Although relatively few Peninsular artists seem to have worked abroad, the spread of Saracenic ideas into northern Europe must derive mainly from Spain, and about 1500 there was a specific link with England at the time of the marriage of Catherine of Aragon to Arthur Tudor. The use of the prism of star-polygonal section as an architectural feature constitutes the best evidence of this influence, appearing quite suddenly and without English antecedents at Windsor Castle, at the very time when embassies were being exchanged between the two countries. The much earlier vault of the Durham kitchen, clearly of Saracenic origin, may derive either from Spanish or from Persian sources. Other resemblances of detail probably reflect the pilgrimages or business journeys of individual artists.

Regardless of origins, the Spanish achievement in architecture is outstanding. At Seville is the greatest individual work of the whole Gothic period, at Palma the highest expression of Gothic structural ability, at León the best surviving example of a cathedral of fully perfected Gothic complete in all its parts. In addition to these completed masterpieces there are truncated fragments of such vast projects as the new cathedral at Plasencia and Herrera's basilica at Valladolid, each second to none in its surpassing quality, while the completed cathedral at Jaén ranks only after London's St. Paul's as a supreme product of the Roman Renaissance. Spain also contains an immense proportion of the best monuments of the Baroque period, a revulsion from classicism to the dynamic, aspiring and spatial qualities that had become so deeply rooted in Spain during the Gothic period. Among these the exterior of Santiago, the front of Murcia, the whole cathedral of Cadiz and the noble towers of Osma and La Calzada have a far more than national significance.

There has been no space in this consideration of the Spanish cathedral as architecture to deal with its manifold contents. Yet its stained glass provides an array hardly of less significance than that of France, while its riches of wrought ironwork, of tombs and monuments of all periods, of paintings, carvings, vestments and plate are unique. These riches are important, not alone for their own sakes, but for the total atmosphere which they impart to the churches they furnish. In Spain alone is it still possible to see and to appreciate the artistic outcome of the Ages of Faith, and to witness their religious services still in their majestic stride, neither dulled on the one hand into mere routine nor on the other betrayed into a self-conscious over-emphasis.

The reason for this is not bigotry, nor a mere devotional conservatism, but is a part of that capacity for discrimination on which I remarked before. Religious activity is essential to Spain, continuous and all-pervading; yet though it has been and is sometimes accompanied by fanaticism, this is the exception rather than the rule. Its outward expression is almost invariably in good taste, never vulgar; a striking contrast to its counterparts (of whatever church or sect) in other lands at the present day. Most of all this is true of the Spanish cathedrals, where more than anywhere else can be felt the presence of the numinous within the house built by hands and out of inert materials. Here if at all within the western world the skill and genius of man have found their highest expression; here the created has, by the work of his brain and hands together, produced an art of such power that it enforces belief in the Creator.

It is this quality that endows the study of the cathedrals of Spain with an importance that is not merely historical or aesthetic. But it is through a proper appreciation of their historical and artistic background that their transcendent values may best come to be appreciated. For history is the story of man; and art is that story in the form which makes the clearest appeal to man's senses. In considering each cathedral we are facing the works of many men done at many times, yet here in Spain integrated each with the other to an extraordinary degree. And in this contemplation we observers also, affected and acted upon by what we perceive, enter upon this special space-time continuum, a world which was, and is, and is to come.

Historical and Descriptive Notes on Each Cathedral

THIS book is mainly concerned with existing cathedrals which were built as such, and in the following list all these are printed in **BOLD CAPITALS**. Particulars are also given of churches now having cathedral status though not built for the purpose, shown in ROMAN CAPITALS; of cathedrals built as such but not now cathedrals, in *ITALIC CAPITALS*; and of certain other churches commonly reputed cathedrals, or titular cathedrals not in fact the see, in SMALL CAPITALS. Besides the churches named here, which include all those on the mainland of Spain and in the Balearic Isles, there are cathedrals belonging to the Spanish Church at Ceuta in Morocco, Las Palmas on Grand Canary and La Laguna on Teneriffe. The cathedral of Perpignan and the ex-cathedral of Elne, now in France, are included in their respective categories, as they were politically in Spain at the times that they were built. The sites of cathedrals of Roman and Visigothic times have not been included except where the see has survived or was re-established after A.D. 1000.

The total number of cathedrals, ex-cathedrals and titular cathedrals, excluding the two now in France but counting both where two exist, is 77, but at Castellón there is no cathedral-designate and at Cartagena virtually nothing now remains of the building erected before the see was transferred to Murcia.

Dates of foundation have not been given for sees already established in Visigothic times; these are described as "Visigothic" and the ancient name added in parentheses. Dimensions are external, except heights to vault or ceiling and widths of main span; in most cases these dimensions have been taken from drawings and are only approximately correct. The names assigned to each work are those of architects or master craftsmen known from documentary sources, and dates of building based on documentary evidence are given thus: 1458–1472. Where the date is known to lie within a certain period, this is given in parentheses: (1458–1472). Destroyed work is in *italics*, "(F)" indicating that fragments remain. The name of the modern province is given except where it is identical with the name of the see.

ALBARRACÍN (Teruel)
See: 1171–1851; joint with Segorbe 1246–1577.
Dimensions: length about 200 feet.

Building Dates
c. 1531   Church rebuilt
c. 1595   Tower begun
late 18th cent. Neoclassic interior

ALCALÁ DE HENARES (Madrid)
See: shares in the title of the diocese of Madrid-Alcalá; was a Visigothic see (*Complutum*).
Dimensions: length 230 feet; width 95 feet; span 33 feet.

		Architect
Building Dates		
1497–1509	Church	Pedro Gumiel

Algeciras—see Cádiz

ALICANTE
See: titular cathedral (Colegiata de San Nicolás) 1851–; see Orihuela.
Dimensions: length 183 feet; width 95 feet; span 51 feet; dome 148 feet high.

		Architects
Building Dates		
1613	Designs	Agustín Bernaldino
1616–1662	Church	
1627	South portal	Martín de Uceta
late 17th cent.	Cloister	
–1738	Capilla de la Comunión	

ALMERÍA

See: 1490.
Dimensions: length 226 feet; width 128 feet; span 33 feet.

		Architects
Building Dates		
1524–1543	Church	Diego de Siloé
1550–1573	Great portals, chapter-house	Juan de Orea
1558–1560	Choir stalls	Juan de Orea
–1616	Tower	

ASTORGA (León)

See: Visigothic (*Asturica*)
Dimensions: length 190 feet; width 128 feet; span 30 feet.

		Architects
Building Dates		
1471–	Church begun	Simón de Colonia
1524–1527	Chevet glazed	
1530–1559	Nave	Rodrigo Gil de Hontañón
1551	Stalls, pulpit	Roberto
1558–1562	Retablo Mayor	Gaspar Becerra
–1693	West front	
–1704	South-west tower	
c. 1780	Cloister rebuilt	Gaspar López

ÁVILA

See: Visigothic (*Abela*)

Dimensions: length 318 feet; width 164 feet; span 28 feet; height 82 feet.

Building Dates		Architects
c. 1160–1180	Chevet	Fruchel
c. 1200	Ambulatory vaults	
–1211	West front, lower stage	
c. 1269	Chapter-house (now Sacristy)	Varón
(1312–1355)	Vault of crossing	
1458–1472	North porch altered	Juan Guas
1499–1508	Retablo Mayor	Pedro Berruguete, etc.
1536–1547	Stalls	Cornelis de Holanda

BADAJOZ

See: 1228.

Dimensions: length 213 feet; width 125 feet; span 24 feet.

Building Dates		Architect
1232–1284	Church	
1240–1419	Tower	
1509–1520	Cloister	
1558	Stalls	Jerónimo de Valencia
c. 1600	Sanctuary rebuilt	
1619	Main doorway	
1708	Retablo Mayor	

BAEZA (Jaén)

See: Visigothic (*Beatia*); transferred to Jaén 1248. The present church is reputed a cathedral.

Dimensions: length about 200 feet.

Building Dates		Architect
15th cent.	Puerta del Perdón	
1567–1593	Church	Andrés de Vandaelvira
1635	Stalls	

BARBASTRO (Huesca)

See: 1571–1851.

Dimensions: length 211 feet; width 126 feet; span 34 feet.

Building Dates		Architect
1500–1533	Church	Juan de Segura; contractor Baltasar de Barazábal

BARCELONA

See : Visigothic (*Barcinona*).

Dimensions: length 308 feet; width 151 feet; span 41 feet; height 85 feet; towers 170 feet; spire 197 feet.

Building Dates		Architects
1046–1058	Romanesque church (F)	
1298–1317	Transept and bay to E.	Beltrán Riquer

1317-1329	Chevet; E. nave	Jaime Fabre
1365-	West nave	Bernard Roca
1382-1448	Cloister	Bernard Roca
1385-1389	Bell towers	Bernard Roca
1390-	Coro	
1405-1454	Chapter-house	Arnau Bargués
1418-1430	West lantern (base)	Bartomeu Gual
1457-	Stalls, lower	Matías Bonafé
1483-1490	Stalls, upper; pulpit	Michael Lochner
1890-1892	West front	José Mestres & Augusto Font

BARCELONA

Templo Expiatorio de la Sagrada Familia (Church of the Holy Family); included on account of the entirely cathedral character of its architecture.
Dimensions: length 371 feet; width 282 feet; span 49 feet.

Building Dates		Architects
1882-	Crypt	Francisco del Villar
1883-	Church	Antonio Gaudí
1954	Fresh start made	

BILBAO (Vizcaya)
See: 1950. The church was the Colegiata de Santiago.
Dimensions: length 187 feet; width 95 feet; span 30 feet.

Building Dates	
c. 1379-1404	Church
1404-	Cloister
1571	South doorway

BURGOS

See: 1075.
Dimensions: length 379 feet; width 194 feet; span 36 feet; height 88 feet; spires 275 feet.

Building Dates		Architects
1222-43	Chevet	? Ricardo
1243-1260	Transept; nave	Enrique
c. 1290-1324	Cloisters	Juan Pérez
1316-1354	Chapter-house (Capilla de Santa Catalina)	
1442-1458	West towers and spires	Juan de Colonia
1477-1482	Capilla de Santa Ana	Simón de Colonia
1482-1494	Capilla del Condestable	Simón de Colonia
1499-1512	Stalls	Felipe de Vigarni
1540-1568	Lantern	Francisco de Colonia

CADIZ (Cádiz)
Old Cathedral, now Parroquia de la Santa Cruz.
Dimensions: length about 150 feet.

Building Dates	
1602-	Church
1650	Retablo Mayor

CADIZ

See: transferred from Medina Sidonia 1265; to Algeciras 1344; restored to Cadiz 1624.

Dimensions: length 374 feet; width 236 feet; span 51 feet; dome 170 feet.

Building Dates

		Architects
1720	Designs	
1722–	Church begun	Vicente Acero
1753–	Continuation	Vicente Acero
1789–	Upper front	Torcuato Cayón
–1832	Church finished	Manuel Machuca
–1853	Towers and sacristy	Juan Daura

CALAHORRA (Logroño)

See: Visigothic (*Calagurris*); joint with Nájera c. 950–1180; joint with Santo Domingo de la Calzada from 1232; nominally transferred to Logroño 1890.

Dimensions : length 236 feet; width 92 feet; span 23 feet.

Building Dates

		Architects
1485–	Nave	
1561–1567	Chevet and transept rebuilt	Juan
1621–1635	Capilla Mayor and chapels	Juan Pérez de Solarte
1680–1704	West front and tower	

CARTAGENA (Murcia)

See: Visigothic (*Carthago spartaria*); transferred to Murcia in 1291. The church of Santa María la Vieja ranked as a cathedral but was rebuilt in 1904.

Building Dates

		Architect
1266–1291	Church	
1904	Rebuilt	Veltri

CASTELLÓN DE LA PLANA

See: nominally transferred from Segorbe in 1851.

CIUDADELA (Baleares: Minorca)

See: 1798.

Dimensions: length 171 feet; width 80 feet; span 47 feet.

Building Dates

c. 1300–1360	Church
1805–1814	Front

CIUDAD REAL

See: the church is not a cathedral but priory of the Military Orders and head of an exempt jurisdiction equivalent to a diocese.

Dimensions: length 197 feet; width 172 feet; span 52 feet.

Building Dates

		Architects
c. 1490–1514	Chevet and eastern bays	
–1580	Church completed	Antonio Fernández
1616	Retablo Mayor	Giraldo de Merlo
17th cent.	Tower	
19th cent.	Tower altered	

CIUDAD RODRIGO (Salamanca)

See: 1160–1851.
Dimensions: length 235 feet; width 137 feet; span 30 feet.

Building Dates		Architects
c. 1166–1188	Church	
1212–c. 1230	Vaults	
c. 1320–	West and south cloisters	Benito Sánchez
1498	Stalls	Rodrigo Alemán
1525–1538	North and east cloisters	Pedro Güemes
1538–1550	Capilla Mayor	? Rodrigo Gil de Hontañón
c. 1760–1765	West tower	Juan de Sagarvinaga

CORDOVA (Córdoba)

See: Visigothic (Corduba)
Dimensions: length 220 feet; width 144 feet; span 49 feet; tower 305 feet.

Building Dates		Architects
1523–1560	Sanctuary and transept	Fernán Ruiz el Viejo
1560–	Coro	Fernán Ruiz el Joven
–1598	Vault of Coro	Juan Oliva
1593–1617	Tower	Fernán Ruiz el Joven
1599–1600	Central dome	Diego de Praves
1664	Lantern of tower	

CORIA (Cáceres)

See: Visigothic (Cauria)
Dimensions: length 190 feet; width 118 feet; span 55 feet.

Building Dates		Architects
c. 1450–1473(?)	Cloister	
1489	Stalls, first set	
1496–1502	Church	Martín & Bartolomé de Solórzano
1502–1506	Vaults (part)	Bartolomé de Pelayos
1514–1515	Stalls, second set	Martín de Ayala
1536–1570	Porches, tower (lower stage), west front	Pedro de Ibarra
1732	Tower (top rebuilt)	Manuel de Lara y Churriguera
1745–1749	Retablo Mayor	Juan & Diego de Villanueva
1756–1760	Tower (upper part)	? Juan de Sagarvinaga

CUENCA

See: 1182.
Dimensions: length 361 feet; width 128 feet; span 30 feet; height 67 feet.

Building Dates		Architects
c. 1197–1208	Chevet	? Ricardo of Burgos
–c. 1250	Nave	
1448–c. 1490	Ambulatory, etc.	? Hanequín de Egas
1664	West front (F)	
1785	High Altar; Transparente	Ventura Rodríguez
1902–	West front	Vicente Lampérez

249

ELNE (Pyrénées-Orientales, France)

See: Visigothic (*Elena*); transferred to Perpignan 1602.

Dimensions: length 150 feet; width 82 feet; span 22 feet.

Building Dates		Architect
1042–1068	Church	
late 12th cent.	South and west cloisters	
c. 1300	North and east cloisters	
1294–	Gothic chevet (Foundations)	Bartholomeus of Perpignan

GERONA

See: Visigothic (*Gerunda*).

Dimensions: length 284 feet; width 118 feet; span 75 feet; height 116 feet.

Building Dates		Architects
1038–1117	Tower "of Charlemagne"	
c. 1180–c. 1210	Cloister	
1312–1320	Chevet	Enrique
1320–1347	Sanctuary	Jacques Favran of Narbonne
1320–1325	Silver Retablo	Bartomeu
c. 1350–1386	Nave walls	Francesc ça Plana
1351–	Bishop's Throne	Aloy of Barcelona
1357–	Retablo enlarged	Pedro Bernes of Valencia
1394–	South porch	Guillén Morey
1416–	Nave	Guillermo Bofill
1580–1581	South-west tower	
–1604	Nave vault	José Ferrer
1680–1690	Great Staircase	? Francisco Puig
1730–1733	West front	Pedro Costa

GRANADA

See: 1492.

Dimensions: length 416 feet; width 318 feet; span 46 feet; height 100 feet; tower 185 feet.

Building Dates		Architects
1504–1521	Capilla Real	Enrique Egas & Pedro de Morales
1521	Designs	Enrique Egas
1523–1525	Foundations	Enrique Egas
1527	South doorway of Capilla Real	Juan García de Pradas
1528–1561	Chevet	Diego de Siloé
–1640	Transept	
1667–1703	Nave and west front	Alonso Cano

GUADIX (Granada)

See: Visigothic (*Acci*).

Dimensions: length 205 feet; width 148 feet; span 26 feet.

Building Dates		Architects
1549	Designs	Diego de Siloé
–1574	Chevet	Juan de Arredondo
1710–	West front	Vicente Acero
–1796	Interior altered	Gaspar Cayón

HUESCA

See: Visigothic (*Osca*); refounded 1096.
Dimensions: length 174 feet; width 141 feet; span 37 feet.

Building Dates		Architects
1273–	East end	
c. 1300–1313	West portals	
1302–1327	Tower base	
1411–1459	Cloister	
1422–	*Tower pinnacles*	Pedro Jalopa
1497–1509	Vaults	Mestre Gil & Juan de Olózaga
1509–1515	Chapels	Juan de Olózaga
1520–1534	Retablo Mayor	Damián Forment
1587–1594	Stalls	Nicolás de Beráztegui

IBIZA (Baleares: Ibiza)

See: 1782–1851; re-established 1928.
Dimensions: length about 200 feet.

Building Dates	
13th cent.	*Church* (F)
1712–1728	Rebuilding

JACA (Huesca)

See: 1063–1096; refounded 1571.
Dimensions: length 248 feet; width 82 feet; span 26 feet.

Building Dates		Architects
1054–1063	Foundations; east end	
1063–c. 1100	Nave	
c. 1495–1520	Aisle vaults	Juan de Segura
–1598	Nave vaults	Juan de Bescós

JAÉN

See: transferred from Baeza 1248.
Dimensions: length 297 feet; width 135 feet; front 184 feet; span 43 feet; height 72 feet; towers 207 feet.

Building Dates		Architects
1512–1519	*Sanctuary* (F)	Enrique Egas & Pedro López
1534	Designs	Andrés de Vandaelvira
1540–	Foundations	Andrés de Vandaelvira
1545–1550	Chapter-house	Andrés de Vandaelvira
1555–1579	Sacristy	Andrés de Vandaelvira
1634–1654	Sanctuary; east nave	Juan de Aranda
1654–1660	Lantern	Pedro del Portillo
1667–1688	West front and towers	Eufrasio López de Rojas
–1726	Vaults; coro	José Gallego
1764–1801	Sagrario	Ventura Rodríguez

LEÓN

See: 916.

Dimensions: length 315 feet; width 158 feet; span 36 feet; height 95 feet; south tower 223 feet.

Building Dates		Architects
1065–1073	Church (F)	
1255–1277	Chevet, etc.	Enrique of Burgos
1277–1303	Nave, etc.	Juan Pérez
14th cent.	North tower	
–1448	North front	Jusquín
–1458	Cloister walls	Jusquín
1458–1472	South tower	Jusquín
1467–1476	Stalls, first set	Juan de Malinas
1476–1481	Stalls, second set	Diego Copín de Holanda
1492–1507	Capilla de Santiago	Juan de Badajoz el Viejo
1525–1534	Chapter staircase	Juan de Badajoz el Mozo
1529–1538	Trascoro	Juan de Badajoz el Mozo
c. 1538–1540	Cloister vaults	Juan de Badajoz el Mozo
1868–1901	Restoration	Juan de Madrazo & Demetrio de los Ríos

LÉRIDA

Old Cathedral, now disused.

Dimensions: length 192 feet; width 167 feet; span 34 feet; tower 249 feet.

Building Dates		Architects
1203–1278	Church	Pedro Decumbo
1278–	Vaults, lantern and cloister	Pedro de Pennafreita I
c. 1310–1350	Cloister continued	Pedro de Pennafreita II; Jaime Castayls
c. 1350–	Belfry	Jaime Castayls
1386–c. 1400	South nave porch; Cap. de los Requesens	Bartolomé de Bruxelas & Esteban de Gostant
1391–	Belfry continued	Guillem Solivella
–1416	Belfry lantern	Carlí (Carlos Galter of Rouen)

LÉRIDA

See: Visigothic (Ilerda); re-established 1149.

Dimensions: length 279 feet; width 154 feet; span 38 feet.

Building Dates		Architects
1760	Designs	Pedro Mártir Cermeño
1764–1781	Church	Francisco Sabatini & José Prats

LOGROÑO

See: titular cathedral (Santa María la Redonda); 1851, nominally transferred from Calahorra 1890.

Dimensions: length 252 feet; width 77 feet; span 28 feet.

Building Dates		Architect
c. 1480–1510	Church	
1742–1760	West rotunda	
1769	Portal and towers	Martín de Beratúa

LUGO

See: Visigothic (*Lucus*).
Dimensions: length 374 feet; width 148 feet; span 34 feet; height 75 feet.

Building Dates		Architects
1129–1177	Transept, etc.	Raimundo de Monforte
c. 1177–1220	East nave	
–c. 1275	West nave	
1308–	Chevet	Juan Fernández
c. 1530	North porch	? Juan de Álava
1624	Stalls	Francisco de Moure
1708–1714	Cloister	Fernando de Casas y Nóvoa
1726–1735	Capilla de la Virgen	Fernando de Casas y Nóvoa
1762–1768	Sanctuary altered	Charles Lemaur
1769–1784	West front	Julián Sánchez Bort

MADRID

See: 1851, established in the church of San Isidro el Real 1885.
Dimensions: length 207 feet; width 125 feet; span 45 feet; height 79 feet.

Building Dates		Architect
1622–1664	Church	Francisco Bautista

MADRID
See: new cathedral of Nuestra Señora de la Almudena in construction.
Dimensions: length 330 feet; width 180 feet.

Building Dates		Architect
1880–	Crypt	Marqués de Cubas

MÁLAGA

See: Visigothic (*Malaca*).
Dimensions: length 390 feet; width 249 feet; span 51 feet; tower 280 feet.

Building Dates		Architects
1528–	Church begun	Diego de Siloé
1549–1564	Ambulatory	Diego de Vergara
–1570	Transept	
–1580	Sanctuary	
–1588	Completion of crossing	
1592–1632	Coro	Diego de Vergara el Joven
1719–1783	West nave and towers	José Bada

MANRESA (Barcelona)
See: reputed a cathedral (La Seo).
Dimensions: length 262 feet; width 121 feet; span 55 feet; height 95 feet.

Building Dates		Architects
c. 1020	Cloister	
1322	Design	Berenguer de Montagut
1328–1353	Chevet, etc.	
1353–1425	East nave	Arnaldo de Vellers
–1548	Completion	
1572–1590	Tower	Juan Font & Giralt Cantarell

Medina Sidonia—see Cadiz.

MONDOÑEDO (Lugo)

See: 1112–1182; transferred to Ribadeo 1182–1218; re-established 1218.
Dimensions: length 208 feet; width 115 feet; span 30 feet; height 56 feet.

Building Dates
c. 1219–1248	Church
–1603	Eastern chapels
1705	West front altered
1778–1797	Transepts rebuilt

MURCIA

See: 1291; transferred from Cartagena, the titular diocese.
Dimensions: length 295 feet; width 177 feet; span 46 feet; tower 312 feet.

Building Dates
		Architects
1394–1465	Church	
c. 1440	Puerta de los Apóstoles	Alonso Gil
c. 1495–1507	Capilla de los Vélez	? Juan de León
1515–1529	Capilla de los Junterones	Jerónimo Quijano
1521–1525	Tower, bottom stage	Jacopo & Francesco l'Indaco
1526–1545	Tower, second stage	Jerónimo Quijano
1737–1754	West front	Jaime Bort y Meliá
c. 1765–1792	Tower completed	Juan de Gea & Ventura Rodríguez

Nájera—see Calahorra.

ORENSE

See: Visigothic (*Auria*).
Dimensions: length 272 feet; width 188 feet; span 24 feet.

Building Dates
		Architect
1132–1194	Church (F)	
c. 1218–1248	Main works	
c. 1300–	Cloister	
c. 1468	Capilla de San Juan Bautista	
1499–1505	Lantern	Rodrigo de Badajoz
1620–	Ambulatory, etc.	

ORIHUELA (Alicante)

See: 1564; nominally transferred to Alicante 1851.
Dimensions: length 171 feet; width 92 feet; span 26 feet.

Building Dates
		Architect
c. 1305–1355	Church	
c. 1500	Transept	
c. 1540	North doorway	? Jerónimo Quijano
c. 1565–	Ambulatory, etc.	

OSMA, BURGO DE (Soria)

See: Visigothic (*Oxoma*)
Dimensions: length 354 feet; width 164 feet; span 39 feet; height 66 feet; tower 236 feet.

Building Dates		Architects
1232–c. 1300	Church	Lope & Johan de Medina
1258–	Shrine of San Pedro de Osma	
1478–1483	Pulpit	
c. 1494–	Flying-buttresses	
1510–1523	Cloisters	Juan de la Piedra
1550–1554	Retablo Mayor	Juan de Juni & Juan Picardo
1739–1744	Tower	Domingo Ondátegui
1772–1781	Ambulatory and Capilla de Palafox	Juan de Villanueva

OVIEDO

See: (*Ovetum*) 812.
Dimensions: length 259 feet; width 149 feet; span 37 feet; spire 269 feet.

Building Dates		Architects
c. 802–805	Cámara Santa	Tioda
c. 1070–1080	Old tower	
c. 1180	Cámara Santa altered	
c. 1302–c. 1345	Cloister (part)	
1388–1412	Chevet	
1431–	Tower begun	Pedro de la Tijera
1475–1479	Transept	Juan de Cándamo de las Tablas
1487–1497	Nave and cloister	
1508–1512	Narthex; tower	Pedro Bunyeres
–1556	Spire	Juan de Cereceda
17th cent.	Ambulatory	
1705–1712	Capilla del Rey Casto	Bernabé de Haces

PALENCIA

See: Visigothic (*Palentia*)
Dimensions: length 403 feet; width 187 feet; span 33 feet.

Building Dates		Architects
673–	Crypt	
c. 1075	Vestibule of crypt	
1321–1424	Chevet, etc.	
1424–1429	Vaults	Isabrante
1428–1440	Capilla de San Jerónimo; tower	Gómez Día of Burgos
c. 1440–1450	Transept	Pedro Jalopa
c. 1450–1516	Nave, etc.	Bartolomé de Solórzano
c. 1499–1519	Trascoro	? Simón de Colonia
1505–1530	Retablo Mayor	Juan de Flandes & Felipe Vigarni
–c. 1520	Cloister	Juan Gil de Hontañón

PALMA DE MALLORCA (Baleares)

See: 1230.

Dimensions: length 364 feet; width 182 feet; front 197 feet; span 62 feet; height 141 feet; tower 207 feet.

Building Dates		Architects
−1273	Tower	
c. 1306−	Capilla Real	
−1324	Chevet Chapels	
−1327	Nave aisles	? Jaime Fabre
1329−1346	Retablo Mayor	Antonio Camprodón
1368−1406	Nave piers, etc.	Jaime Mates & Guillermo Oliveras
c. 1389−1422	Mirador	Pedro Morey
1420−1529	Nave vaults	Guillermo Sagrera
1497−1529	Stalls	Felipe Fullo & Juan de Sales
1594−1601	West doorway	Miguel Verger

PAMPLONA (Navarra)

See: Visigothic (*Pampilo*); re-established 829.

Dimensions: length 295 feet; width 161 feet; span 34 feet; towers 165 feet.

Building Dates		Architects
c. 1317−1319	Chapter-house	? Juan García de Laguardia
1317−	Cloister, north and east walks	
1397−c. 1525	Church	? Jacques Pérut
1492−1507	Cloister, south and west walks	
1597	Stalls	Miguel Ancheta
1780−1783	West front	Ventura Rodríguez

PERPIGNAN (Pyrénées-Orientales, France)

See: transferred from Elne 1602.

Dimensions: length 270 feet; width 164 feet; span 59 feet; height 84 feet.

Building Dates		Architect
1324−	Church	Jacques Favran
1443−1453	Sanctuary rebuilt	? Guillermo Sagrera

PLASENCIA (Cáceres)

See: 1189.

Dimensions: length 213 feet; width 131 feet; span 56 feet; height 85 feet.

Building Dates		Architects
c. 1250	Chapter house	Remondo
c. 1320−1400	Church	Diego Díaz (1328); Juan Francés (1389)
1416−1418	Cloister begun	Asoyte
1418−1438	Cloister completed	Juan Martín
1492−1520	Stalls	Rodrigo Alemán
1498−	Foundations of east end	Enrique de Egas
1513−1522	Sanctuary	Francisco de Colonia & Juan de Álava
1522−1537	Transept, etc.	Juan de Álava

1537–1548	Works continued	Alonso de Covarrubias, Diego de Siloé & Fernán Ruiz
1538–	South front	Rodrigo Gil de Hontañón
1558–1578	North front, etc.	

Ribadeo—see Mondoñedo

RODA DE ISÁBENA (Huesca)

See: 957–1149
Dimensions: length 107 feet; width 84 feet; span 20 feet.

Building Dates		
c. 1063–1067	Church	
12th cent.	Cloister; crypt	

SALAMANCA

Old Cathedral.
Dimensions: length 208 feet; width 144 feet; span 26 feet.

Building Dates		Architects
1152–c. 1200	Church	Petro Petriz (1163)
1177–	Cloister, etc.	Pedro & Juan
c. 1180–	Lantern	? Dominico son of Juan
1344–1350	Capilla de Santa Bárbara	

SALAMANCA

See: Visigothic (Salmantica).
Dimensions: length 407 feet; width 197 feet; span 43 feet; height 116 feet; tower 361 feet.

Building Dates		Architects
1512–1538	Nave	Juan Gil de Hontañón
1538–1560	Transept	Rodrigo Gil de Hontañón
1588–	Chevet	Juan de Ribero Rada
1705–1733	Dome	José Churriguera
1725–1733	Coro	Alberto Churriguera
1755–1759	Sacristies	Juan de Sagarvinaga

SAN SEBASTIÁN (Guipúzcoa)

See: 1950.
Dimensions: length 220 feet; width 140 feet; spire 246 feet.

Building Dates		Architect
1888–	Church	Manuel Echave

SANTANDER

See: 1752.
Dimensions: length 151 feet; width 92 feet; span 22 feet.

Building Dates		
c. 1217–1219	Crypt	
–1310	Church	
14th cent.	Cloister	
c. 1700	East end altered	
1942–1955	Reconstruction	

SANTIAGO DE COMPOSTELA (La Coruña)

See: transferred from Padrón (*Iria*) c. 858.

Dimensions: length 348 feet; width 233 feet; span 28 feet; height 72 feet; south tower 262 feet; west towers 230 feet.

Building Dates		Architects
1075–1077	Chevet	Bernardo el Viejo & Rotbertus
1088–1102	East nave, etc.	Esteban
–1128	Church completed	Bernardo ? son of Esteban
1168–1211	Pórtico de la Gloria	Mateo
1384–1445	Lantern	Sancho Martínez
1521–1537	Cloister, north walk	Juan de Álava
1527–1538	Sacristy	Juan de Álava
1538–1590	Cloister completed	Rodrigo Gil de Hontañón, etc.
1676–1680	South tower	Domingo de Andrade
1697–1703	Retablo Mayor	
1738–1750	West front and towers	Fernando Casas y Nóvoa
1758–1765	North front, lower story	Lucas Ferro Caaveiro & Clemente Fernández Sarela
1765–	North front, upper story	Ventura Rodríguez

SANTO DOMINGO DE LA CALZADA (Logroño)

See: 1232 (joint with Calahorra; nominally transferred to Logroño 1890).
Dimensions: length 197 feet; width 118 feet; span 26 feet; tower 228 feet.

Building Dates		Architects
1158	First stone laid	
1168–1180	Chevet chapels	
1180–c. 1200	Sanctuary	
c. 1200–1235	Transept; nave	
1513–	Shrine	Felipe Vigarni & Juan Rasines
1513–1529	Presbytery and south transept rebuilt	Felipe Vigarni & Juan Rasines
1517–1550	Cloister rebuilt	
1521–1526	Stalls	Guillén de Holanda & Andrés de Nájera
1537–1541	Retablo Mayor	Damián Forment
1762–1767	Tower	Martín de Beratúa

SARAGOSSA (Zaragoza)

See: Visigothic (*Caesaraugusta*); the original cathedral known as La Seo, though it now shares in cathedral rank with El Pilar.
Dimensions: length 256 feet; width 253 feet; span 36 feet; height 75 feet.

Building Dates		Architects
1119–	Church (F)	
1189–	Further works	
1316–1412	Sanctuary, etc.	
1417	Repairs to lantern	Isembart
1431–1444	Retablo Mayor begun	Pere Johan
1467–1477	Retablo completed	Hans de Suabia
c. 1490	Outer aisles, etc.	

c. 1500	Stalls	Francisco & Antonio Gomar
1498–1520	Lantern rebuilt	Juan Botero
1546–1559	Nave, two west bays and general alterations	Charles de Mendivi
–1683	North-east front	Julián de Yarza
1682–1690	Tower	Giovanni Battista Contini

SARAGOSSA

The Basilica of El Pilar, which has shared diocesan rank from 1675.
Dimensions: length 435 feet; width 220 feet; span 52 feet.

Building Dates		Architects
1509–1518	Retablo Mayor	Damián Forment
1544–1546	Stalls	Étienne d'Obray & Giovanni Moreto
1677–	Church rebuilt	Francisco de Herrera el Mozo
1753–1766	Cupolas, etc.	Ventura Rodríguez

SEGORBE (Castellón)

See: Visigothic (Segobrica); re-established 1176; joint with Albarracín 1246–1577; nominally transferred to Castellón 1851.
Dimensions: length about 200 feet.

Building Dates		Architects
14–15th cent.	Cloister	
1483–1534	Church	Juan de Burgos
1600	Main doorway	
1791–1795	Nave rebuilt	Mauro Minguet & Juan Bautista Gascó

SEGOVIA

See: Visigothic (Segobia).
Dimensions: length 361 feet; width 190 feet; span 43 feet; tower 289 feet.

Building Dates		Architects
1472–1491	Cloister (moved 1524)	Juan Guas
1522	Designs	Juan Gil de Hontañón
1525–1558	Nave	Juan & Rodrigo Gil de Hontañón
1563–1591	Chevet	Rodrigo Gil de Hontañón
1615–	Dome	Juan de Mugaguren
1620–1626	Main doorway	Pedro Brizuela
1620–	Tower altered	
late 17th cent.	Capilla del Sagrario	Manuel Churriguera
1768–1775	Retablo Mayor	Francisco Sabatini
1784	Trascoro	Ventura Rodríguez

SEO DE URGEL (Lérida)

See: Visigothic (Urgello); re-established 1010.
Dimensions: length 185 feet; width 175 feet; span 28 feet.

Building Dates		Architect
c. 1131–	Church	
1175–c. 1182	Vaults	Ramón Lombardo

SEVILLE (Sevilla)

See: Visigothic (*Hispalis*).
Dimensions: length 454 feet; width 295 feet; span 53 feet; height 121 feet; tower 320 feet.

Building Dates		Architects
1184–	Giralda begun	Ahmad ibn Baso
–1198	Giralda completed	Alí de Gómara
c. 1400	Designs	? Alonso Martínez; Carlí
1402–1432	Nave	
1432–1467	East end	Carlín
1467–1498	Vaults	Juan Normán & Simón de Colonia
1498–1506	*Lantern*	
1475–1478	Stalls	Nufro Sánchez & Dancart
1482–1526	Retablo Mayor	Dancart, etc.
1511–1519	Lantern, etc., rebuilt	Juan Gil de Hontañón
1551–1575	Capilla Real	Martín Gainza, etc.
1568	Giralda, top stages	Fernán Ruiz

SIGÜENZA (Guadalajara)

See: Visigothic (*Segontia*); re-established 1124.
Dimensions: length 318 feet; width 154 feet; span 34 feet; height 89 feet.

Building Dates		Architects
c. 1155–1169	Chevet and transept	
c. 1170–1190	*Cloister*; chapter-house	
–1226–	Chevet and transept raised	
c. 1300	South-east tower	
1335–c. 1350	South-west tower, middle stage	
–1491	Stalls	Rodrigo Duque & Francisco de Coca
c. 1500	New vaults	
1503–1508	Cloister	Alonso de Vozmediano
1527	New chapter house	Francisco Baeza
1532–1535	Sacristy	Alonso de Covarrubias
1567–1606	Ambulatory	
1609–1611	Retablo Mayor	Giraldo de Merlo
1665–1688	Trascoro	Juan Lobera
1797	South doorway	Luis Bernasconi

SOLSONA (Lérida)

See: 1593–1851; re-established 1895.
Dimensions: length 164 feet; width 86 feet; span 52 feet.

Building Dates		Architect
1161–1163	Apses, etc.	
14–15th cent.	New church	
c. 1730	West front	
1780	South front	? Francisco Pons

TARAZONA (Zaragoza)

See: Visigothic (*Tirassona*)
Dimensions: length 274 feet; width 115 feet; span 25 feet.

Building Dates		Architects
1152–1235	Church	
1362–1500	Chapels, tower, etc.	
1486	Stalls	Maestros Sariñenas
c. 1500	West doorway	Alí el Darocano
1504–1529	Cloister	
1506	Pulpit	Maestre Pedro
1543–1558	Lantern	Juan Botero
1560	Capilla Mayor	
–1588	Tower completed	
1603	Retablo Mayor	

TARRAGONA

See: Visigothic (*Tarraco*).
Dimensions: length 335 feet; width 187 feet; span 46 feet; height 86 feet.

Building Dates		Architects
c. 1171–1199	Eastern apses, lower stage	
c. 1195–1220	Cloister	
1200–1230	Chevet raised; transept	
1233–1251	Side-aisles completed	Fray Bernardo (d. 1256)
c. 1250–1272	Nave, three east bays	Raymondo de Milian (d. 1266)
1272–1289	Nave, two west bays; west front	Bartolomé
1375–	West porch completed	Jaime Castayls
1426–1434	Retablo Mayor	Pere Johan & Guillén de la Mota
1478–	Stalls	Francisco Gomar
1760–1775	Capilla de Santa Tecla	José Prats

TERUEL

See: 1577.
Dimensions: length 213 feet; width 72 feet; span 26 feet.

Building Dates		Architects
1248–1278	Church	
1257–	Tower	
c. 1260–1314	Wooden ceiling	
c. 1335	East end altered	
1535–1538	Retablo Mayor	Gabriel Jolí
1538–	Lantern	Martín de Montalbán
c. 1596–c. 1614	Side-aisles	
1658	Ambulatory, etc.	

TOLEDO

See: Visigothic (*Toletum*).
Dimensions: length 446 feet; width 207 feet; span 43 feet; height 102 feet; spire 295 feet.

Building Dates		Architects
1226–1238	Chevet	Martín
–c. 1300	Crossing; east nave	Petrus Petri (d. 1291)
–c. 1400	West nave	
1389–1425	Cloisters	Rodrigo Alfonso
c. 1400–1418	North-west tower, bottom	Juan Alfonso
1418–1444	West front, lower stage	Álvar Martínez
1425–1440	North-west tower	Álvar Martínez
c. 1430–1450	Capilla de Santiago	Álvar Martínez & Hanequín de Egas
1448–1452	Spire	Hanequín de Egas
1452–1465	South portal	Hanequín de Egas (d. c. 1471)
–1493	Vaults finished	Martín Sánchez Bonifacio
1495–1543	Stalls	Rodrigo Alemán, Felipe Vigarni & Alonso Berruguete
1498–1504	Capilla Mayor	
1502–1504	Retablo Mayor	Felipe Vigarni, etc.
1504–1519	South tower, etc.	Enrique de Egas
1531–1534	Capilla de los Reyes Nuevos	Alonso de Covarrubias
1606–	Upper west front	Juan Bautista Monegro
1626–1631	Cupola of Capilla Mozárabe	Jorge Manuel Theotocopuli
–1732	Transparente	Narciso Tomé

TORTOSA (Tarragona)

See: Visigothic (Dertosa).

Dimensions: length 236 feet; width 123 feet; span 39 feet.

Building Dates		Architects
1345	Plans	Antonio Guasch
1346	New plans	? Benito Basques
1347–1441	Church to west of crossing	Benito Dalguayre; Andres Juliá (1381); Paschasio de Xulbe (1416)
14th cent.	Cloister	
1441–1568	Coro	
1588–1593	Stalls	Cristóbal de Salamanca
1621–1660	West nave	Martín de Abaria
1705–1757	West front	

TUDELA (Navarra)

See: 1738–1851.

Dimensions: length 200 feet; width 157 feet; span 33 feet.

Building Dates		Architect
12–13th cent.	Cloister	
1194–1204	Church, east end	
c. 1205–c. 1265	Nave and west front	
16th cent.	Stalls	Étienne d'Obray

TUY (Pontevedra)

See: Visigothic (Tude).

Dimensions: length 221 feet; width 128 feet; span 23 feet.

Building Dates		Architect
c. 1170–1225	Church, eastern part	? Reimundo
1218–1239	Transept vaults	
1225–1287	West porch, etc.	
1264–	Cloister	
1495–1499	East end altered	

VALENCIA

See: Visigothic (*Valentia*)
Dimensions: length 328 feet; width 171 feet; span 34 feet; tower 213 feet.

Building Dates		Architects
1262–c. 1356	Church	Arnaldo Vitalis (1267); Nicolás de Autona (1303)
c. 1330–1354	Puerta de los Apóstoles	
c. 1330–1360	Lantern	
1356–1369	Chapter house	Andrés Juliá
1381–	Tower begun	Andrés Juliá
1414–1429	Tower finished	Pedro Balaguer
1430	Lantern repaired	Martín Llobet
1440–1480	Nave, west bay	Francisco Baldomar & Pedro Compte
1566–	Galleries outside chevet	Gaspar Gregorio
1703–1713	West front	Konrad Rudolf & Francisco Vergara
1774–1779	Interior transformed	Antonio Gilabert & Lorenzo Martínez

VALLADOLID

See: 1595.
Dimensions: length 450 feet; width 236 feet; span 49 feet.

Building Dates		Architects
1527–	Foundations	Rodrigo Gil de Hontañón, etc.
1580–1585	Church begun	Juan de Herrera
–1668	Church part finished	
1730–1733	West front, upper part	Alberto Churriguera

VICH (Barcelona)

See: Visigothic (*Ausona*).
Dimensions: length 269 feet; width 164 feet; span 39 feet; tower 151 feet.

Building Dates		Architects
1038–1180	Tower	
12th cent.	Lower Cloister	
1324–1400	Upper Cloister	Ramón Despuig
c. 1340–1360	Chapter house	Bartolomé Ladernosa
1420–1427	Retablo	Pedro Oller
1633–1680	North chapels	Jaime Vendrell
1780–1803	Rebuilding	José Morató

VITORIA (Álava)

See: 1862, established in the Colegiata de Santa María.
Dimensions: length 191 feet; width 125 feet; span 22 feet.

Building Dates

c. 1370–c. 1400	Church
c. 1400	West portals
c. 1500	West porch

VITORIA

New cathedral in construction.
Dimensions: length 387 feet; width 157 feet; span 42 feet.

Building Dates		*Architects*
1906–1914	Church begun	Javier Luque & Julián Apraiz
1946–	Works continued	

ZAMORA

See: Visigothic (*Semura*).
Dimensions: length 240 feet; width 100 feet; span 26 feet.

Building Dates		*Architects*
1151–1174	Church	
c. 1175–c. 1225	Nave completed; cloister	
–c. 1240	Tower	
1490	Stalls	Rodrigo Alemán
1496–1506	Chevet rebuilt	
1591–1621	Cloister; north front	Juan Gómez de Mora

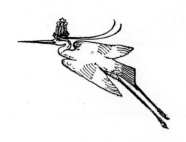

Bibliographical Note

The important works in English are:

BEVAN, B.: *History of Spanish Architecture*, 1938. Later revisions are included in the Spanish translation, 1950.
CLAPHAM, A. W.: *Romanesque Architecture in Western Europe*, 1936.
CRUMM-WATSON, W. : *Portuguese Architecture*, 1908.
HERSEY, C. K.: *The Salmantine Lanterns* (Harvard University Press), 1937.
SITWELL, S.: *Southern Baroque Art*, 1924.
STREET, G. E.: *Some Account of Gothic Architecture in Spain*, 1865. Revised edition by G. G. King, 1914; but the original should be consulted for its larger and better-printed illustrations.
WHITEHILL, W. M.: *Spanish Romanesque Architecture of the Eleventh Century*, 1941.

In French are two works of special value for the Gothic period:
LAMBERT, E.: *L'art gothique en Espagne aux XIIᵉ et XIIIᵉ siècles*, 1931.
LAVEDAN, P.: *L'architecture gothique religieuse en Catalogne, Valence et Baléares*, 1935.

The standard work on Spanish Baroque is in German:
SCHUBERT, O.: *Geschichte des Baroks in Spanien*, 1908. Spanish translation, 1924.

For the most part the literature of the subject is in Spanish, and the following is a select list of the principal works only.

ARS HISPANIAE, V, *Arquitectura y Escultura Románicas*, 1948.
—— VII, *Arquitectura Gótica*, 1952.
—— XI, *Arquitectura Siglo XVI*, 1953.
Volumes on different periods by various authors, in progress.
GASCÓN DE GOTOR, A.: *Nueve Catedrales en Aragón*, 1945. (Albarracín, Barbastro, Huesca, Jaca, Roda de Isábena, Tarazona, Teruel, Zaragoza La Seo and El Pilar.)

LAMPÉREZ Y ROMEA, V.: *Historia de la Arquitectura Cristiana Española de la Edad Media*, 2nd ed., 1930. Includes plans and descriptions of most of the cathedrals.

LOZOYA, Marqués de: *Historia del Arte hispánico*, 1931–34.

—— & L. F. de Peñalosa: *El Arte Gótico en España*, 2nd ed., 1945.

Monumentos Españoles: *Catálogo de los declarados histórico-artísticos* (Instituto Diego Velázquez), 1953–54. The officially listed monuments of Spain (some 1,300) arranged by provinces, with plans, photographs and bibliography of each building; includes almost all the cathedrals.

SARTHOU CARRERES, C.: *Catedrales de España*, 1946. A serious monograph, mainly historical and descriptive, with photographic illustrations but no plans.

TORMO, E.: *Levante* (Guías Regionales Calpe), 1923. (Alicante, Cartagena, Murcia, Orihuela, Segorbe, Tortosa, Valencia.)

For individual cathedrals information will be found in the *Blue Guides* (Southern Spain and Portugal, 1929; Northern Spain, 1930, revised edition in the press), and the French *Guide Bleu* (*Espagne*, 1954). Detailed descriptions of certain cathedrals appear in various Spanish series or in individual monographs. The series of especial value, all well illustrated, are the volumes so far published of the official *Catálogo Monumental de España*, here abbreviated as (CM); the *Guías Artísticas de España*, edited by Sr. D. José Gudiol Ricart (GA); the *Monumentos Cardenales de España* (MC); and *El Arte en España*, published by Editorial Thomas (AE), this last including translations of the short texts in French and English. The relevant volumes, together with a few recent monographs, are here listed alphabetically under the cathedrals described.

ALCALÁ DE HENARES. E. Tormo: *Alcalá de Henares* (Patronato Nacional del Turismo), 1930.

ASTORGA. M. Gómez Moreno: *Provincia de León* (CM), 1926.

ÁVILA. S. Alcolea: *Ávila Monumental* (MC), 1952.

BADAJOZ. J. R. Mélida: *Provincia de Badajoz* (CM), 1925.

BARBASTRO. See below, HUESCA.

BARCELONA. J. Ainaud, etc.: *La Ciudad de Barcelona* (CM), 1947. J. Gudiol Ricart: *Barcelona* (GA), 3rd ed., 1954. *La Catedral de Barcelona* (AE).

BURGOS. J. A. Gaya Nuño: *Burgos* (GA), 1949. L. Huidobro: *La Catedral de Burgos* (MC), 1949.

CÁDIZ. E. Romero de Torres: *Provincia de Cádiz* (CM), 1934.

CIUDAD RODRIGO. L. M. Cabello y Lapiedra: *Ciudad Rodrigo* (AE). M. Hernández Vegas: *Ciudad Rodrigo*, 1935.

CORDOVA. S. Alcolea: *Córdoba* (GA), 1951. L. Torres Balbás: *La Mezquita de Córdoba* (MC).

CORIA. J. R. Mélida: *Provincia de Cáceres* (CM), 1924. M. A. Orti Belmonte: *Cáceres y su Provincia* (GA), 1954.

GERONA. P. de Palol: *Gerona* (GA), 1953. *Gerona Monumental* (MC), 1955.

GRANADA. S. Alcolea: *Granada* (GA), 1951.

HUESCA. R. del Arco: *Provincia de Huesca* (CM), 1942.

JACA. See above, HUESCA.

JAÉN. J. Chamorro Lozano: *Guía Artística y Monumental de la ciudad de Jaén*, 1954.

LEÓN. M. Gómez Moreno: *Provincia de León* (CM), 1926. M. Domínguez Berrueta: *León* (GA), 1953. *La Catedral de León* (MC), 1951. J. Torbado y Florey: *La Catedral de León* (AE).

LÉRIDA. S. Alcolea: *Lérida y su Provincia* (GA), 1955. M. Herrera y Gés: *La catedral antigua de Lérida*, 1948.

LUGO. F. Vázquez Saco: *La catedral de Lugo*, 1953.

MADRID. J. A. Gaya Nuño: *Madrid* (GA), 2nd ed., 1950. *Madrid Monumental* (MC).

MANRESA. J. Gudiol Ricart: *Provincia de Barcelona* (GA), 1954.

MURCIA. A. Noguera y Lorenzo: *Guía de Murcia*, 1952.

OSMA. V. Núñez Marqués: *Guía de la Catedral de Burgo de Osma*, 1949.

PALENCIA. *Provincia de Palencia* (CM), vol. IV, 1948. J. Milicua: *Palencia Monumental* (MC), 1954. M. Vielva: *Palencia* (AE).

PALMA. F. P. Verrié: *Mallorca* (GA), 1948. V. Furio: *The Cathedral of Palma*. R. A. Cram: *The Cathedral of Palma de Mallorca*, 1932.

PLASENCIA. See above, CORIA.

RODA DE ISÁBENA. See above, HUESCA.

SALAMANCA. A. García Boiza: *Salamanca Monumental* (MC). F. Chueca Goitia: *La Catedral nueva de Salamanca*, 1951.

SANTANDER. Simón Cabarga: *Guía de Santander*, 1946.

SANTIAGO. J. Filgueira Valverde: *Santiago de Compostela*, 1950. S. Alcolea: *La Catedral de Santiago* (MC). K. J. Conant: *The Early Architectural History of the Cathedral of Santiago de Compostela*, 1926.

BIBLIOGRAPHICAL NOTE

SANTO DOMINGO DE LA CALZADA. A. Prior Untoria: *La Catedral Calceatense*, 1950.

SARAGOSSA. F. Abbad Ríos: *Zaragoza* (GA), 1952. *La Seo y El Pilar de Zaragoza* (MC).

SEGOVIA. I. de Ceballos-Escalera: *Segovia Monumental* (MC), 1953. A. Dotor: *La Catedral de Segovia* (AE).

SEO DE URGEL. S. Alcolea: *Lérida y su Provincia* (GA), 1955.

SEVILLE. J. Guerrero Lovillo: *Sevilla* (GA), 1952. S. Montoto: *La Catedral y el Alcázar de Sevilla* (MC), 1948. A. Dotor: *La Catedral de Sevilla* (AE).

SIGÜENZA. E. Tormo: *Sigüenza* (Patronato Nacional del Turismo), 1930. A. de Federico: *La Catedral de Sigüenza* (MC), 1954. R. Aguilar y Cuadrado: *La Catedral de Sigüenza* (AE).

SOLSONA. S. Alcolea: *Lérida y su Provincia* (GA), 1955.

TOLEDO. J. Ainaud: *Toledo* (GA), 1947. J. Gudiol Ricart: *La Catedral de Toledo* (MC), 1947. J. Polo Benito: *La Catedral de Toledo* (AE).

TORTOSA. J. Matamoros: *La Catedral de Tortosa*, 1932.

VALENCIA. A. Beltrán: *Valencia* (GA), 2nd ed., 1953.

VALLADOLID. G. Nieto: *Valladolid* (GA), 1954. F. Chueca Goitia: *La Catedral de Valladolid*, 1947.

VICH. J. Gudiol Ricart: *Provincia de Barcelona* (GA), 1954. E. Junyent: *La Catedral de Vich*, 2nd ed., 1949.

VITORIA. C. de Castro: *Provincia de Álava* (CM), 1915.

ZAMORA. M. Gómez Moreno: *Provincia de Zamora* (CM), 1927.

Notes to the Text

References are given only for matters of importance not readily discoverable in the works quoted in the preceding bibliography.

INTRODUCTION

PAGE

41 Mediaeval methods of building—the subject was admirably dealt with by Street and, with fuller information, by Lampérez (see bibliography). For a summary, see J. H. Harvey: *The Gothic World* (1950), chaps. I–III.

42 Simón García's manual of design has been published by J. Camón: *Compéndio de architectura y simetría de los templos. Año de 1681* (1941); and see J. Camón in *Archivo Español de Arte*, No. 45 (1941), 300–5.

43 Tortosa—see J. Matamoros: *La Catedral de Tortosa* (1932), where the plan of 1345 and the elevation by Benito Basques are reproduced, as well as the seventeenth- and eighteenth-century designs for the west front.

46 Las Huelgas—J. González in *Revista de Archivos, Bibliotecas y Museos*, LIII (1947).

60 Short biographies of a number of the most important architects of the sixteenth century are appended to F. Chueca: *La Catedral Nueva de Salamanca* (Acta Salmanticensia, Filosofía y Letras, tomo IV, num. 3, 1951), 209 ff., where the only surviving original drawing of Salamanca is reproduced.

62 Barcelona—the design of 1408 is reproduced in J. Ainaud, J. Gudiol Ricart & F. P. Verrié: *Catálogo Monumental de la Ciudad de Barcelona* (1947), II, figs. 596–7.

CHAPTER ONE

70 Jaca lantern—J. Camón in *Seminario de Arte Aragonés*, II (1945), 17–26.

75 Pamplona east end—see J. H. Harvey: *The Gothic World*, 100, 102.

77 Pamplona paintings—*Exposición de Pinturas Murales de Navarra en la Real Academia de Bellas Artes de San Fernando* (1947).

79 Villaespesa chapel—J. Ramón Castro & J. Esteban Uranga in *Príncipe de Viana*, X (1949), 129–226.

80 Calahorra and Danzig—see Harvey: *The Gothic World*, 123; and fig. 206.

CHAPTER TWO

87 Castilian language—R. Menéndez Pidal: *El Idioma Español en sus primeros tiempos* (1942).

95 León glass—see C. H. Sherrill: *Stained Glass Tours in Spain and Flanders* (1924); L. Pérez Bueno: *Vidrios y Vidrieras* (1942).

96 Rheims palimpsest—see Didron in *Annales Archéologiques*, V (1846), 87ff.; VI (1847), 139; and for reproductions of elevations from it W. R. Lethaby: *Mediaeval Art* (1904), fig. 116; Harvey: *The Gothic World*, fig. 11. Western towers separated from the front, as at León and Astorga, are also found at Rodez, France, in work of *c.* 1500.

106 Osma cloister—E. García Chico in *Boletín* (Universidad de Valladolid, Seminario de Arte), XVIII (1951–2), 135 ff.

CHAPTER THREE

128 Orense, Franciscan cloister—D. Calonge: *Los Tres Conventos de San Francisco de Orense* (1949).

141 Santillana—M. Pereda de la Reguera: *Santillana del Mar y Altamira* (1953), including English text.

CHAPTER FOUR

149 Gerona cloister—C. Cid Priego: *La Iconografía del Claustro de la Catedral de Gerona* (Anales del Instituto de Estudios Gerundenses, 1951).

166 Santes Creus—J. Puig y Cadafalch in *Ensayos Hispano-Ingleses*: *Homenaje a Walter Starkie* (1948), 313–14.

173 Valencia—F. M. Garín Órtiz in *Arte Español*, XIV (1942–3), No. 3, 29–32.

176 Orihuela—P. Gutiérrez Moreno in *Archivo Español de Arte y Arqueología*, X (1934), 21 ff.

CHAPTER FIVE

183 Durham kitchen vault—see J. H. Harvey: *Gothic England* (1947), 55; and figs. 72, 73

184 Tarazona—F. Torralba: *Catedral de Tarazona* (Instituto Fernando el Católico, Monumentos de Aragón, No. 3, 1954).

CHAPTER SIX

205 Toledo west front, etc.—J. M. de Azcárate in *Archivo Español de Arte*, No. 76 (1948), 173–88

211 Plasencia—J. Benavides in *Boletín de la Sociedad Española de Excursiones*, XIII (1905), 40 ff.

CHAPTER SEVEN

223 For biographies of the principal masters of the early sixteenth century, responsible for the major churches of Andalusia, see above, note to p. 28.

EPILOGUE

241 Ogee arches at Troyes: see N. Pevsner in *Architectural Review*, February 1953, where Dr. Pevsner mistakenly attributes to Lasteyrie the untenable view that these ogee arches were insertions of the nineteenth century, whereas (R. de Lasteyrie: *L'architecture religieuse en France à l'époque gothique*, 1927, II, 45) he endorses the revised view of Enlart that this particular block of stone must be a repair of the late fourteenth or fifteenth century. Examination on the spot fully supports Lasteyrie's view that the carved fleurs-de-lys which surround the ogee arch, as well as its crockets, are of a far later character than the original work of *c*. 1261–66. A much better claimant to be the earliest known ogee arch was the outer arch of the "porch" of the now destroyed shrine of Ste-Gertrude at Nivelles, made between 1272 and 1298 according to a portraiture by Maître Jacques, a Benedictine monk; but if this arch was a late afterthought, towards 1298, it would still be later than the earliest English examples.

HISTORICAL NOTE

The chief sources for the architects and other artists named will be found in J. A. Ceán Bermúdez: *Diccionario histórico de los más ilustres profesores de las Bellas Artes en España* (1800; new ed. 1880); the supplementary volumes by the Conde de la Viñaza: *Adiciones al diccionario histórico de J. A. Ceán Bermúdez* (1889–94); and E. Llaguno y Amírola: *Noticias de los Arquitectos de España* (1829). The more recent German compilation of international scope, U. Thieme & F. Becker: *Allgemeines Lexikon der bildenden Künstler*, will also be found useful.

Index

The captions of the figures have been included, and also the names of architects occurring in the Notes; the Glossary has not been indexed. Numerals in *italics* indicate the principal references to buildings; those in **heavy type** refer to the *figure numbers* of the illustrations. Dates are given for Spanish architects and master builders: carvers and sculptors are indicated by S.; painters by P.

INDEX

INDEX

INDEX